WHAT OTHERS ARE SAYING

"(T)he story is about Minnesota people committed to the Church in youth, married to it in fact, who leave the ever increasingly vulnerable structure to live a physical life in mortal marriages...a wonderful source of understanding of those times of the '60s and '70s... founded on so much hope and belief in the power of love among mortals—mythical, really. The telling again of the tale of what happens when one favored by the gods decides to fall to earth and make a life there."

—Vernal Bogren Swift, itinerant artist

"What struck me most about Solem's *Such a Road* is the courage with which Jackie and Phil have lived their separate and their intertwined lives. Reading this book will strengthen any marriage."

—Susan Hawkinson, co-author of *Timber Connection*

"Jackie and Phil Solem are extraordinary individuals. Their life together is greater than the sum of the parts. The Solems' journey, refracted through this stunning joint memoir, conveys the humility and joy of lives lived in gentle pursuit of truth, simplicity, honor, wisdom, and profound creativity. *Such a Road* is a gift to us all."

—Martha Grace Reese, JD, MDiv.,
author of *Unbinding the Gospel*
and *The Real Life Evangelism Series*

for more copies: www.sucharoad.com

OR: Solem/Such a Road
25591 Spruce Drive
Bovey, MN 55709

Such a Road

Autobiography of a Marriage

Philip Solem
with Jacqueline Vesel Solem

wheat/mark

Such a Road: Autobiography of a Marriage

Published by Wheatmark™
610 East Delano Street, Suite 104, Tucson, Arizona 85705 U.S.A.
www.wheatmark.com

ISBN: 978-1-58736-004-6
LCCN: 2007940623

Lyrics from "Going Home (Mythical Kings and Iguanas)" from *Dory Previn–Live at Carnegie Hall*, April 18, 1973, © Liberty Records, a division of Capitol Records, Inc.

Out of Africa, Universal Pictures, 1985, produced and directed by Sydney Pollack, screenplay by Kurt Luedtke, Universal Home Video © 1997.

Going home is such a ride.
Going home is such a ride.
Isn't going home a lo– and lonely ride.
                    –Dory Previn

Msabu! This water must go home to Mombasa!
                    –Farah Aden

Caminante, no hay camino.
Se hace camino al andar.
                    –Antonio Machado

I wish to thank Susan Hawkinson for the many generous hours she gave working with me on the manuscript. Thanks, also, to Vernal Bogren Swift and Pat Browne, the first to read the manuscript and cheer me on. And to Gay Reese who gave most helpful information and direction toward publication. Most of all, my heart's thanks to my wife, Jackie, who, no matter how you read or parse the word, was the "inspiration" for this book.

CONTENTS

INTRODUCTION

Ancud, Chile

*A*ncud is the first town on the island of Chiloe after you get off the ferry, a short crossing from where the Puerto Montt bus stops at the water's edge. This is two-thirds down the skinny length of Chile, almost the end of the highway before the last third stitches its way south to Tierra del Fuego as an uninhabited archipelago pushed up against the diminishing Andes by constant, strong sea winds.

We had not planned to go to the island, but were glad for the chance. The guidebooks say that Chiloe is a fascinating place, unspoiled and rich in folklore. Our plan had been to sail from Puerto Montt on the *Magallanes* that morning and thread our way four days south along the Patagonian inside passage. But when we rolled our backpacks dockside to board the big ship, we were told: No embarkation today. The ship has not come in. Bad weather at sea. So we were stalled in a scruffy port and looking at a second night in a dingy hotel — unless...unless we took the chance of hopping across to Chiloe, spending a cheery day and night in a picturesque fishing port and getting back on time to the ship the next day.

Ancud gets less than a column of print in the guidebook, but we found it relaxing and charming: small, brightly colored fishing boats, sea-weathered people working on nets and engine rehab, good seafood, and nearly all the houses covered roof-to-ground with colored, hand-made, zig-zaggy shingles which give them a light and lacey look. We liked Ancud, and the next morning we were back on the bus right on time waiting at the ferry dock to the mainland.

As we waited for the bus to creep onto the narrow, yellow barge, Jackie and I were happily reminiscing about other travels, conversationally bouncing about the globe, amazed at how many places we had been together, how full of adventure and love and pain and surprise our lives had been. Suddenly she turned a face full of sunshine toward me and, with unexpected intensity, said:

"You *should* write our story! It's been *such* a road!"

We had been told this many times by many people — you two should write a book! Always we shrugged it away, uninterested, shy, even mildly irritated at what was surely meant as a compliment. This time, however, the urging came from Jackie herself. With feeling. And this time, to my surprise, as when a key wiggled and jiggled in a stubborn lock suddenly feels a smooth movement of parts sliding into place, something inside me said: Yes. I think I will.

As soon as we returned home from South America, I began. Our code name for the writing, just between ourselves, was "The Ancud Project." That was because I had no title yet, and this phrase had a certain mysterious flair, something better than "our story" or "our memoirs." I even suggested it as a title to Jackie at one point; but she wisely said, no, that's too odd, nobody would get it.

However we did agree on a subtitle: "stories of the inner life" (which later became "autobiography of a marriage"). The inner life is what has always interested us most. Initially, I tried to interpret the stages of our coming together and living together with little sage essays and thoughtful commentary; but, after a first reading or two, I deleted them all as contrived, sententious, and even wrong. As I worked on the Ancud Project, the telling of the outer life unfolded an inner life; and all I had to do was tell the story which I did not really understand very well until I myself began to hear it.

One morning her sister, Madelyn, called from her ashram in Texas. Jackie was not home, so Maddie and I just chatted as usual.

"So, what are you doing this morning, Phillie?"

"I'm writing our story. Jackie's and mine, the story of our life. I'm on

Chapter Two, which tells about her childhood and growing up years and her years in the convent until we met."

"Oh, no, no, no, no! You can't do that! That's hers to write!"

I explained that I was the writer. I would interview Jackie at length, write a draft. She could correct or veto anything. I was thinking of unity of style, consistency of voice, stuff like that. Yet, the oxymoron Maddie was pointing out stood there: a biographical autobiography? How does one person write an autobiography for two?

I still thought I was right. Even Jackie seemed to agree as she listened to my first and second drafts of Chapter Two, making only a few changes and deletions here and there. Suddenly, one day, she shook her head and said: "Move over. Let me drive this stretch." Her complete rewrite of this chapter brought a freshness and intimacy I had missed, but the style was off. So I tried again, folding her telling into the batter I had prepared. This seemed to work, especially where Jackie said, "Hand me the mike, please."

So it is an autobiography, after all. And the way we worked it out was a lot like our marriage.

ONE

·············

Marriage

*W*e married at two o'clock on Sunday afternoon. August 16, 1970.
It seems now like a strange time of the week to marry. When
we were growing up, Catholic weddings always took place on Saturday
mornings or Saturday afternoons, never on Sunday. Yet those were the
days before the Mass had been changed from Latin to English, before the
altars were turned around to face the people, and before Sunday Mass
obligation could be satisfied by going on Saturday evening. That is, before a lot of things, which had been done a certain way since the days of
Jesus or earlier, began to change.

The peculiar thing is that Jackie and I chose Sunday afternoon for a
complex tangle of reasons ranging from caution to boldness. The problem with *that* Saturday was that August 15 was the Feast of the Assumption, a Catholic holy day of obligation, an inappropriate time to hold
an illegitimate Catholic wedding. So as not to offend, we quietly moved
forward a day–to Sunday? Yes, but to Sunday *afternoon*, 2:00 P.M., when
all morning Masses would be over and people would be home in their
yards getting the barbecue ready or driving out to the cabin; and the
clergy themselves would be sitting back in lawn chairs in casual, colored
shirts for a smoke and a beer. We had carefully scheduled our wedding
to avoid competing with the holy times. The reason for this nicety was
that we were not allowed to marry at all. I was a priest of the diocese,

ordained five years earlier. Jackie had been a nun under solemn, permanent vows–although she had applied for and received formal dispensation from her vows from the Vatican. We were marrying in defiance of church law; therefore the church would not recognize the marriage as valid–even though the marrying clergyman, Joe Selvaggio, was himself a priest. The problem there, however, was that he had his wife with him; and the church did not allow him to have one either.

A tightrope walk of trying to avoid offense while giving offense would characterize much of our life together from this point. A suggestion of this lay in one of the wedding songs written for the occasion by our friend, Art Dale, a Lutheran pastor, who was there with his wife and seven children to sing us into a new era. He had written all of the songs just for us and introduced the first one this way: "From the very moment I met both of these people, I have known them to be very careful people. And their romance has been very careful. This song is about them." Then the Dale family began to sing quietly...

Walk slowly...breathe softly...
Take off your shoes,
When opening any new door.
But once you're inside,
Cast fear away,
And live! Live! LIVE!

....

Jackie had met the Dale kids one winter evening on the skating rink in Virginia, Minnesota, where the Mother Superior had assigned her to teach at the Marquette Elementary School. Of course these were Lutheran kids; and they were amazed at the sight of two nuns, head to toe in billowing black, their rosy, radiant faces pinched, forehead to jowl, in starched, white coif, two panting, ebony swans skittering about the rink, whirling, falling, laughing. The kids brought them home: Mom, Dad, look what we found! So Sister Jacqueline and Sister Jeanine were invited to dinner the following week. After that, Jacqueline continued to go for dinner from time to time, played their games, played their piano, and gradually was taken into their family as a special love.

Was the other Sister there, too? She must have been, much of the time, for in those days nuns went out in public only in twos. I remember a riddle fad that was popular around that time which consisted of posing a complex crime scene with a number of misleading clues embedded in the telling and one true clue which was key to solving the crime. One of these puzzlers gave the clue, "...a nun walking down the street going south..." The answer to the crime, of course, was the nun; she had to be a fake nun because there is never *a* nun, there were always at least two nuns.

My cousin, Marguerite, was a nun named Sister Alanna. I remember once being with her for some kind of family event at her hometown church in southern Minnesota, and our families and relatives had gathered. She was in full habit in those days; and so was I, in a way. I was then in the major seminary studying for the priesthood and was already a "man of the cloth," which meant that, when I went out in public, I was to go in formal dress: black suit, white shirt, black tie, black dress hat, black shoes. Sister Alanna had been allowed to go in public without a sister companion that weekend only because she was surrounded by family. Yet only reluctantly, and with some uncertainty, would she allow me to drive her alone and unaccompanied from her parents' apartment down Blooming Prairie's four blocks of main street to the church, after insisting that she sit in the back seat, with me in full clerical garb at the wheel. She was not unduly fastidious; those were the rules in those days.

Marguerite was my favorite cousin, two years older than I. We looked alike, everyone said. Even I saw the resemblance, although I thought she was quite pretty. We were pals; but I did not see her often when we were kids, since she lived in southern Minnesota and I in the north. Whenever her family came for visits, I was overjoyed. Now, as young adults, our affection was strengthened by a common calling to the religious life and shared attraction to a life of piety, devotion, and service in the church.

The night before this family gathering at the church, she had been allowed to stay at her mother and father's apartment in Blooming. My mother and I also spent the night there. I discovered to my horror that evening that I had forgotten to pack a necktie with my clerical blacks! Our traditional Catholic family members understood the problem, and all pitched in to try to resolve this crisis. But neither my uncle, Chester, nor my cousin, Alan, nor any other male around had a black tie to lend. Dark navy blue with small dots was the closest. But, no, it had to be black. My aunt, Babe, I think, came up with the suggestion of cutting a piece from Marguerite's veil. Not the external veil, of course, but a silky underlayer that covered her hair.

In an hour I had what was needed to complete my outfit, carefully cut, sewn and pressed into a necktie no one would suspect. I remember the wistfully erotic sensation I had putting it around my neck the next morning. I think I allowed myself that awareness, confident in the rigid rules of our religion to safeguard my purity of heart. An hour later I drove the four blocks to the church. Sister Alanna sat in the back seat.

So the other Sister must have come along at times when Jackie visited the Lutheran pastor's family and grew to love Art and Bev, Sarie, Sonja, Tom, John, Carol Sue, Victoria, and Lori. On the other hand, perhaps a companion sister was not always there; for things were loosening up a bit in the Catholic culture. This would have been the early 1960s, and the breezes of change were beginning to be felt. Pope John XXIII had thrown open the widows of a Vatican audience hall in symbolic gesture indicating the need in the Church for fresh air and *aggiornamento*. Belgian Cardinal Suenens had not yet written his energizing bestseller, *The Nun in the World*, but he was thinking about it. So perhaps Jackie–Sister Jacqueline–had begun to venture out alone, negotiating the growing pressures of her inner life against the corset stays of convent culture.

Later that year, Art Dale accepted a pastoral call to a church in Minneapolis and moved his family away from Virginia. The following year Sister Jacqueline was also sent to teach in Minneapolis at Our Lady of Victory School, giving her the opportunity to continue spending time with the Dale family. Years later, when she and I planned to marry and she had been dispensed from her religious vows, Art found her a job with a summer program at Augustana Lutheran Church. He and Bev gave her a room in their house for three months while she waited for me to come for her.

Now here they were on the sanctuary dais of the wedding hall, a room which had formerly been a chapel of the Lutheran Student Center in Duluth, all nine of them singing their hearts out for us: "*...once you're inside, cast fear away, and live! Live! LIVE!*"

....

We wanted to keep the wedding small and unobtrusive; so the guest list was limited to thirty-three; but six others showed up unannounced at the last minute. So there were thirty-nine in all, mostly our family members, special clergy friends and their families. We seated them at long church-hall tables positioned end-to-end to make a large oval, and we stood in the middle to exchange vows in the traditional ritual of the Catholic wedding Mass. Afterward, rather than being served first at a head table, Jackie and I waited tables and served our guests a meal which friends had been preparing in the kitchen. This symbolic gesture said that we wanted to live our marriage as an act of service.

Her three sisters were there, but not her mother who stayed home with her terminally ailing husband. Perhaps it was a relief for her mother to have a reason to stay away, for there must have been a firestorm of gossip in her small town about her daughter, the nun, marrying a priest. My mother was there, but not my father, who stayed home for no given reason. My mother was the Catholic and should have been more threatened by the implications of our wedding. However, she was also more adventuresome than my conservative, sedentary, unchurched father, for whom the seventy-five-mile trip to Duluth was an effort, especially in his chagrin at his priest-son's recent fall from grace, first through his antiwar notoriety and now through his irregular marriage.

There were a number of close relatives, three friends with whom we planned to live in community, and a couple who were providing us with a honeymoon cabin. Six of our clergy friends–Episcopal, Baptist, Lutheran, Catholic–were there with wives and children. Three of them were colleagues in the antiwar movement. One was our counselor who had helped us through months of discernment on the decision to marry. One a kindred spirit in the charismatic prayer movement. During the next several years all six clergy couples would divorce.

Those six pastors and their brides had once pledged to marry for life. Jackie and I had once pledged to remain unmarried for life. The irony of our breaking and making commitments in a single act this day did not escape us. For over a year we had each wrestled with this contradiction and eventually accepted it. It had helped a little that she had been dispensed from vows by a rescript from the Vatican and was no longer bound. I had never vowed celibacy but was bound to it by canon law. I was willing to break the law and accept the penalty of excommunication.

What is more, we had been coming to our decision and resolve during a period of high social turmoil. These were days of tension and conflict–and of eager expectations: the Vietnam War, the resistance movement, the prospect of doing prison time, ideals of voluntary poverty and living in community, renewal of prayer and spiritual life, the crumbling of old religious structures and formation of new.

Our counselor, Jim Price, a Baptist pastor, had warned us that our church would not let us alone if we did not agree to drop out of sight, move away and start life elsewhere. We would be driven off, he predicted. We considered this but disagreed and insisted we were not leaving the church or our town. The church would change soon, we thought. We would stand our ground and wait.

Early that late summer Sunday morning, three of us sat on the shore of Lake Superior to watch the sun rise into a beautiful day: Jackie, my cousin, Marguerite, and I. We sat on the shoreline rocks in silence and prayer for nearly an hour. Then we went up to the old mansion, now a university student center, on Superior Street to begin the bustle of preparations, the food, the arrangements, the changing of clothes, the gathering of guests. I went upstairs to the third floor where Jackie and her sisters were getting ready and saw her for the first time in her wedding dress, a simple, knee-length, white shift which she had sewn herself. I gave her a box of jewels–that is, a velvet-padded silverware case from Goodwill filled with found objects from Lake Superior's beach–shells, curls of driftwood, a weathered thread spool, a feather.... She wept. Our song, "Bridge over Troubled Waters" by Simon and Garfunkel, was playing:

> *Sail on, silver girl,*
> *Sail all night.*
> *Your time has come to shine,*
> *All your dreams are on their way.*
> *See how they shine!*

Then we wept together. I went downstairs to wait. The guests quieted. Jackie came down the broad staircase with Madelyn, Jeanne, and Pat. The Dale family began to sing.

We may have been living in tense and uncertain days, but this was a day of joy for us. Art Dale's last song of the day was:

Isn't this the funnest day ever in your life?
Jackie's got a husband!
And Phil has got a wife!

We ran out the back door to our car in a shower of rice after the reception and drove an hour to Big Sandy Lake to begin our honeymoon. As we nosed the car carefully over a one-lane wooden bridge to where we would find the motorboat to take us to the island, a huge, full, golden moon rose dead ahead, appearing to approach. Of course, we stopped mid-crossing and just gazed. Near midnight we lay on our backs on a tethered square dock floating on the lake. Above, the Northern Lights were in wild display, curtains of colored light rapidly shifting and shimmering. We were sure it was heaven's greeting.

....

Jackie and I have often been asked by people who know we were nun and priest how we got together– curious about the drama, the brazenness, the scandal it must have involved. We answer quite openly with our story, an abbreviation of this memoir's narration. It is fairly easy for us to speak about the atmosphere of turmoil and revolution of the 1960s both in the church and in society at large–the Vatican Council, the Vietnam War, the flower generation, the burning of the ghettos, the mass departures from the convents and rectories–a time of desperation alongside zealous anticipation of an Age of Aquarius. This was the public context in which we left and married.

However, there were other subtler layers of context which we seldom speak of and which influenced the more private movements of our lives. I would like to offer another piece of my answer to the curiosity about how we got together. I think the very constraints of our roles as religious elite in our religion, with all the high-definition strictures on stance, appropriateness, and conduct, paradoxically gave us time and occasion. Let me approach this indirectly–with a story.

While I was still a very young priest, perhaps only a year or two ordained, a young wife came to ask for instructions in the Catholic religion because she wanted to convert. In those days there existed no developed group programs of instructions in Catholicism for small parishes, and the usual procedure was for the parish priest to give one-to-one instructions on the tenets and requirements of the faith. So, with the aid of a user-friendly adult catechism and a curriculum which I had developed, I proceeded to "give instructions." It was a routine duty in my work week, something I did with many people. In fact, as a personable, articulate, compassionate young associate, in a parish which had been run for some time by a gruff, dozing, old pastor, I probably attracted a new wave of interest in Catholicism. At one point I found myself giving instructions to nearly a quarter of the student nurses from the nearby hospital training program.

In any case, this young wife came asking to convert to the church of her husband, perhaps "for the sake of the children," but even more because she was looking for something more in her life, something one might call greater spiritual depth. Not surprising, the emptiness of her marriage was part of this. I knew her husband and found him coarse and dull. She was intense and unusually beautiful.

As the course of instructions proceeded, one hour a week in the parish office, it took on the character of counseling. I was keenly aware of the danger in this development, but counseling parishioners was implied in my job description, and parishioners often came to me in the confessional or at the rectory door for counseling on very difficult problems with which I had no personal experience and for which I had no training: child-rearing, affairs, betrayal, addictions. I simply did the best I could in hearing and advising those who came to their priest for help. When I met with the young wife, I discerned that she was sincerely longing for spiritual peace, was becoming strongly attached to our weekly discussions, and was growing infatuated with me. I carefully monitored my inner world and guarded my response. I did not flirt.

The day came, however, when she began our session of instructions by telling me simply that she had been thinking about me a lot and probably was falling in love with me.

To this day I am ambivalent about what I did next. Feeling relief that it was out on the table, I remained calm and listened to her. I said I thought her feelings were understandable because I had been kind and helpful to her at a time of distress when she was not finding warmth and affirmation at home. I believed she had come honestly seeking spiritual growth, and my own experience was that there often was a fine line between spiritual and romantic excitement; in fact, they flowed into one another when men and women shared thoughts and feelings deeply. I said her feelings of infatuation for me were not wrong, but to pursue them would be. Because of where God had called each of us in life, neither of us was available for anything but a priest-parishioner relationship.

I was gentle with her, yes, but I also rebuffed her. Despite my effort to be kind, did I hurt her with my chaste, reasonable explanation? Yet how could I have done differently? It would have been reckless to discuss her feelings about me further, even more so to tell my own. I found her attractive, but I nursed no fantasies. I had to shut the door on this as carefully as I could.

Hard as this may be to believe, I do not remember how this ended, whether she continued to come for instructions or became Catholic or not. I only recall this episode; and, while for me it did not end in trouble, I wonder what it meant to her and how it did end for her.

What was "my experience" of the fine line between spirituality and romance I spoke of? Although I was only a year or two out of seminary, quite green and not very worldly-wise, I had for years carefully observed the movements of my own heart, emotions, thoughts, and imagination. Seminary training in what was called "the spiritual life" was quite wise and healthy on the whole in my opinion. Adolescent boys and young men were being trained for a life of celibacy, and the regimen of prayer and meditation and regular instruction on how to deal with temptation, meaning sexual fantasies and feelings, was practical and wholesome. A major deficit, however, was the absence of lab work: no permission to date, to flirt, to experiment, fall in love and break up. So we came into the priesthood trained deeply on one level but naive and inexperienced in the ways of seduction, love and the aftermath. I experienced frontal seduction by women a number of times in my early years in the priesthood, in one case pursued so relentlessly with midnight phone-ringing that the senior pastor agreed to have a shutoff switch installed. This sort of sexuality seasoned but did not tempt me.

Sensuality and spirituality were entwined in the religious environment in which I grew up, persistent and never acknowledged. I do not think of this as a devious covering of sexual desire with piety. I believe this entwining is healthy because it is real, a normal aspect of human love. I acknowledge it now in late life, and I think I was acknowledging it in words less understood when I spoke to the young wife who had just told me she was beginning to love me.

Some threads in this twine are yearning, seeking, fulfillment, desiring oneness with the beloved, losing or relinquishing oneself. There is an erotic quality both to sexual mating and to the spiritual journey; yet each has its own expression, severely guarded by high walls. This means that on the other side of the wall is forbidden fruit–not forbidden in order to tempt but truly to keep it out of reach. Nevertheless, these boundaries highlight the attractiveness of what is forbidden and increase erotic energy.

Is there a clearer example of this than the biblical book, *The Song of Songs*? "She is a garden enclosed, my sister, my promised bride; a garden enclosed, a sealed fountain...I sleep but my heart is awake. I hear my love knocking. 'Open to me, my sister, my beloved....' I opened to my love, but he had turned and gone. My soul failed at his flight...."

No mention of God in the poem, no prayers, no rituals, only scintillating Persian love poetry. These passages were the inspiration of the greatest writings of Catholic mysticism, the poems and commentaries of St. John of the Cross. This Spanish Carmelite saint wrote highly erotic poetry on the ascent of the soul to heights of spiritual contemplation. Carmelite nuns to this day are cloistered and hidden, gardens enclosed, bodies concealed in burka-like habits, speaking to men only through an iron grill. Yet their spiritual discourse among themselves is full of love poetry, and they speak of themselves as virgin brides.

When I was a young man at the seminary in Louvain, Belgium, I could look out my fourth floor window across Karmelitenberg Lane at the walls of the Carmelite convent only ten meters away. I could even see into a corner of their courtyard, but in four years I never caught a glimpse of one of the cloistered nuns as I had hoped. I was very curious. Only once were a group of us young men allowed into the visitors' hall to assist at a special Mass, and only then did I see the shadowy female shapes moving in stillness beyond the large grill.

The spiritual friendship of John of the Cross and Teresa of Avila led the great Reform of Carmel in the sixteenth century. There were other models: Saints Francis and Clare of Assisi, Saints Benedict and Scholastica. History or legend, I am not sure, but we only know of Scholastica in the story that says that she was a nun and Abbot Benedict's own sister.

Holy Benedict paid her a rare visit, and they spoke of heavenly things all day into the evening, at which time he indicated he had to return to his monastery. She pleaded with him to stay and prolong their spiritual discourse, but he insisted on leaving before nightfall, being a stickler for following his own Holy Rule. Whereupon she fell to praying to God so earnestly that a terrible rainstorm came up forcing Benedict to remain at the convent; so he and she continued their conversation through the night. In the morning she was dead, and he was given a vision of her soul leaving her body and rising to God like a dove.

Jackie and I were raised on such stories of the saints' lives. She says that, at the end of the family rosary prayed aloud each evening in her home, her parents would add a brief prayer to Saint Maria Goretti that their daughters would remain "good, clean, pure, holy, honest, Catholic girls." Maria Goretti's story was very popular in our youth. She was an Italian teenager who resisted rape and died by stabbing rather than lose her virginity. Her murderer repented, was punished, was converted, and entered a monastery. Not all the saints' tales were in this vein, but there was a noticeable preoccupation with virginity in a good many of them

Over the centuries, the Catholic Church had devised special structures for the encouragement and protection of dedicated virgins, male and female. Men and women lived apart, dressed in full body cover to announce their unavailability, acted under orders from superiors, socialized with their same-sex group, refrained from activities and entertainments seen as perfectly innocent for the laity but unseemly for celibates. This was the world of holiness Jackie and I entered with eagerness and ready hearts, each in our own time. She entered the convent in the middle of her college years. I entered the minor seminary as a freshman in high school. Both environments were similar in separating us from secular lifestyles and directing us to celibate futures.

In the 1960s, when Catholic culture became more liberal–many would say more worldly–these very restraints were retained but reinterpreted. In increments, nuns' habits were abbreviated, still seen as a "sign of commitment," but no longer cloaking their bodies. Nuns and priests, brothers and monks, lived apart but met with one another on relaxed, tree-shaded campuses for summer institutes on catechetics or the liturgy or scripture. Or they teamed up to oppose the war, to enter the struggle for justice, to work with the poor. They went places unsupervised. They spent a lot of time in one another's company and talked passionately about things that really mattered. They mixed freely with their lay peers, but the focused dedication of their lives in religion and the common training and ideals they shared drew them more closely to one another, soulmates.

What distinguished nuns and priests from other people now gave them cover to spend time together. Because of their special dedication to church work and mission and service, fewer eyebrows were raised when they rode in the same car, went to the same meetings, were seen having a good time together. This was the change in the external environment that came with the social shifts of the 60s. What had not changed was the braided strand of sexuality and spirituality that runs through the life of high ideals. When men and women religious had freedom and greater opportunity to share the life of spirit in depth and intimacy, they fell in love. Is that so strange?

How did I know about this when I spoke to the young wife in my office as a new priest? I knew because I had observed myself while in training for celibacy. Because of seminary rules, I did not date in high school and did not miss it. Yet in the major seminary, when I had sacristan duties and had to go for sacristy supplies to a nun twice my age and a severe beauty, I was smitten. The day I wore my cousin's religious veil as a necktie, I might have been a medieval knight, his virtue protected by chivalric rigor, wearing his virgin lady's token as he left on the quest of the Grail. A boy, a young man of high ideals, I was strongly moved by women also in love with high ideals. So I understood very early something about the twinning of sexual and spiritual stirring.

I could warn the young wife in my office about it. Did I listen to my own warning later on?

TWO

....

Gerry / Sister Jacqueline

Summer, 1990. Jackie and I and our two teen-age daughters had been waiting for over an hour on the station platform in Kranj, Yugoslavia, waiting not for a train but for release of our bicycles. We had taken a train across the high Alps; and here, at the first stop beyond the Austrian border, station officials of this Communist country had impounded them. They spoke only Slovenian, and we had no idea what document might be missing or what law we might have broken. My efforts in English, German, French, fragmentary Italian, and energetic gesturing brought no response. The officials had disappeared inside the office and shut the door, leaving us to wonder whether we were to materialize the absent paperwork, offer a bribe, or simply go our way without the four bicycles which had carried us this far from Brussels, Belgium.

Ironically, we were only twenty kilometers from the village of Dvorje where Jackie's relatives lived. As we sat there, an idea came. She rummaged in her money belt and pulled out a folded slip of paper, walked to the office door, held the paper against the glass, and tapped. After a few moments, the door opened wide enough for a hand to reach out and take the paper. The door shut, and we continued to wait. Abruptly the door opened, and a bulky, uniformed guard beckoned to me. I followed him into the office and was dumbfounded when a woman sitting at a desk handed me a telephone receiver. On the other end Vido Kepic,

Jackie's cousin, was shouting very broken German: "I will come right away! How many bicycles do you have?" As I replaced the receiver, the guard put two documents printed in Slovenian before me and gestured toward a pen. Hoping I was not confessing to espionage, I signed. The four bicycles were ours.

Within a half-hour Vido appeared in a white van pulling an open trailer for the bikes. He was a nervous, wiry man with a brush-cut crest of hair, constantly moving with hurried actions. Jackie in tears threw her arms around him. This was her first cousin whom she had never met. Vido appeared awkward and flustered in the embrace, eager to get on with the business of bringing us home to the *gostilna,* the neighborhood tavern which he and his family ran in Dvorje.

We stayed with them for four days and met Jackie's two other cousins, Ivan, a butcher, and Franz, recently retired from work in a German auto factory. There were endless hours of chatting in the kitchen–English via German to Slovenian and back–eating and drinking in the *gostilna* where men from the village and nearby town began gathering in the early morning before work. We were awash in button-box polka music, slivovitz and beer, loud talking and arguing by burly men in handlebar moustaches who would suddenly break into stentorian, maudlin love songs. We ate the same dishes served in Jackie's childhood home in Minnesota. Again and again we would catch them gazing at Jackie, whispering to one another and nodding, and I would quietly translate to her what they were saying: "Amazing! It's like looking at Mama again! Yes, you're right, just like Mama when she was young."

"Mama" was Ivanka, the sister of Frances, Jackie's mother. The two sisters had been born on opposite sides of the Atlantic, had corresponded in Slovenian, but had never met, and now were dead. Frances had lived her final months in our home, passing into a sweet, peaceful death in a tiny bedroom upstairs only a year and a half earlier. In fact, it was the modest inheritance she had left, divided among Jackie and her three sisters, which had allowed us to take this bicycle trip. When the money had come, Jackie had offered her share at once so we and our daughters could spend three months bicycling and tenting in Europe. She had often urged her widowed mother to make the trip to Yugoslavia, while there was still time to meet her sister, Ivanka, and had offered to go with her. But Frances shook her head. She had always lived on an edge of Minnesota called the Iron Range, had never ventured far from Ely or Tower-Soudan, and was no daring spirit like her second daughter.

....

How had this separation of families come about? The key was Grandma Burja–or Grandma Sershen, the same person, named differently depending on which side of the Atlantic was speaking. Jackie's grandmother came from the town of Cerklje, with its tiny satellite village of Dvorje, and had an arranged marriage to a local man, Frank Sershen. Shortly after the birth of Ivanka, their first child, Frank signed on for work in America with a recruiter sent over from the Oliver Iron Mining Company which had desperate need for labor to exploit the dramatic mining boom unfolding in northeastern Minnesota around 1900. This recruitment dragnet swept through the Balkan regions of what was then Austro-Hungary and shipped boatloads of immigrant workers and their families as indentured workers, obligated to the company for repayment of maintenance and ship's passage by a percent of their mining wages. However, when Frank and Frances prepared to sail, their two-year-old Ivanka was ill and not allowed on board. So they placed her with an aunt in Cerklje and left, hoping to return for her some day when times were better.

What drew entrepreneurs from the eastern United States and a wave of immigrants from Europe to northern Minnesota was a one-hundred-mile narrow vein of iron ore lying diagonally just south of the Canadian border. Along this rich formation sprang up a string of mining towns and small settlements called "locations" to make the Iron Range. Seventy percent of the workforce who came to dig the open pits and deep shafts were from Finland, Sweden, Slovenia, and Croatia. They mixed with Italians, Serbs, Montenegrins, and others to form an idiosyncratic culture, unique in the state, and known to this day as "Ranger" for its distinct accent, hard drinking, labor activism, and roughness in talk and behavior.

The Sershens settled in Ely, last town on the eastern end of the Range, where even today one can stand looking north and see only a roadless tract of forests and lakes far into Canada. They began a second family, three daughters, three sons. Jackie's mother, Frances, was the second of these daughters.

An old, formal, sepia-tone family portrait shows her looking very sad beside her mischievous-eyed sisters, between mother and father, with three brothers propped about the edges. Her mother appears darkly beautiful and imperious, her father leaning back in a chair, remote. Perhaps one can read too much into a photograph; but it is a fact that, not long after this picture was taken, her parents divorced–a virtually unheard of scandal in a Catholic immigrant family of that time. Jackie's mother bore the scar of this all her life, telling us more than once, "People would spit on us when they went by our house because we came from divorced parents." The divorced mother of seven became a legend in family gossip. She opened a boarding house in Ely, ran a still, took up with one of the tenants named Frank Burja, then married and later divorced him. She was always known thereafter as "Grandma Burja" (pronounced "Boodya"), who defied convention, ordered the men about, wielded a butcher knife and swore fiercely when her temper was up. In time, matronly and prosperous, she made the return visit to Cerkle in the old country, thinking to bring her first daughter back to America. But Ivanka, now grown into her mid-teens and in love with a local youth, was not interested. Willful Grandma Burja, who was used to getting her way, returned to Ely empty-handed.

Jackie's mother, Frances, carried her own mother's name but was of a milder character, more subdued, witty and good-natured, but often sad. She married her true love, Matt Vesel, sixth of sixteen children from Matthias and Katherine Vesel, who had also immigrated from the Slovene region of Austro-Hungary and had settled in Tower-Soudan, twenty miles down the road from Ely. Matt and Frances were very much in love, obvious in the family photos taken during the early years of their marriage. Gone is Frances's woeful expression in the childhood picture with her parents, replaced by a face radiant and joyful in her pictures as a young woman.

Later, however, this same face looking out of photos above the darling faces of her own growing family becomes scowling and pinched. These were the years of returning suffering. As a five-year-old, she had run and fallen under the wheel of a car driving out of the yard, wrapped about the tire, crushed her nose and broken her arms. She had never fully recovered: a flattened nose, four miscarriages, and separation from her bewildered daughters nine times for surgeries on internal organs. Compounding this pain was her pattern of severe mood swings, which made for a tempestuous marriage and a periodically chaotic home life.

Matt Vesel was a steady father and husband, honest and hard-working, but remote and domineering, insisting on order and control in the house which he built in Soudan. His eleven brothers and sisters had pride of place at his table to which many of them came visiting most Sunday afternoons, and his Frances was expected to cook and clean and cook again whenever they appeared. At times his wife, usually submissive, would erupt and rail at him for treating her as a servant. But he was the man and men ruled. They had four children who, resentfully and perhaps unfairly, claimed that Matt had really wanted a Pat, Jerry, Matt, and Gene instead of the Patricia, Geraldine, Madelyn, and Jeanne that he got.

....

It was the second daughter that I married in 1970. I knew her at that time as Jacqueline, but she had been born Geraldine Ann Vesel on September 27, 1940, in the house her father had built in Soudan. She had always hated the name Geraldine and was happy to change it when she entered the convent in Duluth.

As I set about the task of writing our story, I have been able to describe her beginnings from historical accounts and family legend. However, when it comes now to describing what it was like to be Gerry Vesel, how could I tell what has always been most precious to her, the story of her inner life? Of course I did not know Gerry nor did I know Sister Jacqueline during most of her years in religious life; and, even if I had, my account would only have been my impression of the outer life. So, after thirty-six years of marriage to me, she agreed to sit for interview. Interestingly, the place we chose for the five-hour telling of her tale was Ely. It was happenstance, not pilgrimage, which brought us there for this discussion.

We are grandparents now, almost fully retired. We had towed our little second-hand popup camper to the Kawishiwi River, just beyond Ely, for five days of beautiful June-July weather in the peaceful north woods. From the edge of the river, just below our campsite, I could look upstream a hundred yards at the old, overhead-steel-girder bridge, built during the Depression, from which my own family had fished before church many Sunday mornings when I was four and five years old. Now, a lifetime later, Jackie and I drove in to town from the campground for Sunday Mass and then had coffee and muffins on the veranda of The Front Porch coffee shop overlooking main street and meandered through the story of Gerry Vesel and Sister Jacqueline. I think this is what she told me —

....

It was a miserable start. Soon after birth, Gerry developed a severe case of eczema, a furiously itching skin rash. The doctor could do nothing for it. Katie Russ, their next-door neighbor, sewed a little baby strait jacket from striped feather ticking that looked like a chain gang uniform in the old movies. Every night Gerry's mother tugged this onto her, its sleeves sewn fast to the sides and leggings sewn together, to bind her tight and keep her from scratching the weeping sores. Every morning her mother was distraught to find that the baby had worked her arms free and left blood spatters on the wall from thrashing and scratching. This went on for three years. Every night Frances redoubled her efforts with up to twenty-six safety pins, but every night baby Gerry would break out. One morning, at her wits end, Frances held her baby up and cried out: "Take her! Take her, God! I can't do anything with her!" Years later she told us she was sure this prayer was heard; for within three days the eczema began to clear completely.

The relatives told Gerry as she was growing up, "You were a bloody mess. We didn't think you were going to make it." They said she spent so much time bound up those first three years that she didn't crawl. One day she just stood up and became a toddler.

Her mother seemed to like retelling this story of Gerry's dramatic entry into life and the healing. She saw it as a sign of God's favor to her daughter and herself. One day, when Gerry was about seven, her mother called her upstairs and ceremoniously took down a cardboard box from the closet. Sitting on the bed with the box on her lap, she pulled away the tissue wrapping and showed the mythic strait jacket.

Recalling this moment as we sat on The Front Porch in Ely sipping coffee, Jackie told me: "This was Mom's ritual. This jacket was a symbol of our shared suffering, and it created a bond between us. I began to understand then this story that I had always been hearing about myself when I saw this thing. It freed me, in a way, because I had become fixated on her pain which often drew her to the cliff edge of sanity. Later I began to realize what a dangerous place this was for her."

Jackie went on to tell me once again what I had often heard her say–

"I was a sad and lonely little girl. The repercussions of all the trauma in Mom's own early life rippled into her adulthood, and she began having severe depression and extreme mood swings. She nursed her melancholy with long periods on the couch. Or she would be washing walls and windows, hanging clothes, cleaning floors, putting flowers on the dining room table and having a meal cooked by the time Dad came home from day shift at the mine.

"I liked the house feeling so full of energy those days. But on the dark-mood days I felt such loneliness and foreboding. We could feel a storm coming.

"Mom seemed to do better when Patsy and Maddie and I started grade school. So did we. We had more structure then, and Mom had more space. I remember us hurriedly walking a mile home from school for lunch in winter through heaps of snow, and she would have a wonderful lunch ready. My favorite: thick tomato soup with toasted cheese sandwiches, topped off with homemade potato donuts. But a lot of the time I would come home to find Mom on the couch. I would stand there asking, 'What's the matter, Mom?' but she wouldn't answer me. I would try to bring her out of it, but I couldn't."

Her father's response to this disorder was to redouble efforts at controlling it. It must have left him desperate. At times her mother would comply, at times fight him wildly. At times she would go off to the hospital–Gerry did not know why–and her grandmother would come in to take care of the girls. Although a woman's place in this culture was under male authority, when fierce Grandma Burja appeared, adding yet another layer of control, even Matt Vesel would move over and defer.

"No one spoke openly in our house about the pain we each felt," Jackie continued. "Janie was my best friend all through my school years, but I couldn't even tell her what it was like at home. I often wished a social worker, like Janie's aunt, would come to our house to help us out. Patsy and Maddie and I kept the shame at feeling so raw and helpless to ourselves. We never talked to each other about it.

"Mealtimes were especially tense and short. Most evenings we had

supper together with Dad at the head of the table, each of us in our places. I was so eager to please and not say the thing that might cause upset
that I was always spilling my milk. I never did it on purpose, but it did
redirect the tension. Sometimes Mom would flare-up, angry or fearful.
Dad would ineffectively try to control her by dismissing her feelings or
making demands, even when she had no energy left. I loved Mom intensely and had compassion for her vulnerability; but, as I grew into my
teen years, I hated her cruelty when her erratic behavior embarrassed me
and made me ashamed to bring friends home."

Patsy, the firstborn, responded to the tensions at home by taking on
the toughness of Range attitudes as she grew up. Gerry's younger sister,
Maddie, coped by remaining silent and invisible. When Patsy became a
teenager, she started to run wild, provoking her father's rage and ever
tightening control, which became abusive. At one point, even stubbornly
silent Maddie butted in between them and stood up to him with a feroc-
ity which shocked him.

Gerry's way was to become the sensitive good-girl, empathetic toward her mother's suffering, not giving her father trouble, showing a
friendly, cheerful face.

"I was told, 'You need a tougher skin, Gerry!' I was always trying to
figure things out. I decided I needed an invisible shield around my skin
like the one in the Colgate toothpaste magazine ad that protected the
smiling model's pearly-whites. I imagined a plastic shield around me.
Kids used to chant, 'Sticks and stones may break my bones, but names
can never hurt me!' Well, I knew that wasn't true. I knew names and yelling and swearing and mean looks *could* hurt me.

....

I have been part of Jackie's large extended family for more than thirty-five years now. It was not the first time I had heard the surface of these
stories. However, as I interviewed Jackie on The Front Porch that day,
something new began to come clear for me.

When I wrote "she became the sensitive good-girl," I did not mean
that niceness was her cover. I think little Gerry's strategy for self-care–
formed with a child's wily wisdom in developing a personality–was
this: She absorbed the deep values of her culture and lived them to extremes. That is how she coped in that family. That is how she stayed on

good relations with those about her while maintaining her own freedom. The reason I say this is that I think I have observed this about Jackie all through the years I have known her.

Plainly put, people in Tower-Soudan saw this kid as "different." Now, I know a good bit about the Iron Range. I am from there, have a Range accent myself, and know the culture. When Rangers say, "Boy, *that's* different," they imply suspicion, mild dissent, but not outright disapproval. They tend to mutter this in the presence of something or someone showing originality, daring, or creativity. They don't follow it with much elaboration; they have said just about all that needs to be said. Well, Gerry made her way, I think, by being different, not to the extent of seeming odd, but rather by carefully playing it out in a manner that won respect.

Even her sister, Pat, would taunt: "Oooh! You're so-o-o-o sensitive!" She was talented in art, loved to read, spent time alone in the woods up behind the house or in the tiny library above the Community Club Store, sitting on the floor behind the stacks.

"In kindergarten," she said, "Miss Kitto told my parents: 'All she wants to do is paint all day.' Exactly! That was where I discovered how soothing paints and colors and shapes were to me. My inner world opened when I touched the tip of a paintbrush to paper; and that bright little painting room closet at the back of our classroom brought an unusual sense of ease. My parents recognized my need and squeezed their tight budget to provide paper, crayons, and paints where I could find hours of peace at home.

"Life could be rough, raucous, and sarcastic in Tower-Soudan. I managed it by not letting on how this affected me–maybe with my invisible, plastic shield–staying engaged, staying cheerful and outgoing. I had a paper route and got to know many of the people in town, knew who lived where and who was related to whom. They liked me, I think, and found me an outgoing, interesting kid. Schoolwork was not difficult, and my teachers saw me as curious, artistic, eager to learn.

"They would not have thought of me as sad or lonely. I showed this side only to three special women in my life outside my home: my godmother Ann Yapel, Aunt Ange 'Jackswife,' and Aunt Joan."

Aunt Joan was an English war bride her uncle Ed had brought home. Joan was from outside the Range culture and could see into what was going on in this town and family with keen intelligence and caring. She held a special warm place for this niece who was suffering at home and so full of yearning. Aunt Joan was open and forthright, not afraid to ask questions or face conflict. Her high-pitched laughter, English accent, and boldness were refreshing; and Gerry felt safe at her house.

She told me: "Joan had not had an easy time being accepted there either. She was compassionate to me and to Mom. 'Franny,' she would say to Mom, 'don't let them bother you!'"

These ways of being "different" were mild and acceptable. The extremes to which she would take them in time were these: She would become an artist. She alone in her family would complete college and earn post-graduate degrees. This sensitive kid would become a psychotherapist.

....

And then there was religion. This is the best example of how Gerry/Jackie embraced the deepest values of her family and society and lived them out in startling–even shocking–ways. She would become a nun, marry a priest, and live a life of evangelical simplicity with her eyes on Jesus. She would especially take *this* value to extremes–as the rest of this book will tell.

Religion of the Catholic flavor was a deep and strong value in the Slovenian culture and Vesel home. Her dad and his friend, Moonk, would talk about it during lunch breaks on the twenty-seventh level of the underground, trying to figure out how to bring up their kids. Every evening at home they all knelt in the living room to pray the family rosary–

"...And the rosary always ended with an add-on prayer that Patsy, Maddie, and I would grow up to be 'good, clean, pure, holy, honest Catholic girls.' They prayed we would become saints. I hoped we would, too! I thought I might feel a whole lot happier than I did."

When she tells of the role of religion in her childhood, there are two faces, one harsh and dark, the other turned toward the light. Listen:

"Despite the heavy-handedness of some of my religious training, where guilt was a primary motivation for being 'good,' something seemed clear to me. The harsh, punishing, never-not-looking-God, whose representatives resembled Him, was not the one I looked to for refuge when all hell broke loose at home. Much more attractive to me was the beautiful, trustworthy, strong, powerful Mother Mary, who could help us out in place of the social worker that we needed so badly. The people I saw around me did not inspire hope. I saw how children were treated, how wives were discounted, how alcohol and anger and rough words wounded. We needed someone to take charge, hold things together and maintain order and safety; but, when I saw someone mistreated, abused and unable to protect themselves, something inside me registered, 'Wrong! Something's wrong here!' Since I was taught that the Holy Mother did not die but was raised, body and soul, into heaven, I thought she was a safer advocate to look to than Jesus, who got crucified.

"I worried about God's punishment, since that was threatened whenever we misbehaved. We often heard–sometimes in Slovenian: 'God punishes!' Yet there was another awareness working its way through. I was always pondering, and a sense of mystery awoke as I sat alone on the grass alongside my family home, with the sun-warmed basement wall at my back and the sun on my face. I listened to the quiet, wondered about my life and tried to figure out how it worked.

"I remember one particular day like this when I was probably about ten. Our next-door neighbor, Mary–Katie's sister–had been killed suddenly in a car crash. She had been my beloved babysitter. No one seemed to think about the impact this would have on us children, and I couldn't imagine a way of telling anyone about the confusion of my feelings. Kata, Rosie and Mom would gather over coffee and go over every detail of the crash, the blood, the closed casket, the preparations for the wake. I was stunned. How could this be? Where is she? Who will take care of us now? I missed her. Imagining what life would be like without her, grief stuck in my throat. The summer sounds around me, the lowing of the cows a few doors down just in from pasture, the buzzing of bees and sounds of birds all formed a consoling backdrop to the quandary that her death presented for me.

"Maybe it was that same summer, I don't remember, but I was awakened one morning by an inner invitation while everyone was still asleep in the house. Someone down the street was already mowing their lawn, and birds were warbling their welcome to the daylight. I crept to the window, leaned my chin on my hands and just listened. An invisible presence filled the atmosphere. Everything seemed exceptionally beautiful and shimmered with light. Kneeling there in awe, I sensed that this ordinary moment became an embrace, a communication of love and of being known which spilled into my heart like soft rain. This presence surrounded me and held everything in its loving embrace. I had no words for this experience and told no one. And, though it did not completely remove the usual tightness in my throat or stomach, a new horizon opened beyond the fence enclosing my world.

"I did not know if anyone else had this sort of experience, though I suspected my devout godmother, Ann, might have, and maybe a few other women I loved. Keenly aware of my mother's agony, I guessed that she would have had a desperate longing for that 'other' reality. I began to take it as my task to be something like this faithful presence to her as well. I recognized our bond as wounded females. I had, after all, created years of grief for her by my birth.

"Fifteen years later, in a moment of recognition while studying religious psychology, I was able to name that numinous moment 'a religious experience.' It seems that I grew lighter at that moment."

Townspeople were church folk and had been brought up on lives of the saints and gospel stories, but those were stories about another land, another time–different. There were few books in her home with which to escape other than a huge red-leather illustrated family bible, seldom opened. One day, all alone in an empty house she opened it and read the story from the Gospel of Luke about Mary's virginal conception. She was incredulous.

"Nobody believes this," she said to herself.

....

"As I grew, I knew there was more to life than what was being offered here and I wanted it. My eyes and heart stayed open; and, when I discovered anything positive, anything at all, I would go for it. I wanted to live my life at a deep level, which left me vulnerable to dissatisfaction and disappointment many times. The story of my infant years, bound in a strait jacket, struggling to wrench free and break out, restrained from crawling then abruptly standing up and toddling, became the myth of my life. Again and again I would want to do that which was deepest in me, to break out, not to toddle but to fly. I wanted to fly!"

Yet this was still Tower-Soudan, where she played with her friend Janie in the woods and down at the spring, walked to the elementary school in Soudan, a mile from her house, on sub-zero winter days when the snow banks had been ploughed to twice her height. Her family went fishing and swimming in Lake Vermilion and picnicking and berry picking. Every day her father and his brothers, descendants of the Slovene miners brought over by the Oliver, went down in the steel cage to the twenty-seventh level, 2341 feet underground, to dig and dynamite and load in the half-dark. On Sundays the family might go for a drive in the country or to visit relatives in Virginia, if other relatives didn't pile into the house after church first. As she grew older, she could walk past the tall mine headframe to McKinley Park to meet friends, swim at the beach, and look out at a most beautiful scene of sky-blue water and islands. There was only one small store, The Club, in Soudan, two Protestant churches. The businesses, shops, grocery store, Catholic church, high school, were all in Tower, two miles away. In high school she was a cheerleader, played the clarinet in band, dated, went to the prom, had a lot of fun. The last two summers of high school she worked at Birchwood Lodge on Lake Vermilion cleaning cabins and was the acknowledged local artist chosen to paint the large billboard sign on the highway advertising the Lodge....

"....And one of the most important events in our lives happened when I was a junior in high school: We had another sister! Jeanne was born on a wintry day when trips to the basketball state tournaments were cancelled because of a blizzard. She grew up alone when Patsy, Maddie, and I were pretty well on our way–but she is still one of my best friends in all the world."

....

Finally came the class of '58 graduation day at Tower-Soudan High School–cap and gown, commencement address, families, diplomas, congratulations, handshakes, hugs, tears. She was conscious of how separate she felt. Some of her friends were going on; but many were staying around here in town, getting jobs, no big plans. Some were already planning marriages. She knew what she was going to do; she had to get out, to travel.

For three years she had been saving her money, first from a paper route, then from the summers at Birchwood Lodge. She had three hundred dollars. Her father had let her know he could not afford to send her to college and that, if she wanted it, she would have to earn her way. She had applied to Gale Institute whose brochure advertised itself as: _"The foremost Communication training center in the United States. Located in the beautiful lake district of Minneapolis, Minnesota. 'Gale' students receive complete specialized training in airline and railroad communications—preparation for a career position."_ She was on her way to a four-month airline school preparing to be an airline stewardess. She was going to fly.

Her father and mother dropped her off at a boarding house for men in Minneapolis, where Gale Institute had lined up a job for her cleaning and cooking in exchange for an apartment in the basement. Her father said, "I've taught you all I know. From now on, you're on your own."

"I wasn't lonely or scared anymore. I was eager! I fixed up the dark apartment, made it pleasant, and decked it out with quotes on paper slips stuck up everywhere from Norman Vincent Peale's best seller, _The Power of Positive Thinking._ I wanted to remember I wasn't going to live in the old way. On Sundays, my day off, I learned how to use the metro buses, find the art galleries, the interesting places to eat, the churches I liked. I took my Brownie camera along and snapped whatever caught my eye.

"Vivian, my landlady and my boss at the boarding house, was kind to me. But she was alcoholic, and sometimes I would come back and find her out of commission. So I would just take over and cook for the guys. There were eleven of them, working or going to college. They were good to me and treated me respectfully. They really liked me and gave me a lot of attention. You know, they made me feel safe and taken care of, like lending me a car or giving me rides to where I needed to go. Things like that. I still think of them—Roland, Mel, Whitey, Bill—especially Skip. I had a crush on Skip."

She says she liked the Gale Institute, made friends right away, and was excited about learning new things. There were classes in teletype, stenography, reservation booking, and charm—that is, how to sit properly, arise from sitting, walk gracefully, and put on makeup. One day she came down the stairs at the boarding house after diligent homework with powder, eyeliner, lipstick, and rouge hoping to catch Skip's eye. He simply said to her, "Gerry, go wash your face. You look better without all that stuff." She says she was not hurt but had to agree. She just turned and did as he said.

The four-month program at Gale ended with a Certificate of Proficiency on January 9, 1959. Only then did she learn that she was too young to be hired by an airline for stewardess training. Even if she waited, she was told, she would not get in because she wore glasses.

So Gerry left Vivian's boarding house, got a full-time job as a secretary at Archer Daniels Midland, and took an apartment near the Art Institute with two friends. The guys from Vivian's would come by at times to hang around or ask them out. Mel dated her at times and was getting serious, but she was not interested. She was interested in Skip, who had just gotten out of the army and was starting college on the GI bill. Skip, however, did not lead her on. Instead, he told her, "Gerry, you are smart. You can do better for yourself than Gale Institute and working at ADM." It was a very important thing for her to hear.

Still, she liked her job at ADM. She knew shorthand, and could type and file. Her bosses let her know she was doing well. Her first boss was Mr. Good, a man true to his name. Late one Friday, however, instead of "Good night," he said "Goodbye, Gerry." That weekend he died. She was aware that he had liked her but was surprised when his family members, who she had no reason to think knew of her existence, came and specifically invited her to the funeral and had her sit with them at the front of the church. The following week, another executive in the office, Mr. Blessing, fired his secretary, who was filing more of her fingernails than her paperwork, and asked Gerry to come work for him.

In September she left Archer Daniels Midland and enrolled as a full-time student in the University of Minnesota. She found her way asking questions, following up on leads, scanning bulletin boards in the halls on campus and lined up part-time jobs tallying data from research questionnaires and holding a desk-job at the university hospital.

She followed wherever her interests led: taking a class on the Bible, ushering at Northrup Auditorium in order to hear live classical music free of charge, joining the Rovers, an outdoor adventure club. The part of her education hardest to negotiate was collegiate sex life 101.

"My classmates and roommates would tell these steamy stories that left me feeling amazed and naive," she told me, smiling and shaking her head. "I wasn't prudish or judgmental–just curious. But I thought, 'That's certainly not the way I am!' And I had a certain sense of shame in recognizing my own lack of experience, a sense of missing something and not knowing enough.

"I observed a *lot* of sexual activity on my outings with the Rovers. I was fascinated, but I was not attracted to join in. There was this one guy that kept coming on to me. I didn't give him any encouragement. Finally he gave up in disgust with a parting insult: 'You're gonna be a nun!'"

"I kept changing majors at the university, trying to find out what I liked, where I wanted to go. I tried interior decorating, dress design, occupational therapy; and, finally, I landed on art–my first love. I just trusted I was being guided. It seemed that there were the right people there at the right time to support me and direct me to the next step, like Mr. Good, and Mr. Blessing, and Skip, who told me I was smart. Then I could take it from there. But what I wished for during my two years at the U was more personal guidance in my education, advisors with whom to talk over what I was learning. It was very hard to get in to talk to a teacher, the university was so huge."

....

In that second year she began to receive unsolicited letters from a Sister Prudentia at St. Scholastica Priory in Duluth, long, personal letters in graceful script. It was puzzling to get these, discretely inquiring whether Gerry might ever be interested in looking into the religious life. She was not interested in being a nun, had never considered such an option. She was enjoying her life at the university, continuing to scan the environment and the horizon for what was next.

She was dating and enjoying being with one man with whom she just clicked. They could talk freely, laugh together, go dancing, have fun. They were both faithful to religious and moral values and could be relaxed with each other. However, that was the problem–religion. He was Seventh Day Adventist, she Roman Catholic; and they saw that there would be no future for them. Reluctantly, they agreed to break it off. She dated another after that who would have pleased her family–stable, traditional, the right religion–but her heart was not in it. He did not come out and say so, but he assumed they were on a track toward marriage. She did not feel it, instead was beginning to feel tense.

The letters kept coming. Gerry answered them politely. Then her date actually mentioned marriage. She felt panicky and told him suddenly, "But I have to go on this retreat in Duluth. I have to go and find out if I should be in the convent!"

She was feeling overwhelmed by the intensity of her life. She did not know how to say no to this guy, did not know what to say on another date with a preacher's son who threw at her, "Don't you know about your church? Don't you know about all those popes who had mistresses and kids?" She didn't. She didn't know how to continue being good in this world, didn't know if she was majoring in the right thing at the U, but did know she didn't want to marry, at least not now!

At the end of the retreat at St. Scholastica Priory, she signed up. When she told her date, he glumly replied, "Well, at least I didn't lose you to another man."

She finished out that quarter at the university and, on September 8, 1961, entered the convent as a postulant. "Postulant" is convent-speak from a Latin word, *postulare,* meaning to request. It is the application stage for a woman inquiring into a career of a lifetime under religious vows. Her parents were very happy. Prayers for "good, clean, pure, holy, honest Catholic girls" seemed on their way to being answered, at least in this daughter. She was safe now, and her relatives were proud. In Tower-Soudan people were saying: "You hear about Gerry Vesel? She's going for nun."

She joined a group of twenty-five postulants that fall, all young women about her age. They wore black dress uniforms with white collars and metal cross pendants, calf-length skirts, black stockings and shoes. They were not yet nuns, but college girls attending classes with all the female lay students at the College of St. Scholastica. Gerry completed her junior year this way and found her true academic home by continuing to major in art. Sister Cabrini was their Postulant Mistress, a gentle, good woman, who oriented this group to the convent culture and oversaw the early stages of their spiritual formation. Gerry responded with eagerness and soon began having strong spiritual experiences. She was much taken with a thin book, *Mr. Blue,* by Myles Connolly, a 1928 novel about "...a gent who is so happy he is almost crazy." The foreword says,

Some years ago it was written of Mr. Blue:
It is impossible to be with him an hour without breathing a new wholesome
air, charged with beauty. It is impossible to be with him and not catch the
spectacular glory of the present moment. At the power of his presence, be-
fore the eloquence of his eyes, poverty, neglect, and such trifles become as

nothing. One feels bathed in a brilliant and even tangible light, for it is the light he sees, and which, he would have us believe, is about us on our gallant journey toward death. All the scales of pettiness fall off the soul. The spirit stands up, clean, shining, valiant, in an unconscious effort to match his. But then he is gone, with his tears and laughter and his dazzling glory. 'Come, come' his eyes say. 'Behold the perilous road!' No one follows, I believe. And sometimes I wonder if he cares. 'You will die, stifled with comfortability and normality, choked by small joys and small sorrows.' Such is his warning as he goes. What can a man do with a fellow like that?

....

This was the life she wanted. This spoke to her soul. In this, she knew, lay the answers to the melancholy of her childhood and the excited uncertainties of life in the city. She began to feel herself breathing "wholesome air, charged with beauty," and to experience a new sense of belonging. Here was a new family, and not only a crowd of sisters with aspirations like her own but a mother who guided and directed them under the fifteen-hundred-year stability of the Rule given by Father Benedict. She had indeed embarked on her own "gallant journey toward death," and her frequent thoughts about death now took on transformed currency. She thought she would die young like St. Therese the Little Flower. Postulant Mistress Sister Cabrini, a very practical woman, was dismayed at such strong feeling, uncertain about how to direct it.

At the close of the academic year in June, the postulants' request for admission to the order was granted. In a joyous ceremony, all twenty-five filed into the chapel in flowing, white dresses with gauzy wedding veils pinned to their hair to signify that they would now be "brides of Christ." During the ceremony dedicating them as novice nuns of the Order of Saint Benedict, they left the sanctuary to lay aside the wedding dress in a private side-room, then re-entered the chapel wearing shoe-length black dresses and long, white veils, which completely covered their hair, along with wimple and coif–stiffly starched fabric wrapping forehead, ears, and neck.

They were given new names. Gerry had been attracted to the biblical prophet, Jeremiah, and was inclined to choose his as her new name in religious life. It was common for nuns to adopt male names. The prioress herself was Mother Athanasius. Others in this group chose Stephen,

Edward, John Bosco, Justin, and one even took the Italian family name of the late pope: Pacelli. Gerry almost went from Geraldine to Jeremiah; but one of the other nuns from a family of artists suggested her own sister's name: Jackie (Jensen, later Dingman). To be named for an artist rather than a prophet was more appealing. She took the name Sister Jacqueline.

It was a gala affair with singing and feasting and the cheer of family afterward, a gloriously happy day. Sister Jacqueline's parents were there with her sisters, Pat, Maddie and Jeanne, her relatives, and her childhood friend, Janie, with her new husband, Bill. Maddie herself would be following her into the convent in the next few years. Eight-year-old Jeanne was thrilled with this strange place, a vast, grey, stone building like a towered castle on a hill, high above Duluth, looking down over the city and out to the glistening expanse of Lake Superior. There were beautiful grounds, flowers, shaded paths into the woods, long, polished hallways, formal sitting rooms with elegant furniture and even a three-lane bowling alley in the basement. But Jeanne hated the strict rules that would not let her sister wear some colorful clothes or come home for visits. In fact her sister would be entering cloistered seclusion for the next twelve months, a period called "novitiate."

Novitiate was a time for reflection, spiritual education, and deeper adaptation to the monastic disciplines. Novices took the year off from college and focused on religious studies: Benedict's Holy Rule, the Benedictine tradition, the meaning of the vows, Scripture, and lives of the saints. They were assigned daily tasks of manual labor–cleaning, laundry, gardening, assisting in the kitchen. They surrendered possession of personal property, did not leave the monastery enclosure, submitted in holy obedience to the directives of superiors. They were instructed to confess infractions of the rule, no matter how small or unintended, by "going before the cross," which meant kneeling and publicly naming wrongdoing before the assembled sisters.

They also developed warm friendships, laughed and sang. They had time for long walks on the lovely grounds, past the cemetery, where plain headstones in rows marked the passing of a century of nuns, along an outdoor stations-of-the-cross, past Our Lady's grotto shrine, to the brink of a hill above The Valley of Silence, which marked the boundary of the priory grounds. They were a lively group of young women, not easy for the Novice Mistress to bring to heel. They put on plays for the benefit of the older nuns and sometimes slipped in cheeky messages as a protest against stodginess and formalism–like their skit based on the gospel story of The Man Born Blind.

Novices entered the novitiate ready to adapt to the convent system and eager for its program of spiritual formation. As they became more comfortable, they began to assert themselves. Some remained docile and embraced its comforting Catholic piety. Jacqueline, however, experienced there a heightened spiritual awareness which broke into the religiosity of her early life and was drawn to sisters seeking an adventurous spirituality more suited to the times.

Yet the regimen of convent life, with its stress on self-abnegation and conformity, imposed such uniform structure that she would later tell me, "You go in as a grownup and they infantilize you." Had this been a developmental strategy, a form of boot camp on the way to seasoned competence, it might have been an effective approach to the formation of mature women. However, conformity was too often an end in itself. The conflict between adaptation and exploration left her once again disquieted, unsure about how she fit in this new home.

That tension was relieved once she entered the next stage. Juniorate was a trial period of living the vows for three years. It began with the day of First Profession, the first time they took vows to live as nuns in the order. The white novice veil was replaced by a black veil indicating that they were now fully monastic nuns. Jacqueline resumed her studies in the College of Saint Scholastica, and a world of opportunity, resources, and mentoring opened to her.

"I had excellent teachers," she told me with evident joy at these memories that day I interviewed her in Ely. "I had terrific courses: Art, American Lit, Music, Western Culture, Philosophy, Biblical Studies. All the things my soul longed for–which I had never been offered before. I drank it like water!

"I had a regulated life, time to study, small classes. I could just walk down the hall from the priory to get to the classrooms. All our meals were provided. I didn't have to juggle two or three jobs to stay in school. I was out of the dating game and could focus on what I truly loved."

Her goals were clear; she knew what she would be when she grew up. It was a time of deep satisfaction and joy. Her favorite subjects were Art and Sacred Scripture where she had some of her best teachers.

Sister Mary Charles, a highly gifted woman, who already at that time was gaining a national reputation in religious art, was her primary art teacher. She recognized Jacqueline's passion and potential very early and began a mentor relationship that would last more than forty years. Until Jacqueline lost this dear friend, only a few months ago, the two of them still worked side-by-side in Sister Molly's (Mary Charles) Subiaco Studio in Duluth, painting religious icons in the traditional styles of the Eastern Orthodox Church.

"And at Scholastica I had art materials and studio space provided free–just like when my mom and dad provided me with art materials at home because they could see how much I loved it! I would lose myself in the studio, absorbed in painting and sculpting so that I did not notice the bells and forgot to go to meals and prayers."

One day Mother Athanasius called her in and said that Sister Noemi Weygant wanted her for an apprentice. Noemi was a unique character in this place. She had married, raised children, divorced, converted to Catholicism, and entered the convent. A professional photographer with a body of published work, she was assertive, dramatic, and unconcerned about tidiness or decorum. Jacqueline found her a breath of fresh air, someone who had lived a full life out in the world before settling here. Soon Jacqueline was learning camera equipment, darkroom techniques, setup, style, framing, selection of shots. They went on extended nature shoots equipped with the best cameras and an unlimited supply of film. "Shoot, shoot, shoot," she was told. "Don't worry about how much film you burn; that is the only way to learn!"

One summer Noemi took her along to spend a week on the Minnesota-Canada border doing a photo study of old Fort St. Charles for a book she was working on. By this time Jacqueline was in a modified habit-short veil, hair showing, white blouse, black skirt. She met a young man her age, nephew of a priest who was there.

"His name was Jim," she said. "We spent a lot of time talking. I took his picture on the dock. My hormones were active. He invited me to see him again at his sister's wedding later in the summer. I got permission to go–in full habit. When he saw me in full habit, he was shocked, and he got drunk. Then *I* was disgusted, and the bubble burst. It was probably good for me, this brief revisit of the life I thought I had left behind."

There were two other sisters who were very influential in Jacqueline's life at this time. Sister Elodie was their Juniorate Mistress, and Jackie says she was "a lifesaver." Elodie was wise, cultured, and inspiring. She had just returned from a year of study at Lumen Vitae in Brussels, one of the centers of theological renewal in Europe. She brought back the excitement of reform that was coming from the Second Vatican Council in Rome. The sisters of her order in Duluth were negotiating an uncertain transition from the cautious style of enclosed religious life toward a more daring engagement with the modern world. Some of the sisters, however, were resisting this and struggling to reassert custom and rigidity.

"We saw Elodie as our hope," Jackie said. "Her death was a great sadness."

The other influence was Sister Ambrose. Her given name was Annette Marsnik, and she had entered the convent as a postulant only a few months after Gerry and was part of her group. However, when other sisters were still taking college classes, Sister Ambrose was on the college faculty in the philosophy department. She had a superb philosophical education, a brilliant mind, and an engaging personality.

"Ambrose and I were drawn to each other from the outset. We were both Slovenian, she was from Ely and I was from Soudan. We just liked each other. She offered these philosophy seminars and invited her favorite people. I was one of them. Ambrose taught me a great deal and gave me books to read and encouraged my own natural idealism with her own. Elodie, you know, did not approve of Ambrose–worried about her enthusiasms and seductive influence. But her strong intellect and her charisma protected her from censure by some of the older nuns."

It is interesting about these two nuns who were so important to Jacqueline. I had met them both before I knew her. Sister Elodie I had met briefly when she and I were both studying in Belgium during the Second Vatican Council. Sister Ambrose and I had become good friends and colleagues soon after I was ordained. Sister Ambrose had the makings of a reformer. She was a paradoxical figure, calling for high thoughts and noble actions to address the needs of the world, while urging a return to the basic teachings of the gospel and to the contemplative ideals of her order's sixth century founder. She eventually did lead the beginnings of a reform and was granted leave to found a small contemplative branch of the order with two other nuns three miles north of her hometown, Ely. I was part of that endeavor briefly. However, that will be told later when I give my own story.

....

Entering the convent had closed down Jacqueline's outer life so that her inner life could thrive. However, during her third year in the Juniorate, she was suddenly sent out to replace an elementary school teacher in Virginia, a small town seventy miles north.

Stepping in at midyear, she was to teach fourth grade at Marquette School, sixth grade art and eighth grade French. She had not been trained in elementary education. She had not yet graduated from college. She did not know French. God, she was assured, would give the necessary graces.

So she went north from the vibrant, expansive priory to join a few nuns in a small house and began to teach. She liked the children, taught them with play and music and art, and stayed one chapter ahead of her French class. However, she told me, it was a very stressful move:

"I developed severe allergies and asthma. I had to improvise without training. I felt pushed beyond my abilities in replacing a nun who had been a crackerjack teacher. And I missed the energy of the College and being able to spend time in the art studio. In a matter of a week or so I had been sent, without experience, into a tight space with a group of highly focused teachers, who were helpful but busy with their own full schedules. We were in the public eye in a small town, and I felt I didn't fit. But that changed when I met Art and Bev Dale and their multi racial family. They felt like home to me. As important as that relationship was, I could never have guessed how important it would become later–a stepping stone to life far more open and unpredictable.

"I returned to the priory that summer to graduate from college and make my Final Profession. I made permanent vows as a Sister of the Order of St. Benedict. I was given a ring to wear as sign of this lifelong commitment.

"Then, after a second year at Marquette School, I was transferred to Our Lady of Victory in Minneapolis. Art Dale was now an associate pastor at Hope Lutheran Church down there, so I got back in touch with him and his family. They seemed *real*–less formal and contrived in the way they went about a life of religion and service.

"At that same time I continued my friendship with Ellen Kean, a young psychologist I had met at my Aunt Ann's house in Tower the previous summer. Ellen also lived in Minneapolis, and we became very good friends. She was open and creative and curious about the world. This is what she wanted to encourage in me, giving me books, as Ambrose had, but of a different sort, taking me to avant-garde theater, nudging me during our long conversations into a more psychological analysis of who I was and what I wanted. When we had come to know each other well and were very close, Ellen said to me one day: 'Jacqueline, you don't belong there.' I calmly answered: 'I will never leave!'"

....

The following year she was transferred to St. Rose of Lima School in Proctor where she taught first, second, and fourth grades, and fifth and sixth grade art. Proctor was an old railroad town not far from Duluth, and the nuns who taught there commuted daily from St. James Convent in West Duluth. By this time she had developed skill and confidence as a teacher and greater freedom of movement in her personal life–although this brought her into conflict with the house superior at St. James.

The lifestyle of nuns had changed dramatically in a few years. For a while they wore modified black habits, later short colored suits with short colored veils. Eventually, no veil, printed blouses, plain skirts, and a cross pendant to indicate that they were sisters. Formerly they could expect to work either as nurses or teachers. Now some were pastoral workers or chaplains; others were going into social work. This required more specialized education, and many went away for a season by themselves for training. They had colleagues, friendships, and social life no longer restricted to the sisterhood. Although these changes were never completely adopted at the priory up on the hill by the older nuns, who were still in long black veil and ankle-length habit, most sisters out in the field, like Jacqueline, had taken to the newer dress and lifestyle. At St. Rose School, she was indistinguishable from the female lay teachers, except for the Benedictine cross pendant and ring she wore.

She had become good at working with children. By this time, she had taught every elementary grade in some capacity and was a relaxed, fun, and caring teacher. However, during that second year at St Rose, she was having problems with a few out-of-control children in her class-room. She couldn't settle them–impulsive, running around, in and out of their seats all the time. Someone suggested the local mental health center. She phoned for help.

A week later a worker from the center's Child Team came to observe Sister Jacqueline's classroom and advise. Connie Burdick taught her about attention deficit and hyperactivity, then teamed with her to set up effective group work, integrating the problem children into the class-room activity. Jacqueline took to this approach at once, and it worked.

It was the beginning of another relationship whose later importance she could never have imagined: Connie would remain her friend for years, would one day get her a job, babysit her daughter, and eventually support her through a crisis in her marriage.

....

Meanwhile, Jacqueline's father was slowly dying:

Dear Sister,

I'd better write to you and let you know that Maddy is coming up the 8ᵗʰ of Nov to take us to Mpls–Daddy has to have cobalt treatments on his neck. So I don't know how many or how long we'll be gone–he's in good spirits and he eats well so that's a good thing Jeanne has to have her eyes checked again, got a slip from the school so Ann will take her the 20ᵗʰ we'll be in Mpls then–Tona will stay here at our house as he did last time–I just don't know how I hold up I'm so blasted nervous–Maddy said she has an ulcer in her stomache–I hope it doesn't turn into anything serious–worry worry all the time....write to Jeannie cheer her up. Write to Ann & Tona & thank them for taking care of the house & Jeanne–pray for us–I'm really a nervous wreck–but I won't crack as I need to keep daddy's spirits up–he's doing great...Julie takes us down to get the treatment–she's been wonder-ful–thank her for being so kind also Morrie...Well Sister God bless you and write Julie a letter thanking her for going through all this for us all–cheer her up–Love from us both–Mom & dad X X X X

....

There was a lot of other dying. 1968 opened with the Tet Offensive in Vietnam, the long, bloody turning point in the war. In March President Lyndon Johnson almost lost the New Hampshire Primary to anti-war candidate Eugene McCarthy; and, by the end of that month, Johnson announced he would no longer seek reelection. On April 4th Martin Luther King was assassinated, on June 5th Robert F. Kennedy. The cities were burning: Detroit, Newark, Baltimore in 1967, Washington, Chicago, Cleveland in 1968.

She heard the news as an onlooker, not grasping the forces and issues of the national paroxysm. Her friend, Ellen, was going to Chicago that summer to work with gang youth in the inner city and wanted Jacqueline to join her. Ellen was urging her to learn about what was happening in the country, to get involved, at least to photo-study the crisis. Jacqueline wanted to go and asked permission:

"Oh, no, Sister, that's much too dangerous!"

....

So she spent a safe and quiet summer–and in the fall continued the every-bit-as-dangerous inner journey by attending a weekend Welch Center Seminar.

The Duluth Diocese owned a large, old building in West Duluth which had been remodeled as a live-in retreat center, primarily for church youth programs. Recently, however, the Welch Center had also begun to bring in adult church leaders to catch the popular wave of T-groups, also called "sensitivity groups," a social psychology movement pioneered by the National Training Laboratory over the preceding twenty years. There was no formal religious content to these weekends for twenty participants; rather the focus was on group dynamics and experiential learning. In break-out small groups, the emphasis was on getting in touch with feelings, sharing of innermost thoughts and disclosing vulnerabilities, giving and accepting confrontation, reconciliation and bonding. Participants were nudged into dropping masks and moving past their roles toward personal truth-telling . "Authentic" was the buzzword.

Although she had been denied permission to go to Chicago, perhaps her superiors were underestimating the consequences of the venture into her own inner-city. She continued to participate in Sister Ambrose's exciting philosophy seminars. She read J. B. Phillips's *Your God is Too Small.*

She was reading the existentialists and taking in a compelling new view of the world.

She and a few other sisters would occasionally go across town for Sunday Mass to hear a young priest preach who was causing a great fuss with his outspoken opposition to the war in Vietnam. He talked about resistance to the culture, the radical message of the gospel, oppression of the poor and even mentioned in church that the great cities of America were on fire. She found his sermons interesting–he was saying something....

.....I had met Sister Jacqueline several times in passing but did not really know her. The first time was in 1966. She came into my seventh-hour religion class when I was a first-year priest teaching at the Catholic high school in Duluth. She appeared at the classroom door at the end of the day asking if she might take a few photos for the yearbook. She was in full habit, black and white head to toe. Gordy Hautaoja was hunched over in a front-row desk, head down on his crossed arms, sleeping. Gordy and I had an understanding: He was Lutheran not Catholic, he said, and his parents weren't Catholic. He was the only kid in my class of sophomore boys who wasn't Catholic. So he did not have to learn this stuff. I saw his point and, day after day, let him snooze. After all, it *was* the seventh hour, and I was completely wasted myself. So after getting my okay, this nun sweeps into the room and the first thing she does is go close up to sleeping Gordy and–flash! Gordy rears up, squints around, glares at her and shouts: "Get that dame out of here!" (No Catholic kid would have said that.) That was Sister Jacqueline.

I met her a few more times here and there. I remember sitting across a table from her once or twice in Sister Ambrose's philosophy seminar. I remember giving Ambrose and Renata a ride from Ely to Duluth once; and, as we passed Soudan, Ambrose told Renata, "This is where Jackie is from." I did not know who Sister Jackie was, couldn't place her. That would change.

THREE
·············

Philip / Father Solem

My mother told me this story about her father:

Ed Quinn sat on the porch reading a newspaper he had just received in the mail from a town at the other end of the state. He had written three weeks earlier requesting a current issue and had sent money. What was the character of this Ely, he wanted to know, this place so far into the backwoods of northern Minnesota? His daughter had applied there, so far away, for a teaching job. Eddy Quinn had always been protective of his three girls, a strict guardian of their faith and morals. He especially wanted to know if Mildred would be among Catholics up there. That was important.

The porch was the striking feature of the big house, running around three sides in the Southern style, built by his father after moving to south-ern Minnesota from Alabama at the end of the Civil War. Ed Quinn's Irish immigrant father, Michael Quinn, had been a Confederate soldier in the First Alabama Mounted Cavalry and later was transferred to a gunboat in Mobile Bay. Just before enlisting, Michael Quinn had married Margaret Shea, but the marriage had almost not taken place, not because she was unwilling but because she was lucky to be alive. When Margaret was arriving from Ireland as a young girl in the company of an aunt and three children, their ship had foundered in a storm as it approached Mobile and began to sink. She fought the captain who was trying to put her into a lifeboat, separating her from her aunt and cousins; so he pushed her back onto the ship and put someone else in her place. That lifeboat capsized in the storm, and all on it were drowned. The ship itself managed to hold together.

My mother always told me I was "a bit of a rebel." Did I, Philip, inherit some of the rebel streak of my great-great aunt? Combined with that of her husband, the rebel soldier? Well, if Margaret Shea had not rebelled, if she had gone along with the captain and gotten into that lifeboat, I would not have inherited anything. I would not be here.

So Ed Quinn was scanning the paper to see if this Ely showed any signs of Catholicism. His concern was understandable. Mildred had a teaching certificate from the Mankato State Teachers College and already had three years experience, first in Butterfield, then in Blue Earth. However, finding jobs was not easy. She was told: "We have a hard time placing Catholics in southern Minnesota." Once she had received a call expressing interest in her; but, when they asked her religion and learned she was Catholic, they turned her down. She had been hired in Blue Earth because "it is a Catholic town."

Her father was trying to guess the nationalities of the names he came across in the Ely paper and noticed that many names ended in *a* and *i* and *o*, the way Italian names do.

"Maybe it'll be all right, Mary," he called in through the open window to my grandmother. "No Irish names, but it looks like there are quite a few of these Roman Catholic Italians there. I see here a Salo–and a Lampi, Rautio, Koppala, Jussila, Maki...lots of Italians."

Mildred went north to Ely where the pay was good and the mining companies built fine schools. She had been making $100 a month in Blue Earth, now $125 a month in Ely. She married Art Solem, a Norwegian Lutheran mining engineer.

....

My sister and brother were born during the Depression. My dad used to tell me, "We didn't know where our next meal was coming from," which I thought an outrageous exaggeration, for he was an engineer and captain at the Zenith underground mine and never was out of work the whole time.

I was born at the end of the Depression, November 6, 1939, when World War II was only two months old. I have a lot of memory fragments about the war, which continued for the next six years. I can still hear my dad strolling through the house singing slightly off-key "Coming in on a wing and a prayer..." and "Underneath the lamppost by the garden gate...with you, Lili Marlene." Years later, when I was a seminary student in Bavaria, I learned that our enemies had been singing this song at the same time: "Vor der Kaserne, vor dem groszen Tor, stand eine Laterne... wie einst, Lili Marlene...."

I can still see the cartoon drawing of Japs–Tojo, Hirohito, others–with their narrow, slanty eyes and foolish buck teeth. I remember my mother flattening tin cans while she cooked; later we would call this recycling, but then it was called the war effort. One of my favorite toys went to the war effort. At three years of age I sat alone in the yard in my rusty mini-car, which had a working steering wheel and push pedals. It had been thrown up against the scrap metal pile to be hauled away and melted down for victory. Later, when I taught English in Japan, I would tell my adult students this story, tell them that perhaps portions of my childhood car were now in their country, having arrived as bomb casing. Their eyes would widen. "O-o-o-oh," they would say.

And still today–the sound of bells, church bells ringing all at once all over Ely, and a young woman sitting on the stoop in the back yard sobbing.

"Why's she crying, Mom?"

"She's happy, dear. She's crying because the war is over."

V-J Day–Osaka, Tokyo, Hiroshima, Nagasaki–sixty-one years later, and I am having trouble seeing these words on the screen as I type–my chest shakes, my eyes blur, and my face is wet with tears.

On Sunday mornings very early my mom and dad would take us fishing, always it seemed to Half-way, the overhead-metal-girder bridge on the Kawishiwi River. I did not like fishing. I never caught any. I read comics in the car. When we came home, Dad would clean the fish and lay the walleye steaks out on wax paper, pepper and salt them, and wait for Mom and us kids to come home from Mass. Dad was Lutheran, and they did not have to go to church unless they wanted to. We were Catholics; it was a mortal sin if we didn't go.

During the week my dad worked as captain at the mine, which could be a nerve-wracking job. Once the mine caught fire and he spent seventy-two hours without sleep coordinating the fight. He said that fire took a good ten years off his life. He was always being called out in the middle of the night because the pumps were down and pockets of the mine flooding. One month he was sent over to the Tower-Soudan Underground to fill in for their captain who was out sick. It is likely that he worked with Matt Vesel, the father of the woman I would marry.

My mom was not teaching school anymore; she was raising us kids. We went to the ice cream parlor called Buffalo's and snuck into the basement of the Methodist church. I had playmates with funny names: Erickson (no first name), Billy Bunny (actual name) and Dickie Dollar (Methodist Pastor Dollar's son). My brother, Quinn, took me to the show often, and we watched Charlie Chan movies, but he complained to our parents: "I don't know why I have to take that guy (me) to the show! He always wants me to explain it to him on the way home. He never knows what it's about!"

When I was almost seven, we moved to Fraser Location, a different part of the Iron Range. My dad had been promoted to be superintendent of the Fraser Underground. There were only thirty-four houses in Fraser, no stores, no businesses. It was two miles to town. I was greeted by the neighborhood boys about my age, who hung around the yard silently as the movers shifted our furniture and boxes into our new house, leased from the Oliver Mining Company.

They asked if I wanted to join their club. I said I did. They took me two blocks away, behind Hooper's barn, and said I had to fight them if I wanted to join their club. So I fought them, one at a time. We hit each other in the face, punched in the chest, grabbed and choked and thrashed and rolled around on the ground. Then the oldest one said, "Okay, now get up and shake hands. That's the way we do it." So I shook hands all around, and I was in the club.

These were my best friends with whom I roamed the woods, built shacks, lit grass fires, stole apples and broke into the basement of the Fraser Clubhouse.

Fighting continued to be part of my life; but, unlike this initiation, I did it in anger. I was quick to flare up and often flailed at boys older and larger. I nearly always lost. Quinn complained to our parents: "I don't want to take this guy (me) to the basketball games in town anymore! He's always picking a fight with some bigger kid, and then I have to stick up for him." When I came home scraped, chest reddened from punches, my mother would wail, "Oh, Art! He's hurt!" My dad would say, "Did you lick him?" And I would start to blubber, "He got me down and pinned my arms, and I couldn't move!" Then Dad would show me how I should have pulled my arms to my sides while quickly twisting my body face-down so I could push up against the kid with my back, and so on.

Stevie Boubon was my best friend, and I am sure I did not fight him. I think I tried once when he swore at me, but he ran away before I could get hold of him. Too bad, because I might have won that fight. Stevie stuttered, and he was blond and short and cute, and he could spell "Czechoslovakia" in a rapid-fire, non-stuttering performance for the older girls in the bleachers at basketball games, who would laugh and clap and tell him to do it again! and I would yell that I could do it, too, and would loudly spell it out; but they did not even look at me.

Charlie Lund was my other best friend; for, in addition to being Tom Sawyer-Huck Finn boys, Stevie, Charlie, and I were aspiring scholars. We spent nearly as much time tracing maps of countries around the world, memorizing capitals, and reading encyclopedias, as we did exploring the woods and constructing rafts on ponds left behind by mammoth mining machinery. Our games of acted-out warfare were taken from history. The covered deck attached to my house, with its low railings on three sides, made a perfect pirate ship from which we could attack or be attacked and fall to our many deaths with lingering groans. In the winter we were Athenians fighting Spartans and vice versa, hurling sharp-pointed spears into the high snow banks mounded up by the snowploughs and pulling our spears out of the slain as we ran to the top (ten or twelve feet high) to finish the job and yell victory! We were Indians. There were never any cowboys, just Indians, but we were Sioux or Ojibway or Algonquin or Cree or Huron and that also meant warfare; although it more often meant living peaceably in the woods and fashioning shelter out of supple branches and fire pits and bows and arrows and containers out of birch-bark. We fancied ourselves great trackers, moving silently through the woods, scanning, scanning. But always we returned to the books and the Classic Comics which fed this play. We spent a lot of time with one another in silence.

My mother would say, "It's a beautiful day. Why don't you boys go outside and play?" and we wouldn't look up, wouldn't answer, just kept scanning, scanning, turning pages.

My hero during these days was Thomas Edison. I read his biography from the grade school library and thought it the best book I had ever read. I wanted to be an inventor, that would be a fine job to have, so I was always making things like Blue Beauty, a boy-size push car cobbled together out of slats, reminiscent of the metal one I had as a three-year-old which probably went to Japan. And I made puppets and a dog cart so my dog could haul the newspapers I delivered and rapiers and spear-heads and wooden dueling pistols like those used in Alexandre Dumas's *Corsican Brothers* Classic Comic.

There were actual inventions. The best one was a hand-held wooden base with a tiny compass swivel and a sighting tube. I took it to my dad, who as usual, was playing solitaire at a card table beside his large floor-model Zenith radio, which had a circular glass dial face the size of a dinner plate with lots of Hz numbers and short wave bands with actual names of overseas countries.

The surprise in his voice, as he examined my device, was the best praise I could have received. "This is a surveying instrument!" he exclaimed.

My poor brother, Quinn, had to share the bedroom with me and complained there was no room for his stuff. I had a fleet of model airplanes bobbing from the ceiling on string, one wall covered with flags of all nations copied in color crayon from the encyclopedia, a museum collection of clam shells and railroad spikes and layered stones–and, covering the dresser-top, an altar–a replica of a Catholic altar with a gothic high-back of steeples and spikes and niches for statues of saints. There was a tiny open missal book on a miniature book stand, three altar cards with Latin words on them propped against the back, an awkward wooden chalice on a white linen altar cloth which my mom had sewn for me. Beside the altar I had carved a faceless statue of the Blessed Virgin Mary out of balsa wood.

I do not remember when I started getting religious. When I made the altar I had no idea that I wanted to be a priest. It was just one of the many things I was interested in, like drawing, and painting and writing stories and reading everything from Herodotus to books on first-aid and etiquette. When grownups asked what I wanted to be when I grew up, my standard answer was: "Either a miner or a monk or an inventor." But I do not recall having any fantasies of being a priest until I was about ten.

I went to public school in Chisholm, and the nuns came for the first two weeks of summer vacation to teach "religious instruction." I liked that; they told interesting stories about saints and miracles and taught us hymns, and we walked into church in procession. During the school year, the public school let us out early on Wednesdays to go for "release time" to the church of our parents' choice, and we Catholics had to memorize the Baltimore Catechism, things such as the definition of the Sacrament of Extreme Unction. I did not like that so much, but I was pretty good at it.

Religious discussion was very big in my home. My mother and my sister and I talked for hours about church beliefs and rules. My brother, Quinn, had other interests. My dad had his own religion called Lutheranism, but he only practiced it at home and never once went to a Lutheran church. He liked to get up early in the morning and say his prayers at the kitchen table, did not like anyone to bother him at that hour. He recited the Our Father in Swedish, learned from his mother. He had a long list of people he prayed for every day, and the list only got longer as he got older because he was rather superstitious about dropping anyone off the list.

Dad was a thirty-second-degree Mason and had been Master of the Lodge in Ely, but he did not have anything to do with Masons after we moved to Fraser. Dad and I talked a lot about religion, and I tried to convert him to Catholicism, because I knew that was my duty. He had respect for our beliefs and our church. At times he was quite sentimental about the songs like "Lovely Lady, dressed in blue, teach us how to pray," and he wished he could pray the rosary. It was strange, because we had learned that Masons were the enemy of the Catholic Church, and masonry was forbidden to us because it was a secret society. A masonic magazine called *The New Age*, published by the Scottish Rite in South Carolina came to the house every month or two. It looked a bit like a *National Geographic*, about the same size, always a yellow border around the cover. Dad threw it in the trash at once when it arrived; he was ashamed of it because nearly every other page had the words "Roman Catholic" and "pope"on them, never favorably. Some of his thick-bound masonic books were on the bookshelves along with novels and encyclopedias.

We were not to read them. Surprisingly I obeyed. I must have looked once or twice, but not for long. There was a lot of Egyptian stuff there and pictures of carpenter's squares and an eye on top of a pyramid such as you see on the back of a dollar bill. I asked Dad to tell me about the Masons. He insisted they did only good and that he would never belong to an organization that would hurt the church of us kids or our mother. I asked what they did at his initiation and at the lodge meetings. He said solemnly: "That, my boy, is something you will never know." I was awed by that place of mystery withheld, that part of my father's life under oath taken long ago.

When I was ten I knew I wanted to be a priest. No one suggested it to me. I told my parents and said I wanted to go to the seminary after I had finished high school. They said all right. I was not thinking monk any more, I was thinking to be a parish priest. The idea stayed; it did not waver. Then, one winter evening–I was twelve or thirteen now–while I was doing my paper route, the thought came to me: I don't have to wait. I could go to the seminary next fall. I went home and told my mother. An expression of deep sadness dropped across her face. She quietly asked me some questions, then called my dad in and told him what I had told her. He was not happy, but he did not object. I don't remember what happened next; but on September 8, 1953, they delivered me to the Crosier Seminary at Onamia, Minnesota, about a hundred miles from our home.

....

This was the first step of a twelve-year program. The first six years (four high school, two college) was the minor seminary, a prep school for boys interested in becoming priests. Major seminary would be two years of college philosophy plus four years of postgraduate theology. The Crosier minor seminary was run by a religious order from the Netherlands, and the building–a monastery wing for the priests and brothers and a prep school wing for the boys–looked as though it had been flown over from old Bruges or Rotterdam. It was a peaceful place with open spaces and sport fields, next to a lake and a small town. Seventeen priests ran the school. The fifteen lay brothers were, in effect, servants.

There were forty-four in my high school freshman class. Of these, only five of us would be ordained priests twelve years later. This is not surprising, given the reality that we forty-four were only thirteen or fourteen years old when we started, faced a very demanding academic gauntlet, and would have to forego marriage and offspring if we were ever to make it to the end. Our days were tightly scheduled from early rising to lights-out at 9:30 P.M. We slept in two large, open dormitories, bed-locker-bed-locker down long rows. Once we left the dormitory for early morning meditation and Mass in the chapel, we were not allowed back there until "the grand silence," a half-hour of total quiet before bed-time during which we moved about as in a silent film, brushing teeth, washing up, putting on pyjamas, until the dorm lights went out and only the stealthy shadow of the Father Prefect slowly patrolled the aisles.

The weekdays were spent in classrooms and study halls with plenty of time for outdoor sports, indoor hobbies, school clubs and casual fun. We did not wear uniforms, but there was a dress code requiring dress pants, a shirt and tie, and a sport jacket or sweater. For the most part the atmosphere in the school was open, energetic, and sunny. The priests supervised closely but without a heavy hand, and most of them were young-to-middle-aged, friendly, available, and attractive role models.

We were given a first-rate classical education with strong stress on both the humanities and the sciences. Of course, Latin, "the language of the Church," was daily fare during all six years, with both classical and biblical Greek added in our two college years. With enrollment between 150 and 200, it was easy to get to know the entire student body and to make special friends quickly. We were only allowed to go home for visits during Christmas and Easter breaks and summer vacation; so the seminary became our world.

What made this form of prep school unique was the emphasis on religion and spiritual formation. All of us had come there of our own choice to become priests. It was assumed we all shared a common goal. Most would eventually change their minds and leave; but those who stayed were there for one thing, the priesthood. So we were introduced to daily spiritual reading–books on prayer, virtue, the lives of the saints, but seldom the Bible. We were taught various modalities of mental prayer–the Ignatian method, the Sulpician method, the Carmelite method. Frequently during the day, we would pop into the chapel for a "visit to the Blessed Sacrament," that is, a short period of silent prayer. Indeed, so much time was spent kneeling in chapel that we developed what my family members laughingly called "seminarian's knees," when they saw me at vacation time. I had developed pronounced calluses on my kneecaps, tough, scaly formations.

There was strong focus on devotions to the Blessed Virgin Mary; and the clubs one could join at the school included the Sodality of Mary, the Marian Committee, and a sub-group of "slaves of Mary," who studied the *True Devotion to the Blessed Virgin,* a book by a seventeenth century French saint. There was group and private recitation of the rosary and reminders of "the first Saturdays: confession, communion, rosary, and fifteen minutes meditation to console the Immaculate Heart of Mary." Nearly everyone belonged to some chapter of the Apostleship of Prayer and the Catholic Students Mission Crusade.

There was no Pep Club, no prom committee; but there were intramural and extramural sports, and the Crosier Knights basketball team did very well against public high school teams. We had road trips with our chorus and our speech competition teams; so we were not entirely isolated.

I experienced Crosier as a happy, wholesome world. However, girls and women were not part of it. There was little freedom to develop our sexual awareness and desires. I do not recall that this was even a covert part of the conversations among us boys. The priests gave us talks about how to deal with "temptations" and "impure thoughts," and generally counseled keeping busy, daily examination of conscience, and going to confession weekly. We had no opportunity to fall into actual sexual sin with a girl; however, the sin of masturbation was a danger that was always at hand. Occasionally they would warn against "particular friendships," the codeword for homosexual activity; but this caveat was so obscure and featureless that I hardly knew what they were talking about.

It is safe to say that wholesome sexual development was not one of the strengths of our happy, wholesome education. The priests themselves had been raised in a church and a clerical tradition with entrenched, negative attitudes toward women and sexuality. Much of the sexual sickness at the heart of Catholicism would eventually spill out onto the front pages years later in revelations of horrendous Catholic clergy sexual abuse of minors. In retrospect, I have found myself wondering how much of this might have been going on in my high school and college years at the minor seminary. I truthfully do not know. I saw no signs of it. But, of course, secrecy and darkness would have been the *modus operandi*.

....

I should think it difficult for someone not raised in the Catholic world to appreciate how commanding the image of priest and priesthood is. This was our life aspiration in the seminary, and even the word seminarian meant priest-to-be. For Catholics priesthood is not a job title or a career, it is a metaphysical phenomenon. "Once a priest, always a priest" is a saying that slides easily off the Catholic tongue; and in childhood we were instructed that ordination to priesthood was one of the seven sacraments which, like baptism, placed "an indelible mark on the soul." Once a person is baptized, she or he can never be "unbaptized"; so also, a man can never stop being a priest once the bishop lays ordaining hands on his head. "*In aeternum*," we were told, a priest forever. He can lapse, walk away, turn against the church, renounce his faith, become an atheist or enemy of the church: he is still a priest forever. No matter the condition of his soul, he can absolve sins and say the words of consecration that transform bread and wine into the actual body and blood of Christ. He has fundamental magic, the power of words. He is another Christ, one of the saviors of humankind. This, I believe, was the mystique which consolidated the spiritual formation in which I was trained in the seminary–but even before that, trained in my home and in my parish. I think this mystique is foundational to the conviction and staying power of Catholicism itself: The structure and authority of the church from the top down is rooted in the concept of priest. First Christ, the High Priest. Then the Apostles whose successors are the bishops of the Church down to this very day. And what is a bishop but one who has "the fullness of the priesthood." Priests in the parish, missionaries, and others, "share in the priesthood of the bishop." Mostly everything else is commentary.

I would be one of these. This would define the shape of the inner life for me, poured in childhood catechism instruction and set in these seminary years. For me to be a priest meant to be a different kind of human, one with supernatural power, to be guarded by saintliness and imparted with zeal and competence. This would require advanced education, intelligence, and a commitment to excellence. During my sixth and final year at Crosier I had been appointed editor of *The Echo,* the school magazine of essay, fiction, poetry, art, photos, humor, chat and gossip, which appeared bimonthly. Each issue began with my editorial, which I used as a kind of urgent homily to my fellow-seminarians. Here are a few excerpts which reflect these ideals.

From October, 1958, "Kruschev and the Priesthood":

Behind a huge desk in some office in the Kremlin sits a bald, paunchy man... clutched in his hands he holds the throat of half the world. The amount of ink with which he signs his name can drown a generation...He can rain fire from heaven...He can tear up the earth...He can crumble cities...He can raise a peasant to a seat in the Presidium, and he can send a high official off packing to Mongolia...He exalts the humble and humbles the exalted. Before a marble altar in the chapel of Crosier Seminary stands a man... He looks as ineffectual as the man behind the desk. Then he bends forward; slowly and precisely he whispers five words–and he works a miracle. By his word a flake of bread becomes Almighty God...whispers words through the screen which save a man from an eternity of self-destruction...bends over the traffic casualty to administer the last rites...Power has been given from above to the tyrant whose skull-shaped footprints track across cities. He has the power to smash brick and earth, to strew human flesh about. But the power of a priest is the tremendous force. Through the lips of a man at the altar, in the quiet of the confessional, through the simple words of a sermon it does far mightier things than the tyrant ever did. The priest has the power to save, to mold, to build souls. The priest is the most powerful man in the world.

From May, 1959, "What are We For?":

There have been many things said and written in our times about the lack of direction and purpose in modern man....(An) example is the common man, who works at his job only to keep alive, marries only because he is old enough to marry, and dies only because all men die. Very many Christians– very many Catholics– are like this. They never deeply consider why they are in this world, why they do what they do, where they are going in this life. They are too preoccupied with material things...We who are in the seminary are very fortunate. We know what we are for. We know that we have meaning. Some of us will become priests. There is tremendous meaning and purpose in that. A life dedicated to worshiping, blessing, instructing, con-

soling is not a waste. Some of us will drop out of the seminary. The life of a
good ex-seminarian can have a great purpose. Everything he does can have
a powerful meaning. He has a seminary training and education behind him.
The strength of the Catholic Church is in a solidly Catholic laity. But the
whole seminary course, every moment of it, is geared toward making good
priests. With a little thought we can see how every minute of prayer, study,
work, and recreation is to be spent in preparation for ordination.

....

When I left Crosier at the end of the year in which I wrote those editorials, I went shopping for my first clerical clothes–black suit, dress hat,
several ankle-length black cassocks studded with about thirty black but-
tons down the front, and a plastic band of Roman collar at the neck. After
yet another summer vacation at my parents' home keeping the seminary
discipline of prayer, reading, and abstinence from social life in mixed
company, I entered the major seminary in Saint Paul, Minnesota.

The seminary was a compound of red brick buildings positioned in
precise, foursquare arrangement amid ample greenspace alongside the
Mississippi River. Early in the twentieth century, railroad magnate, J. J.
Hill, had endowed the school; and student wags claimed that he must
have dictated the layout so that three boxcar residence halls lined up in
front of the train station, the *Aula Magna* (Great Lecture Hall). Seminar-
ians dressed as priests and were required, when outside their rooms, to
be in cassock and Roman collar and, when walking about the grounds,
to wear a peculiar black hat called a biretta, which had three rounded
flanges resembling Mickey Mouse ears and a feathery pom-pom atop.
We were addressed by the faculty members as "gentlemen" and were
expected to tip our birettas when meeting one of them on the walkways.

New arrivals were called first philosophers, indicating that we
were in the first two-year segment of the curriculum, a highly specialized course of studies: Metaphysics, Epistemology, Logic, Ethics, Theo-
dicy, History of Philosophy, with Hebrew and Gregorian Chant on the
side. It was a demanding program requiring unfamiliar effort to work
with abstractions and ancient ways of seeing the world. For example,
I had difficulty understanding how the Thomistic-Aristotelian concept
of hylomorphism, the metaphysical description of all phenomena as a
composition of prime matter and substantial form, accorded with mod-

ern scientific atomic theory of matter and energy. And for a semester we read, not Aristotle's *Nicomachaean Ethics* (4ᵗʰ century B.C.), but St. Thomas Aquinas's *Commentary on the Nicomachean Ethics* (13 century A.D.)–and read it in Latin! Wondering aloud how this intellectual regimen would prepare us to be good parish priests, we were given the rationale that a solid foundation in philosophy based on natural human reason was necessary preparation for the next four years of theology based on faith and the supernatural.

Despite this claim for human reason, the presentation of philosophy was doctrinaire. We were given to understand that there was a Catholic view on what was true philosophy with its foundation in Aristotle and its culmination in the thirteenth century Scholasticism of Aquinas. Past the Middle Ages, our philosophical education consisted largely of refuting errors, primarily the errors of the Enlightenment. The writings of nearly all philosophers from that time to the present had been placed on the Catholic Church's *Index of Forbidden Books*. For Catholics willfully to read writers such as Kant, Hume, Spinoza, Nietzsche, without permission from a bishop, was considered gravely sinful.

This attitude reflected the deep traditionalism of the Catholic Church during the first half of the twentieth century, authoritarian, elitist, self-confident. Loyal Catholics would know "the mind of the Church" on issues facing the modern world by consulting a periodical called *The Pope Speaks*, which carried the latest encyclicals and Vatican pronouncements. We were safe as long as we stayed together within "the bark (boat) of Peter," which sailed stormy seas in a world generally hostile to our message. "Holy Mother the Church" wanted all men (sic) to be one, which meant not ecumenism but conversion to Catholicism and the "one true Church." Priests were the purveyors of this way of seeing things, and I, a true believer, was training to be one. From the inside, this did not appear to me as arrogance or obsession with control. I saw my training for the priesthood to consist of two things: knowledge and holiness. I saw it as truth and humility. Truth would convince; sanctity would attract.

So I was loyal, a true believer, and yet...and yet, did this not also imply that I would need to be as knowledgeable about the world as possible? And did this not mean I should remain open to whatever people were thinking and saying, not to refute their errors, but to try to understand how they saw things? I asked my History of Philosophy prof when we were going to get to Kant and Hegel and Sartre. "Stick with St.Thomas," he told me. I especially wanted to know about existentialism. I had been in intense correspondence with my best friend from Crosier, Trenk. He had gone on to the Crosier House of Studies to join that order when I came to this seminary; and he was writing me with excitement about Sartre and Camus (even though they were atheists!) and about authenticity and the burning questions of our time, not about being and essence and prime matter but about "How, then, are we to live?" There is even something called Catholic existentialism, Trenk wrote. I pressed my prof: "But what about existentialism? Catholic existentialism?" "It's junk," he grunted. I looked for a second opinion from another of my profs, a revered old monsignor whom I liked. "It's wacky!" was all he said.

I distrusted the door-slamming and continued to read, even the forbidden authors, continued to write long, intellectual letters to my friend, Trenk. I saw I would have to fill in many holes on my own if I were to become a highly educated priest.

I had not always been so confident. I remember a conversation I had with my mother when I was thirteen years old–not long after I had told her and Dad that I wanted to enter the minor seminary at Crosier in the fall. I was very worried. I was not sure that I was smart enough to make it. I was afraid I would flunk out. I can still see her face. Her soft, brown eyes held me for a long moment. Then she said fervently, "Oh, Philip, you are very smart." She went on to tell me something she was not supposed to tell me. Our elementary schools did routine intelligence testing on the children but the results were kept confidential, even from their parents. As a teacher in the system, she had been able to gain unauthorized access to the scores of her own. "You and Marilynn and Quinn all tested high. Don't worry. You will do all right in the seminary." She told me my score level and how I ranked with my sister and brother. Shortly after that she began to drill me in Latin from a text she had studied as a girl. *Porta, portae, portae, portam...amo, amas, amat, amamus...*not so much to give me a head start as to give me the experience of what I could do.

I entered Crosier encouraged, nevertheless haunted by the possibility that I might not be of high enough caliber for the legendary rigors of the seminary. In November the first quarter grades were posted on the wall of the rec room. I approached in trepidation and could not believe what I saw. Solem, Philip: A, A, A, A-, A, A. And so it continued, every quarter, every school year.

....

That was my orientation toward knowledge. My understanding of the second requisite for the priesthood, a desire for holiness, also carried my mother's influence. Primarily from her, I think, I recognized that there was another face to Catholicism, neither authoritarian nor boastful, but closer to the personalities of Jesus and of the saints we admired, like Francis of Assisi and Thérèse of Lisieux and the Curé of Ars. In those days, of course, it was not yet customary to call Dorothy Day a saint; but my mother often brought home from church after Mass a copy of *The Catholic Worker* newspaper founded by Dorothy and Peter Maurin. They preached and lived pacifism, voluntary poverty, simplicity of life, conscientious objection to war, and unstinting service to the poor. My dad thought it was a Commie paper. I leaned toward my mother's view. I had no understanding of their anticapitalist politics, but I could see that these were Christ-like Catholics.

When I was at Crosier, I met a man like them. Returning from a Catholic Students Mission Crusade national conference at Notre Dame, I had car-pooled through the night to Minnesota with a man named Gerry Mischke, a lay missionary in Mexico. All the way he talked about serving the poor and living as they did. I was aflame with zeal for this.

I sought people like him wherever I went. At the seminary in Saint Paul I would use afternoons off to find and learn from people like the Franciscan lay brothers on Nicollet Island ministering to the street people. I believed then, I believe now, I have always believed that the little way, the non-acquisitive, non-judgmental, and nonviolent way is what is most truly holy or most nobly human. I have always been attracted to poor people more than to rich people.

The head prefect at Crosier Seminary told my mother, when she came for a visit during my final year, that the faculty thought her son was bishop-material, in his words, "episcopal timber." She was delighted to pass that on to me; and, although I was flattered, I felt no desire for a successful clerical career. I did not want to teach, did not want to be assigned to bigger and wealthier parishes, did not dream of being a bishop. I simply wanted to be a parish priest, to work with the people.

I was busy getting to know them, that is, to know their world and the way they lived. Our isolation was an obstacle, yet the Saint Paul Seminary had a curious rule which provided an opportunity during my junior and senior years of college. All students had to leave the grounds for the entire afternoon on Wednesdays and Saturdays. Where we were to go, what we were to do was not specified–only that we had to dress in our black suits and hat and go somewhere in Minneapolis/St. Paul. Perhaps this was to nudge us out of our isolation, I was never sure. Most of my colleagues used the time to go shopping, go for walks, go for coffee. I saw it as a golden opportunity to learn about the real world. I visited Protestant churches, arranged to meet pastors, explored Luther Seminary, was given a tour of Temple Aaron on River Road by the rabbi. I learned the metro bus system and went downtown to the courthouse to watch civil and criminal trials in progress. I arranged to audit classes in modern philosophy at the University of Minnesota, toured the art department, and once was allowed to observe open-heart surgery at the University Hospital. I was dismayed that none of my fellow students were interested in going with me; they had shopping to do, dry cleaning to pick up.

One afternoon I returned a bit early from one of these outings and stopped to pick up my mail before going to my room in Cretin Residence. There was a letter return-addressed "Office of the Bishop, Duluth Diocese." My heart jumped. I had never received a letter from my bishop but had imagined this moment many times, imagined it in the nourishing of a secret dream, scarcely a hope, that I might be sent abroad to study. Only once before had my diocese ever sent a seminarian to Rome. So, then, it was possible. I took the letter to my room to open it in private and conceal my trembling. It was a short paragraph: "...and I have decided to send you to complete your theological studies at the University of Louvain in Belgium. Please get in touch with Monsignor Popesh at the chancery soon after you get home for summer vacation. He will help you to make the necessary arrangements...Sincerely in Christ, Francis J. Schenk, Bishop of Duluth."

....

I was twenty-one, a college graduate. I would leave the United States for four years. It was time to begin a journal:

I did not dare dwell on what the moment would be like when Mother and Dad left me on the train. Hour after hour dragged. The three of us said very little as we waited for the time to begin the drive to Duluth. We just sat, taut with dull, emotional tension, getting sick on cigarettes.

They put me on the train in Duluth for the long trip to the east coast. I stopped in New York City to find the Catholic Worker community on Chrystie Street in the Bowery area and volunteer for a day, cutting vegetables for the soup kitchen and binding for shipment the current issue of their newspaper, still "penny a copy," which my mother had brought home from church when I was a boy. Next day I was on the *Statendam* of the Holland-America Line, sailing out of Hoboken, past the Statue of Liberty, eight days to Rotterdam.

Louvain is a famous university town twelve miles east of Brussels. Walking the cobblestone streets and narrow alleys among churches, guild halls and convents from the time of the Crusades, I could imagine that I had just stepped into the Middle Ages. The university had been established in 1425. In my century, it still boasted one of the most prestigious schools of theology in Europe. The Duluth Diocese paid my board and lodging at the American College, but the Belgian government funded my education, and my dad sent spending money. I knew that I had begun a great adventure and felt my world opening in all directions.

The stuffy clerical attitudes to which I was accustomed were behind. Here all was in transition, and the school of theology was forward-looking, eager for the reform coming upon the Catholic world. Many of our professors were on leave for months at a time to serve in Rome as *periti*, theological experts, consulting with bishops from all over the world who had gathered to begin the Second Vatican Council. They would bring back to us in the lecture hall news of the latest developments, reports of the fierce struggles between the liberals and arch-conservatives. They were presenting cautious reconsideration of many points of doctrine, moral teaching, liturgical practice, and the relationship between the Church and the modern world. When the council ended four years later, the year I would be ordained, the book-length collection of official documents issuing from Rome reflected much of what I had been taught in these lectures.

We took our classes in lecture halls with seminary students from other countries and, during the first year, strained to grasp the language more than the content. I had only begun to study French on my own; and, although I had spent years translating Latin texts of Caesar's Gallic Wars, and Cicero's orations, I had never known anyone who could speak Latin fluently. One-hour lectures were delivered from a podium in French and Latin. At the end of the hour, the professor would step down and leave; ten minutes later, the next professor would mount and begin. Some spoke only Latin. Some preferred French. Some would begin a sentence in one language and finish in the other. It was an ironclad tradition that there would be no response from the students, no hand-raising, no questions, no discussion or request for clarification. These were lectures.

The only exception–no doubt also sanctioned by centuries of tradition–was comic. Students were permitted to express agreement or disagreement, pleasure or offense, at something that was said from the podium by waves of hissing, loud desk-knocking, or–if the offense was egregious–a filibuster of deafening foot-stomping on the floorboards. This, of course, was carried on by the European students who understood the bizarre practice, while we Americans looked on in amazement. The professor would pause during the outburst, looking mildly amused, and wait for it to subside. Then, without comment, he would continue.

We were assigned no textbooks, were given no assignments. It was assumed we would be doing theological reading on an independent study basis. We were given open-ended written permission by the rector emeritus of the university, who was a bishop and our next-door neighbor, to read any books we needed; so the *Index of Forbidden Books* was no longer an obstacle. There were no examinations during the year, no requirement to account for progress. However, the academic year ended with a terrifying period called the *bloc*, a solid month without classes, a marathon of silent study and cramming followed by individual oral exams with each professor. The way we survived was by a semi-official system of note-takers. In each subject, two students were selected to take down the lecture notes, one in an English version, one in French. Each professor would review these notes toward the end of the year to assure he was being reported accurately; then the notes would be printed and bound. We could purchase copies of whichever version we preferred in order to get ready for the *bloc*. In effect, our textbooks were being composed on the spot.

At Louvain I learned one invaluable life skill that could not be taught in the lecture hall. I learned how to travel. The American College presented two inconsistent characters. One was the old-system, protective enclosure; the other, adventure on the open road. The College was administered by three American priests: a rector, a vice-rector, and a spiritual director, all on loan from East Coast dioceses. They were not teachers, they were wardens and chaperones, nervous, cautious men, not scholars, who had been trained up in the old school. They kept us on a short leash during the school year. We could go out into the town only in full cassock and broad-brimmed black clerical hat, were not allowed to socialize with lay students, were required to keep strict hours, and had to go about in pairs.

However, when Christmas, Easter, and summer vacations came, they turned us loose. We traveled all over Europe wherever we chose, by whatever means we could arrange. There were few restraints: only that we travel with a companion and, during the three months of summer, that we spend at least six weeks in "parish time," that is, in a fixed location assisting in a parish or working at a camp or the like. The other six weeks we could roam at will, as long as we mailed back a weekly postcard letting them know we were still alive and where. One more: we were not allowed to return to the States.

From our elder schoolmates we learned the ropes–how to travel cheap, where to find lodging, where to find contacts for "parish time," how to negotiate the basics in countries where we did not know the language. For seventy-five dollars I bought a small German motorcycle from an older student, who had bought it third-hand himself. As I was learning to ride, I piled it and myself into a tree and had to wheel it back to the repair shop, hobbling with a badly bruised knee, to have the cracked frame welded. I did not really get the clutch maneuver down until two days into Easter vacation while speeding in fast traffic through a highway tunnel in Rotterdam. There, in a desperate flash of insight, I finally figured out how to shift!

The first Christmas I learned where to go skiing in Switzerland, how to order cheese fondue, where to get low-budget lodging at a hostel run by nuns. That first summer, Jim O'Donnell and I rode our motorcycles the length of France in two long travel days to take a six-week job as counselors for tough inner-city kids from Bordeaux at a camp called Les

Coqs Rouges, five miles from the Atlantic shore littered with sand-drift-ed cement bunkers placed by the Nazi army to repel an Allied invasion. We were each assigned to supervise teams of a dozen insolent, combat-ive teens the entire session. How could we supervise, when we could scarcely speak French? We learned French quickly that summer! I spent the last days of the session in the camp infirmary. I told the nurse I had the flu; I knew the symptoms, had often had them before. She said, "You don't have *la gripe, Monsieur.* You are exhausted."

After I recovered, we hit the road and wound through the Pyrenees. My cycle kept breaking down, losing spark. I figured how to keep it going by wedging twigs and fragments of popsicle stick into the electric box to hold bushings in place. We limped to Lourdes, but there was no miracle cure for the cycle there. On to the ancient castles and walled cities of Car-casonne and Nimes. Finally a mechanic made a proper repair. We stayed ten days in Marseilles living with the worker-priests who were sharing the lives of the unchurched dock workers. Only a day in glittery Monaco. North to Grenoble, and the high mountain redoubt of La Grande Char-treuse, home of the Carthusian hermit monks, severest contemplatives of the Catholic Church. There I visited a former classmate from Crosier who had become a monk, living secluded in a cell, growing his food in a little patch of garden. At Crosier he had been almost pathologically pious. On this visit he looked happier, even vibrant. I would meet him one more time, twelve years later, when he would come to visit me back in Duluth, accompanied by his wife. He and she would be enthusiastic sales reps for a self-help program called Silva Mind Control.

We stayed in youth hostels, camped in fields among sheep, begged lodging at churches and monasteries, rarely took a hotel. In Geneva, Jim lost his passport, so he went on to Paris for a replacement at the embassy, while I continued cycling alone. A few villages later, on a remote back road of Burgundy, my motorcycle took its last breath. I rolled it to the nearest railway station and shipped it back to Louvain.

By hitchhike, train, and bus, I worked my way to the village of Ars, where the incorrupt body of John Vianney, patron saint of parish priests, lay behind clear glass beneath the altar (I did not think he looked good). I made my way to Taizé, an ecumenical monastery of Protestant monks living according to the Catholic Benedictine tradition. They housed me in the wooden barracks recently vacated by German volunteer workers who had just completed the beautiful new monastery church called Church of the Reconciliation. They had built it as an act of reparation for crimes of the World War. I would be back here again, first with Jackie, then again with Jackie, Sara and Maria.

Finally I hitchhiked up to Paris, where the Louvain men were gathering like blackbird flocks in the fall, rolling their cycles into the courtyard of the crumbling Hotel Raspail, sleeping five or six to a room for a dollar or less a night. From Italy, Germany, Austria, Spain, they were coming in for a festival of storytelling, wine-drinking, and strolling down the Champs-Elysees at night. At the end of that week, we were glad of the short train ride north into Belgium, through the Ardennes, to Louvain. We were happy to be home.

....

This was how I learned to travel, a set of skills which I, in turn, have passed on to my wife and children. Jackie and I have always traveled this way, more or less.

That was only the first year. There were shorter Christmas and Easter trips to England and Ireland. During the second and third summers I lived in a Bavarian village named Seeshaupt and learned to speak German. Side-tripping from there, Dave Mahon and I meandered through Austria and Italy, and I began to learn Italian. The final summer, my travel partner backed out at the last minute, so I went on alone to study Spanish in Avila and Madrid.

Meanwhile, bishops passing through Louvain on their way to or from the council were ordaining us to the preparatory stages leading to priesthood. First came a ceremony called tonsure, in which a snippet of hair was clipped in token of head-shaving, signifying that we were now clerics, no longer laymen. Later we were ordained lectors, commissioned to read the word in worship, acolytes, commissioned to handle the instruments of the altar, exorcists, empowered to cast out evil spirits. These were symbolic, but the next one had teeth: subdeacons made a lifelong commitment to celibacy and were required in conscience to recite the Divine Office daily. Deacons (ordained in the middle of the last seminary year) actually assisted at the altar, preached, gave communion. We were on the home stretch.

During the final year, I decided to attend the major school. Our four years of pre-ordination theology were conducted in the university's *scho-la minor*. The *schola major* was an advanced department, three or four additional years postmasters leading to a doctorate. I was not interested in higher degrees, but I felt that the minor school had given me all the theological intellectualizing I would ever need for parish work. I was a little bored and ready for a change and thought it would be interesting to observe how theology was done in the stratosphere. Besides, I could skip a tedious fourth year of Canon Law, and that alone almost made it worthwhile.

I was permitted to skip my fourth year and go on to the first year of the major school by cramming hard from the previous year's lecture notes in October, the beginning of my last year, and scheduling individual oral exams with the professors on courses I had never taken. In this way, I tested out of my fourth year and transferred to the major school curriculum.

I now had a schedule different from that of my classmates, came and went with more liberty to a different lecture hall across the city, and associated with a new group of students from all over the world, many of them already priests . Much of the course material was beyond me, but I did not worry about it, for I was not there for the theology but for the experience. I had already completed my requirements for ordination by testing out in October, and the abstruse theorizing that went on in major school would be no less relevant to the real work I would be doing in a parish than what I would have continued to get in the minor school.

Abstruse it was. For example, one prof, Rev. Frans Nierynck, announced that this year we would study the Gospel of St. Matthew. Good, I thought, that will be interesting. However, he lectured in Latin, four hours a week until Christmas, on two Greek words, *ta logia*, written in the second century by a certain Papias. It seems that Papias had claimed that Matthew had written *ta logia hebraiadi dialecto*–"the words in the Hebrew dialect," suggesting that the original Matthew was written in Aramaic rather than Greek. Well! We explored many nooks and crannies. At one point I think we were hearing about Moses and angels, I was not sure why. When Professor Nierynck read us opinions of other experts, he read them in their original language, so that in one hour we might hear him lecture in Latin with biblical citations given in Greek and Hebrew, commentary in French, and scholarly interpretations read in Spanish, German, Dutch, Italian, and English. He told jokes in Flemish. I knew they were jokes because only the Flemings in the hall laughed.

I was having a good time; but I was concerned that no one in either major or minor school, nor even our American guardians, were doing anything to help us get ready to do priestly work. We had no real training in giving sermons; in fact, the three priests who ran our college were themselves deadly dull preachers. There were no courses in counseling. One would think none of us in the priesthood would ever be called upon to visit the hospitals, teach in high schools, baptize babies, give instructions to converts, work with youth, prepare people for marriage or console the grieving and bury their dead. We had to study on our own what prayers to use for the dying, where to find the baptismal ritual, how to hear confessions, how to celebrate Mass. But if anyone should want a knowledgeable speaker on religious topics, no matter how technical, we would be ready.

....

On June 26, 1965, my sixteen classmates and I were ordained to the priesthood in the hospital chapel across the street from the American College. One of us, the only non-American, was missing. As we were vesting for the ceremony, someone whispered:

"You hear about John O'Leary?"

"What about him?"

"He's gone."

"Gone? What you mean, gone?"

"He's left. Gone home. Gone back to Dublin."

Hours before the final step. After all that! There was not time to process the news; we were lining up to file in.

Our families were there, having arrived on a chartered plane two days earlier. I knew my mother would make the trip, but I was astonished that my dad had come, too. He had grown so sedentary and risk-aversive that it was a big deal for him to drive to Duluth, much less to cross the ocean. His health was bad, I did not realize how bad until I saw him for the first time in four years at the Brussels airport. Overweight, flushed, breathing hard. He was alcoholic, and I had known that since I was a boy. It was a misery in our family life, a demon that he had fought repeatedly, always losing. I did not mention this about him earlier in this chapter, because it is not the primary portrayal of him I wanted to lead with. His alcoholism was very serious, however, and very damaging. In my view, alcoholism was not his identity, it was an affliction he had–and therefore, of course, which all of us in the family had.

So an hour after filing into the hospital chapel I was a priest and giving the First Blessing to my mother and father. The next morning my sixteen classmates and I were concelebrating our First Mass in the college chapel. After farewells, my mother and dad and I made a brief tour of the Europe I had come to know.

We flew to Paris. Mom went with me all over the city to see the sights, but Dad found a place to buy cognac and stayed in the hotel room. He was sadly open and gracious about it: "You two go on. I don't care to do all that walking."

We flew to my second home in the Bavarian parish of Seeshaupt, and I had another First Mass in a packed church with orchestra and chorus. My dad joined the festivity and feasting there–it was a small village, and there was nowhere else for him to be–and I think he enjoyed himself with these warmhearted people who were so good to the son he was so proud of.

We flew to Ireland. Again, Dad stayed in the Dublin hotel, while Mom and I drove down to Tipperary and Cork in a rental car, asking about Quinn family ancestors along the way.

Then we flew home. There was yet another First Mass in my home parish in Chisholm. After the accolades died away and the relatives dispersed, I received another letter from the Office of the Bishop. I was assigned to assist the pastor of St. Anthony's Church in Duluth, and I would also teach religion classes full-time at the Duluth Cathedral High School.

....

When I arrived at St. Anthony's, the pastor, an obese, peevish man in his sixties who spoke rapidly with a clipped brogue, showed me around and let me know the rules. I was to start a youth group, start an adult education program, type and print the Sunday bulletin, take confessions on Saturday afternoons and evenings, talk to the parish grade school classes once a week. I was *not* to visit parishioners at the hospital, that was his job, and I was *not* to disturb him in the early afternoon of any day. He showed me my bedroom with office attached. I was not to use the kitchen nor the dining room nor the living room. If I had to see people for counseling or instructions, I could do that in a room in the basement where money from Sunday envelope collection was counted on a ping pong table after Masses. I was also to help count it. This man was obviously not offering to be my mentor. I was to do my job and stay out of his way. I was appalled, but not disheartened; for, after all, he had left me the most important work. Besides, I had lived in lodgings more austere than this in my traveling days.

The first Monday morning I was getting ready to go out the door for my first day of classes at the diocesan high school. He appeared at the top of the stairs and looked down at me.

"Where are you going, Father?" he demanded.

"To Cathedral High School, Father. It's my first day."

"No! You're not to go there! You are assigned to this parish. There's plenty of work here for you."

"But, Father, the bishop has assigned me to teach there all day. I have to go."

"I'm telling you, you're not to go! That's an order. You understand me?" And with that he turned and went into his room.

I phoned the chancery office and talked to Monsignor Popesh. He told me to go ahead up to the high school. I did. The pastor did not say a word more about it that day or any other.

Apart from that welcome, I loved working in the parish. It was all I had hoped for. What the seminary had not taught me about pastoral life, recruiting volunteers, organizing programs, I learned from the people and made up the rest with common sense. The people made me feel at home, and let me know they were glad to have me. We worked together to start Bible studies, educational programs, outreach ministries. I celebrated Mass in their living rooms, became friends with the nuns who taught in the grade school, gave dramatic little talks to grade-schoolers with sweeping chalk-pictures on the blackboard.

The area I was most earnest about was preparation of the Sunday homily. This was the moment when I would speak to most people. It was for this that had I wanted to become highly educated, not only in books, but in everything. In my experience, most Sunday sermons landed somewhere between harmless and godawful. I decided from the start that I would spend at least ten hours each week preparing the sermon. I would begin on Wednesday by reading the upcoming Scripture texts, then go somewhere quiet for an hour or two–often down to the shore of Lake Superior–to meditate and search for a theme, some focus that had to do with the everyday concerns of people, often issues in the papers or local problems in our city. Fragments of poetry would find their way in, passages from Rabindranath Tagore or Shakespeare or Schwartzbart's novel about the Baal Shem Tov. Then I would write and rewrite, trying to condense and simplify so the homily would not run too long. Then I would type out a complete text and set myself to memorizing. Then I would practice, reciting aloud as I paced back and forth in my room. It was always a good ten hours. I knew I was not a fine orator; but I wanted to give them something worth hearing.

On the other hand, teaching religion to tenth-grade boys at Cathedral High from the first period to the seventh, five days a week, was my nemesis. The textbook we were assigned had a year-long focus on liturgy. Liturgy? Sophomores? Boys? I was a disaster. I had no idea how to maintain discipline. They were bored, insolent, uncooperative, noisy and outrageous. I taught nothing, had no success in getting them involved. Without authorization, I abandoned the textbook and its theme after a month and every week tried to think up some way of interesting and engaging these boys; but I had lost them. I absolutely dreaded going up to the school every morning and rejoiced when I could leave at 4:00 P.M. to begin working in the parish. I asked for help from the administration, got suggestions, but nothing worked. It was the first major failure of my life, and I began to feel ill as I drove into the parking lot each morning, worse when I pulled open the front door. By midyear, I knew I would not make it. I went to the principal and told him I would have a nervous breakdown if I had to continue. I just could not do this. He saw I was right. Soon my classes were assigned to a more experienced teacher and I was given fewer classes, all junior and senior girls. I made it to June.

With two full-time jobs, I was working very hard, six-and-a-half days a week. I only took time off on Sunday afternoons following the morning Masses to go to my parents in Chisholm, an hour or so away. This was my refuge. As Sunday evenings approached, Dad would be urging me to be on the road because it was getting dark. I resented him and resisted leaving because it meant returning to face a looming week of classes. I gagged with fear at the thought.

Unexpectedly, one of these Sunday visits back home was different from all the others. My dad had something else to tell me: he had quit drinking. All three of us were guarded and distrusting, himself included. This had not been the first time. He announced that he had quit several weeks earlier and had gone through "absolute hell" but now was hopeful that this time it was for good. It was. He lived five more years and did not drink again. He dropped a good deal of weight; color returned to his face. I found myself wanting to spend time with him for the first time since I was a boy.

One Sunday I was doing just that. Dad and I were sitting in the living room watching television. Mother was in the kitchen. We were watching a documentary on the alarming buildup of the Red Chinese military machine and the potential for the Vietnam War to draw America toward war with China. I was deeply troubled and asked myself: What do I say about this, and what do I tell them when I preach? What do I say the *gospel* says about this? What *does* the gospel of Jesus say? In a flash I knew the answer; and, in that very moment, I became a pacifist.

What did I know about Vietnam? Almost nothing. I knew that the president had received authorization from Congress to expand our attacks to North Vietnam because their gunboats had attacked our ships in the Gulf of Tonkin. I knew we had to stop the Communists there, otherwise Southeast Asia would fall like dominoes and we would be stopping them on our soil, too little too late. Even in the major school in Louvain, when European and South American clerics were pressing me, asking what business Americans had fighting the Vietnamese, I had indignantly answered: "Every reason in the world. We are fighting Communism." And, now–just a week or so ago–when a letter of support to the president for his Vietnam policies had been circulated among the students and faculty at the high school in response to unpatriotic antiwar demonstrations, I had readily signed it along with everyone else.

Suddenly, I knew I was wrong to have done that. I had spent years reading and meditating the Christian gospel; and here, in the living room, sitting next to my sober dad, who did not have any idea what was going on with me, I was experiencing *metanoia,* a total change of heart and mind. I was no longer episcopal timber.

FOUR
....

Antiwar

I still have the Smith Corona typed text of homilies I delivered on Sundays at St. Anthony's. By the Fifth Sunday after Pentecost, 1966, about a year after I was ordained, new themes were appearing: references to Stokely Carmichael, black power, Martin Luther King, Gandhi, nonviolence. That Sunday I said, "We are a people willing to consider war and violence as a possible solution to our problems...Christ's way of dealing with problems, with injustice, with oppression was nonviolent. *Never* did he endorse war, violence, retaliation. *Never* did his Apostles." This would be a steady drumbeat the congregation would hear from me from that point onward. I was already receiving mailings from the local chapter of SANE, a peace organization about war and nuclear policy. I was going to meetings, making a new group of friends, developing a support community which I would very much need in the months ahead.

One Sunday morning, the pastor came into my office after Masses and sat himself down facing me, something he had never done.

"Father, the people are saying you are preaching we shouldn't be fighting in this war!"

"Yes, Father, that's what I have said."

"You can't be saying that! You're not to be telling them that."

"I have to be telling them that, Father. It is the teaching of the gospel, the way of Jesus."

"You're not to be saying the things you are. Jerry Sheridan talked to me. You know Jerry was at Pearl Harbor when it was bombed?"

"Yes, Father, I have talked to Jerry about that."

"Well, I'm your pastor, and it is my duty to tell you that you are not to be saying these things! So now I have told you."

With that, he got up and left and never mentioned it again. I did not stop, but continued to educate myself about the Vietnam War and attend meetings, gradually becoming an activist. That summer we wrote letters to the editor, held public meetings, began to form a speakers bureau, spoke on call-in radio. Most of my friendships formed around these activities. I was often in meetings and at meals in the Jewish home of Rhoda and George Dizard, in conference with Rabbi Wolfgang Hamburger, drinking beer into the early hours of the morning with my best friend, Evan Ferber, who took me to synagogue on Saturday morning. I was often on the university campus to meet with Ed Flaccus, a Quaker, Brooks Anderson, Lutheran campus pastor, Dick Nelson, Presbyterian chaplain, Bill Brice, Baptist pastor. There were no other Catholic priests in these gatherings, but my most intimate and most intense support came from a few Benedictine sisters at St. Scholastica Priory. One of the sisters organized the speakers bureau, and Sister Ambrose was one of her speakers. These two nuns would become my closest confidants and strongest moral support in the days of crisis that lay ahead.

I had no real friends among the Catholic clergy. I had been out of the country for four years of seminary and returned to the diocese a virtual stranger. We had been told at the American College in Louvain that "the fraternity of the priesthood will be your greatest gift and strongest mainstay," but I did not find this to be the case. I lived in a loveless rectory. I did get together with fellow priests for bowling on the three lanes in the basement of St. Scholastica on Monday evenings. Afterwards we would hang around for small talk in Bernie Popesh's apartment, but I found in this weekly relaxation little comfort for the agony I was going through in my failed assignment as a high school teacher or interest in my growing concerns about war and social issues.

In the parish, on the other hand, I found close friends among the lay people I recruited to teach religion classes and start a youth group. We were peers and co-workers–Mary and Ed Fleege, Roseanne and Bill Galinski, Jack and Gerry Hayden, Art and Charlene Jacquart, and others.

And their children. I was often in their homes for hours at a time, planning, organizing, eating, laughing, pausing so the kids could be put to bed, carrying on. It was a warm and loving world I found among these people–as I had expected it would be. No wonder I did not spend much time at the rectory or hang out with priests. No wonder I could say I loved being a parish priest.

Of course a good deal of time was spent in the church: weddings, funerals, baptisms, and daily Mass. I heard confessions for two hours every Saturday before supper and for two hours after. There was an odd practice in the Catholic culture I did not approve of and tried to resist: Mass stipends. People would come to the rectory door or stop us after Mass with money "to have Masses said" for their dead. The going rate was $3.00 per Mass at that time, not a charge but an "offering," of course, for the priest to say Mass for the soul of the departed loved one. Every time I encountered this, I feared the ghost of Martin Luther would rise from the grave in indignation and rage to haunt us; and these offerings came in bulk orders, thirty, fifty dollars at a time. Which meant adding the name of the departed loved one with repeated dittos to a preposterously growing schedule months into the future. I tried to decline the money and assure the petitioner that I would include the loved one's name in all Mass prayers in the coming days, even tried to decline money for baptisms, weddings, and funerals, arguing that, really! this is my job; you don't need to pay extra for this service; this is what I am here for; I get enough salary! It did no good. I saw I left people not enlightened, but frustrated and bewildered, thwarted in their efforts to take care of their dead or complete the wedding or funeral transaction.

I did get enough salary, $180 a month, I think. Health care, food, and housing were already taken care of, as well as life-long job security. All I had to pay for were clothes and car. I had used ordination gift money to buy a used Plymouth with automatic drive, push-button shifting. It was a good car, but within two years I had enough money from my paychecks to trade it for a brand new, light green Plymouth. This was a rite of passage into full manhood in my mind.

So was taking up fishing. I carried a pole and tackle box everywhere in the back of my car and would stop along the highway as I passed a lake and cast a few times and then drive on. I was crazy about fishing those first few years, but no good at it. I caught very few fish. A real

Iron Ranger, brought up on fishing and hunting, would know what he was doing–would know about seasons and water temperature and lake-bottom topography and proper bait. I had spent too much time on books and foreign languages, so my way of fishing was to choose a plausible shiny lure, one I would go for if I were a fish, and cast and reel repeatedly on the lottery-ticket-method of reducing the odds from 50,000 to 1 down to 1,562 to 1 by casting five more times before getting back into my Plymouth, in hopes that YES! I just might be a winner today!

That summer the pastor was transferred elsewhere and Fr. Dick Partika took his place. He was a dedicated priest, open-minded and fair. He was friendly and treated me as a colleague. I doubt that he agreed with my pacifism and outspoken position on the war, but I sensed no tension between us over it.

My involvement with the small peace movement community increased that fall, and we formed a local group called Clergy and Laity Concerned about Vietnam (CLCV), affiliated with a national network with a similar name. We scheduled teach-ins, leafleted, organized church services of concern, brought in antiwar speakers. I wrote to Senator Wayne Morse from Oregon, one of the only two senators who had voted against the Gulf of Tonkin Resolution, pleading with him to come to Duluth and awaken our community to the realities of Vietnam. I became chairperson of our CLCV group. The membership list was growing. We started focusing on draft counseling, because young men were being inducted at increasing rates to meet soaring troop commitments, already at 429,000 in Vietnam. Operation Rolling Thunder was sweeping all of North Vietnam with wave after wave of bombing daily, including repeated bombardment of Hanoi and Haiphong Harbor, which had previously been off-limits. Antiwar demonstrations in America were beginning to grow. In August a protest disrupted a session of the House Un-American Activities Committee in Washington as it began to investigate Americans deemed to have aided the Viet Cong enemy.

Our small Duluth antiwar group was easily dismissed as a fringe element. Letters to the editor appeared in the newspaper, complaining that we were godless, unpatriotic demoralizers of the soldiers and supporters of the enemy. It was an unpleasant experience for most of us who had taken social esteem and a good reputation for granted. We were finding ourselves increasingly unpopular in the community. I imagined eyes averted and heads shaking when I looked out to the people in the pews on Sundays. However, I continued to question the morality of American war policy from the pulpit and to speak frequently, not about just war theory, but about Jesus's example of nonviolence and the Christian Church's universal doctrine and practice of pacifism during its first three hundred years.

One Sunday morning, as I prepared for the ten o'clock Mass, something happened that nearly knocked me to the ground. I had the vestments on. I looked out the sacristy door at the packed church to see if the music ministry was ready to go. Suddenly from a back pew, on the side aisle, came a loud screech and a prolonged wailing. Every head in the congregation jerked around to see what the disturbance was. There appeared to be a scuffle, then a small clutch of people moved toward the back of the church, holding someone, and edging out the door. After the whispering subsided, Mass began.

Only after it was over did I learn what had happened. Someone, a friend or family member, had quietly approached a woman in the pew back there and asked her in a whisper to step out of the church for a moment. That was all it took. She knew what it meant, this mother. She screamed and clung to the pew and would not follow the messenger of death, would not hear what was going to be said to her outside. Her fingers had to be pried from the wood of the pew; she had to be dragged outside.

Her family lived just two blocks up the hill from the church. I knew what they thought of me and of what I had been saying about the illegitimacy of the cause in which their son was serving. I would not be welcome in their home. I was their priest, but I could not go to them. Thank God, Dick Partika could go, did go to them. I felt horrified and filled with shame.

....

We were not godless nor unpatriotic, and we trudged on. We had no wish to demoralize, only to communicate and to open a serious dialogue. Our group needed greater visibility and impact. We decided to place an ad in the *Duluth News Tribune*–a type of manifesto.

The statement appeared as a quarter-page ad in the January 10, 1967, issue of the paper. It read:

PEACE IS POSSIBLE–BUT NOT THROUGH WAR

We, the undersigned, after much study, reflection and discussion, feel com-
pelled to avow publicly our conviction that the war in Vietnam is unjust,
immoral, and self-defeating. We claim that citizens have the right and the
duty to question and , if necessary, oppose government policies in times of
peace and war. We insist that the greatest betrayal of our American soldiers
now engaged in battle would be failure to question the activity to which
their lives are committed. We believe that the first commitment of Ameri-
cans is to live in peace with all men, for all men are our brothers–even those
who would harm us.

It went on to suggest ways of seeking peace and to "invite all men of
good will" to join us in this public witness. It was signed by ninety-one
people from the Duluth area.

Bishop Schenk let me know that he certainly did not appreciate my
making this public statement without consultation. One other priest of
the diocese had signed, Father John Whitney Evans. So had Father Larry
Rosebaugh and a colleague, both non-diocesan priests. A year and a half
later, Larry would burn draft files as a member of the Milwaukee Fourteen and be sent to a federal prison.

The ad had its desired effect. The media were now very interested in
Clergy and Laity Concerned about Vietnam. Letters to the editor flowed
in. A rebuttal ad of the same size declaring "Disunity Is Not the Way to
Peace" was placed by a Richard Griggs a few days later, earning him a
letter of commendation from President Johnson himself. The paper carried our reply: "We appreciate the action (of Mr. Griggs) which brought
to the attention of the President and the Vice President the Jan. 10 adver-
tisement placed by Clergy and Laity Concerned about Vietnam. We are
pleased to know that our brief statement has not only been responded to
from within our own community, but now has brought forth a response
from the White House." The official newspaper of the Catholic diocese,
The Duluth Register, began carrying news, letters, and balanced editorial and commentary on our activities. Our local group moved into high
gear, sending clergy representatives to a national antiwar mobilization in
Washington, bringing in national organizers and speakers, activating a
speakers bureau to handle sudden interest with topics such as "Historical Background of the Viet Cong" (Evan Ferber), "Freedom, The Task of

Man" (Sr. Ambrose Marsnik, O.S.B.), "The Democratic Foundations of Permanent Peace" (Rabbi Wolfgang Hamburger), "Impact of the Vietnam War on Christian Conscience" (Rev. Whitney Evans), "Economic Disturbances Caused by the Vietnam War" (George Dizard). We joined a national education project called Vietnam Summer, set up a draft counseling service, and began a half-hour silent Vigil for Peace every Wednesday noon at the Civic Center in front of the court house and the federal building.

Disastrous reports from Vietnam fed this energy; the situation grew steadily more dire. More people opposed to the war were coming out into the open, and we were no longer such a fringe group. In addition to Senators Wayne Morse of Oregon and Ernest Gruening of Alaska who had refused to vote for the Gulf of Tonkin Resolution, Senators Eugene McCarthy of Minnesota and J.W. Fulbright of Arkansas were now opposing the war.

As the most visible spokesman for our local group, I continued to learn all I could about the details of this war in order to speak knowledgeably about it as I was increasingly called to do. At the same time I deepened my pacifist convictions by reading Gandhi, Martin Luther King, Thomas Merton, Dorothy Day, A. J. Muste and studying the experiences of Gandhian satyagraha, the Danish and Norwegian resistance to the Nazis, Albert Luthuli's Defiance Campaign against South African apartheid during the 1950s, the farm workers' movement organized by Cesar Chavez, the land distribution campaigns of Vinoba Bhave in India. Many of these examples involved resistance against the oppressive power of the state. Consequently, nonviolent resistance often implied civil disobedience, and there were many prison tales.

Toward the end of 1967, I began to think that the next stage of the antiwar effort would require civil disobedience. I began to think about prison. There was one more example I meditated. Jesus only spent one overnight in jail. But his disciples were regulars. My critics would often quote to me the Apostle Paul's words in Romans 13: "Everyone is to obey the governing authorities, because there is no authority except from God and so whatever authorities exist have been appointed by God. So anyone who disobeys an authority is rebelling against God's ordinance; and rebels must expect to receive the condemnation they deserve." I would, however, point out to this objection that the man who wrote these words had himself done a hefty amount of prison time.

All along, our effort had been to communicate. We strove to open a dialogue about alternatives. Nonviolent ways of resolving whatever we were fighting for or about. We had tried to communicate by sermons and town meetings and teach-ins and speeches and literature and argument and, finally, through a paid ad in the paper that minced no words–and that time we connected. Enough of us (ninety-one) stood together and said things that got the ball rolling, started a wake-up dialogue that, since then, had only gained momentum. Now, I thought to myself, it is time to communicate again and take it to the next level for the same purpose. Now had come the time beyond words for action: a nonviolent, unambiguous action which spoke a meaning hard to ignore. This would be the classic act of soul-force, the breaking of an unjust law and acceptance of the consequences. What would it be? What came to mind was another classic method at the founding of the American nation: pamphleteering.

It was not my custom to keep a journal, but I thought it might be time to start. I knew I would be heading into heavy waters and suspected I might need some documentation to account for myself. I am glad I did, because I would be unable to recount this next part without those few pages of a journal which I started at the beginning of 1968. Not only has my memory blurred much of what I did and thought and felt during that next crucial six-week period, I even forgot that I had ever made notes about it. I came across these pages, very mildewed, among my papers in a box in the attic just the other day. I think they give an immediacy to the narration that today's attempt at recollection would miss.

January 6, 1968 - Feast of the Epiphany. I have been trying to recall where the germ of the idea came from and when it first came, but I can't quite place it. I suppose I could trace the roots of the idea back quite a few months, or even for a few years. But what puzzles me is that it has not been much more than a week that I have seriously been thinking of engaging in civil disobedience.

I suspect that the immediate conditioning for my idea came from an article in the Nov. 24 Commonweal, "A Non-violent Christology," which Sr. Ambrose gave me when I visited her at the hospital just before Christmas. Then there was the time I spent with Marguerite in Rochester on Dec.

28 & 29. On the long, lonely drive back to Duluth, I thought intensely, as I am accustomed to do after a moving experience; but my thinking was dull, diffused, troubled, which surprised me, because Marguerite gives me strength. Perhaps it was on that trip back that the first dire thoughts of civil disobedience began to emerge. If so, they were feelings rather than thoughts. On Sunday (Dec. 31) or New Year's Day I read an article by a revolutionary Black Nationalist called "America Will Burn!" and I went to church in the afternoon, extremely keyed-up and bewildered. I paced around wildly in the church for a full twenty minutes praying, "Christ, Christ, Christ Jesus, what will become of us!" Finally I was calm. Later the same day I read The Catholic Worker which George Dizard had given me, and that brought back the panicky apprehension.

I must have had a vague idea of civil disobedience as early as Sunday when I took part in a planning meeting of Concerned Democrats at Robert Owens' home. We were drafting a proposed slate of officers for the Concerned Democrats and I was suggested for the steering committee. Before leaving I told Bob Owens I might not be an asset, for I was feeling drawn to some less conventional action in the peace movement.

By Wednesday I knew what I should do. But I felt very unsure. I needed to talk with people who would understand and help. At the Peace Vigil Wed. noon I thought of jail. I wanted to talk to Brooks or Ed Flaccus, but I did not just then. I tried to call one of the sisters, but she was out of town. I was afraid to ask for Sr. Ambrose, for I did not know if she had yet recovered from her eye surgery. I needed to talk badly.

Friday morning–yesterday–after my First Friday communion calls, I went to the Villa and talked with Sr. Ambrose and another sister. I told them that I felt called to civil disobedience against the war and that I was preparing to go to prison. They helped me a great deal. They clarified my thoughts and purified my feelings and did not urge me to ask less of myself. It was in those hours with them that I made my decision. That evening the first item on Huntley-Brinkley news was the indictment by a federal grand jury of Benjamin Spock and William Sloane Coffin for illegal draft resistance...What lies ahead, I do not know. I want to talk with Evan Ferber who is home in Detroit for the holidays. I plan to go to Washington in early Feb. In between I must consult with friends and study to fortify myself intellectually and spiritually for hard times ahead....

Jan. 8, 1968. ...Evan and I talked for about 45 minutes. He was full of news from Detroit and Minneapolis, where he attended a conference on the draft. Met many resisters. Some planning to go to Canada...He is behind me all the way on this....

Jan. 9, 1968. I have been using all the free time I have to research my new position. I am beginning to work toward the writing of a pamphlet urging draft resistance which could be sent out to high school seniors.

It is difficult to give myself to my routine work now that this whole matter is obsessing me...thinking that I don't know what my situation will be a month from now–whether I will be in this parish, on leave of absence, suspended, or in prison. Jack Hayden was talking about the trip we had planned for this summer–a weekend fishing. I said, Yes, I still planned on going. But in my mind I was thinking that, instead of fishing in a north-woods lake, I might be in jail.

Jan. 18, 1968...I drove to Chisholm worrying how I would talk to Mother and Dad about this. How would I tell them? More important, how much? I was inclined to think I should tell them everything and prepare them for the worst. I worried about this; but, strangely, I felt at peace, not at all scared. All through this time–from Jan. 5 on–I have felt great peace and conviction about what I am doing. I have felt no fear and no substantial doubt about the rightness of my decision...Mother and Dad and I sat in the kitchen. I was drinking beer. I began to talk about going to Washington. I said things were getting serious, even dangerous. I mentioned fears of wire-tapping. They were concerned and a bit worried by my talk. But they did not stay with the topic and did not press me on what I was saying; and I knew they had not caught the impact of what I wanted to say. However, I wonder if maybe Dad did understand a bit more than he let on–for at one moment he suddenly said in an abstract and fretful way: "Oh, I wish this damn war were over!" ....In the evening the three of us were sitting in the living room. Dad was absorbed in the TV and Mother and I were half-watching and talk-ing. I mentioned the problem again and said I was sending out a pamphlet to high school kids. What would be in it? Urging them to resist the draft. Suddenly she realized fully what I had been talking about! Her face was drawn with worry and fear and she pleaded, "Don't do it! Philip, please don't do it!" I tried to respond but I couldn't say anything. I did not want to go into it here and now in competition with the TV. I told her I would talk to her later about this.

That night she and I stayed up till 2:30 at the kitchen table drinking coffee. I explained why I was doing this–that it was a question of conscience, that I was doing it as an act of priesthood and that I was doing this out of faithfulness to what Jesus taught us. I quoted the New Testament a bit...I said that my greatest worry was how this would hurt her and Dad. But Jesus also had something to say about the disciple's relationship with mother and father.

And then she said something which touched me very much. She suddenly looked not so much worried as soulful and wondering and she said, "You're a true believer! You really believe, don't you?' I did not know what to answer. I wanted to say yes, but I fumbled with words. And at that moment, I felt that I was a good son.

By the end of the evening–or rather by the early hours of the morning–she seemed resigned to the message I had brought home. She shuddered from time to time and looked painfully worried, but I felt that she had accepted.

Jan. 19, 1968. I waited for a time to bring it up with Dad in the morning, but Mike and Jo Sullivan and Francis came over. When they left, we had lunch before I left for Duluth, and then I brought it up to Dad and he got the message. Immediately he became very agitated, but remained very logical; and what he had to say surprised me very much. He seemed horrified by the thought that I might talk some kid into doing something he would not have the strength to carry out and it might ruin his life. He did not plead for me to stay out of trouble, as I had expected. His argument–although very emotional and, in fact, impassioned–he was on the verge of tears and he several times abruptly stood up from the table and left the kitchen and returned seconds later to continue–his argument was very noble and carried great dignity. He told me he couldn't approve of what I was doing. He told me again and again, "Phil, don't tamper with people's lives!" And all I could do was reply quietly that, in my situation and at the point at which I had arrived, to do nothing would be to tamper with people's lives. It was an extremely tense half-hour that we talked. Mother sat silently, listening and suffering. But it was a beautiful half-hour, painful as it was. I don't remember ever having felt such deep respect for my father as I did that day.

On the drive back to Duluth I decided to re-think my whole resolve, to start from zero and work up. My conclusion was the same. I would continue on the pamphlet.

A small group of us flew to Washington for the February 5-6 Mobilization sponsored by the national Clergy and Laymen Concerned about Vietnam. We heard from some of the great figures of the day: William Sloan Coffin, Harvey Cox, Rabbi Abraham Heschel, Andrew J. Young. Our Minnesota contingent met with Senator Walter Mondale (who would be Vice-president). A year earlier he had written me: "You may be sure that I am as troubled as you are about our involvement in Vietnam. You may also be sure that I will seek out and support any reasonable means of relieving a situation which is deeply disturbing to me as a person and to every thoughtful American citizen." We urged him to oppose the Johnson war policies, but he was not ready to do that.

The next day all the Mobilization participants assembled at Arlington National Cemetery. At the last minute the government had rescinded authorization for a march and a memorial service. We were only allowed to assemble for a period of silence. Dr. Martin Luther King (who would be assassinated two months later) was allowed to say: "In silence let us pray." After fifteen minutes, Catholic Bishop James P. Shannon (who would marry a few years later) was allowed to say: "Amen. In silence let us depart."

I returned to Duluth, finished the last steps of stapling the ten-page pamphlet, already run on the church mimeograph machine, finished stuffing, addressing, stamping. On Saturday morning I drove around the city and stuffed eight hundred envelopes into mailboxes in six scattered locations. The pamphlet said:

TO A HIGH SCHOOL SENIOR

At the risk of my personal freedom and at the cost of personal reputation, this pamphlet is addressed to you. I am Philip M. Solem, a Roman Catholic priest, stationed in a parish in Duluth, Minnesota, at the time of writing.

This topic must be of deep concern to you and to all high school seniors, because you are vitally involved in it. It is of deep concern to me because it touches my most fundamental convictions as a human being and a man called to the service of God and God's People. Please hear me out, for what is said here is not said lightly. For saying it I can be, and very likely will be, sentenced to prison for five years.

The message is simple: I urge you in the name of humanity not to serve

*in the armed forces. I urge you to resist induction. I urge you not to cooper-
ate with the military. I urge you not to fight in Vietnam.*

The pamphlet went on to make the case for the illegality of the war
under international law and to address the usual reasons given for its
necessity. It spoke about morality from the perspective of our common
humanity. It quoted a poignant poem by a 33-year old Vietnamese and
spoke of the savage and dehumanizing effects of the war. It put forward
a number of choices available to every young man facing the draft.

WHAT TO DO?

*Please react to what I say, not out of the way you have been trained to react,
nor out of instinct, but out of your own personal freedom. I would have
you resist the draft only if you can come to the conclusion that I have that
it is right to do so. Remember that many of you who read this will soon be
drafted into the armed forces. You will be told to take human life and you
will be told to be ready to die. Before you mindlessly snap to salute, I ask
you to stop and think. Remain a human being. Respond to the envelope
marked "Selective Service" from the depth of your freedom.*

*Everyone must do his own thing. There are many ways a man can
refuse to cooperate with this war; some are perfectly legal, others are acts
of civil disobedience. You can apply for conscientious objector status in the
Selective Service system. If denied, you may be able to hang up the draft
process through appeals. You may refuse induction when drafted or you
may refuse to cooperate with the Selective Service by refusing to register or
by returning your draft card or by destroying it. Some men are driven into
exile from their homeland and feel they have no choice but to go to Canada.*

*If you should decide that you must not enter military life, be fully
aware that the penalties for violation of the law are severe. Do not carry out
such a decision without first becoming fully aware of its consequences and
without seeking reliable counsel and advice.*

*If you should come to the conclusion that you must resist service in the
armed forces, make your decision out of strength, not out of fear. I will aid
and support no one who refuses to serve because he does not love his country. I will encourage and counsel no one who refuses to serve because he is
afraid to suffer and die for his brothers and sisters.*

But if you should decide that your own conscience forbids you to serve

in the armed forces at this period of our national history, I pledge to you my
aid, support, encouragement and counsel–as long as I remain at liberty.
Rev. Philip M. Solem
P.O. Box 373
Duluth, Minnesota 55801

....

The phone at the rectory began ringing Monday morning, February 12, and scarcely stopped ringing for the next two weeks. The first calls were from the newspapers and television. Then a mix of angry calls from parents and appreciative calls from supporters. The next morning it was front-page headlines in all Minnesota papers and within days supporters began mailing clippings from newspapers across the country–Denver, Richmond, Milwaukee, Los Angeles, Dubuque–even one from England.

The *Duluth News Tribune* reported: "Malford Eid, agent in charge of the Duluth bureau of the FBI said Monday afternoon he had conferred with the FBI's Minneapolis office. 'I talked with Richard Held, agent in charge there, who said the matter would be referred to the U.S. attorney general's office for examination,' Eid said."

The diocesan chancery office issued a remarkably even-handed statement on February 14: "Bishop Schenk is not contemplating any kind of disciplinary action in the case of Father Solem. The fact that Father Solem is a priest neither deprives him of his civil and moral right to act according to the dictates of his conscience, nor does it excuse him from the **duty of thus acting** when he considers it **morally imperative.**

"Nothing in his statement contradicts traditional Catholic moral teaching on conscientious objection. Bishop Schenk, in his new role as pastor of the Catholic community, is concerned with the moral and doctrinal aspects of the situation, not primarily with its civil dimension. If Father Solem has violated any civil laws, it is up to the appropriate authorities to take due measures.

"Father Solem's evaluation of the war and his methods of disseminating his personal opinions are open to question and the validity of the one and the judiciousness of the other are debatable."

I spent the rest of the week talking to reporters, talking to an angry delegation of war veterans from the Iron Range, facing cameras, answering the phone, opening mail (1200 pieces in the following two months), scheduling speaking engagements. The Sunday editions of the local and the St Paul newspapers carried lengthy articles exploring my background and motivation. They described me this way:

"In private conversation about his convictions, the Duluth priest's words flow fluently. But he is not yet accustomed to the glaring television studio lights nor the barrage of questions fired at him by newsmen, the result of his sudden entrance into the national limelight.

"He responds to most inquiries with an earnest, sincere attitude, markedly reserved when the topic approaches an area in which he prefers not to comment.

"At times, he bluntly states, 'I am not prepared to speak about that.'

"But he is ready, willing and cooperative in discussing the events which prefaced his controversial action of recent days."

On February 23 the diocesan paper, *The Register*, carried the full text of the pamphlet I had sent out, along with a disapproving but respectful editorial and a spate of letters pro-and-con. The mainstream press carried excerpts of the pamphlets, editorials, letters, and one very funny cartoon in the *St. Paul Dispatch* which showed two wide-eyed teenage boys hulking over a church pew with a confessional in the background and a sign panel over its door reading "Father Solem." One is saying to the other: "He urged me to say six Our Fathers and six Hail Marys here and one 'Heck no, I won't go' at the draft board."

In the following week I was caught up in giving speeches around the state, some focusing on the illegality of the war according to the Geneva Conventions and international treaties, some on the history of Christian pacifism. At the same time, I tried to carry on with routine parish duties and teach my religion class at the high school, now cut back to one hour a day.

Late one afternoon I answered the door at the rectory. A man I did not know stood there, hat in hand. He wanted to speak to the priest, he said. He appeared a bit past middle age, somewhat hollow and dejected. I invited him in, offered a seat in the front office, shut the door, and sat facing him waiting to hear his trouble. He did not speak at once, so I asked what it was that brought him. He continued to look at me a moment longer.

"I've come to shoot you."

A ten pound block of ice slid down slowly inside me and landed hard. Perhaps I said something, I don't know.

"You seem like a nice man," he continued. "I wish I did not have to do this," and at that he slid his hand into the pocket of his topcoat, " but they have sent me and I have to do it."

I have no memory of my side of the conversation; but I am sure I asked who "they" were, what their reasons were, what had I done to him–trying to appear calm while gripped in such white fear that I could scarcely breathe. I was looking at the bulge where his hand had gone to the pocket. He repeated that he was reluctant but would have to shoot me before he left. The gun was pointing at me, he said. I know I pleaded, argued, ordered him to stop this, anything I could grasp at, because I felt certain that this was it. I would die now. I do recall one thought clearly: How shabby, how ugly for this to be happening! Empty, meaningless, the beginning of despair. As he spoke quietly to me without malice, it did not occur to me that this man was crazy. I took him at his word, that he was a hit man, and he would do his job. How long we sat there, no more than six feet between us, impossible to say. Ten minutes perhaps, but I had no hope I would talk him out of it.

I calculated the position of the hand in the pocket, abruptly glanced away to the side of the room, and at the same moment lunged across to him, clutching his wrist and pinning the hand against his hip, throwing my body against him in the chair. He struggled briefly, then relaxed. I worked my way down the wrist to the hand. Through the fabric of the coat I felt nothing hard. It was only a hand. I did not release him.

"Stand up."

He meekly struggled to his feet. Keeping my eyes on his face, I ran my hands over his body, repeated the search.

"Sit down."

I phoned the police. When the squad arrived, the two officers asked their questions, searched his car in the parking lot, scarcely spoke to me except to get my story. They took him away. The officers did not disguise their disgust. As they left, one of them said to me, "You get yourself in trouble, and then you call in the men with guns on their belts. I hope I am not on duty the next time you call."

When they left, I had to go in to supper. I'm sure I told Dick Partika what had happened. I probably had a parish meeting that evening. I had been hearing from a number of people that FBI agents had been asking them about me. I told Dick I needed to go on retreat for a few days. I was very tired. I needed to pray.

One of my friends at the Villa said I was looking tired. Right. I said Father Partika was okay with my taking a few days to go on retreat—somewhere out of state, maybe to the Trappist Abbey in Iowa. She said, "Why don't you go to talk to Thomas Merton?" Merton was a Trappist monk at the Abbey of Gethsemani in Kentucky. He was a famous contemplative writer and poet who had been publishing insightful essays on race riots, nonviolence, and Vietnam. Remarkably, his most active engagement with the crisis issues of the day had taken place since he had begun a solitary existence in a hermitage on the abbey grounds in 1965. He seemed to know everything that was going on in America and was one of the heroes of the peace movement. I agreed with her: Yes, Gethsemani would be an ideal place for a retreat. I had spent a night there in my college days when a friend and I had been passing through Kentucky on our way to Birmingham, Alabama, to do summer church work. I would like to go back there. I could not expect to meet Merton, though. He was a hermit now and shielded from public curiosity.

At the end of February I flew to Louisville, took a bus to Bardstown and a cab to the Abbey. The guestmaster received me warmly and showed me my room, the private dining room, the guest area of the cloister chapel and went over the *horarium* (the day started with the chanting of Divine Office at 3:00 A.M.). No, there was no chance of speaking with Father Louis (Merton's monastic name). Every visitor wanted to see him; but he was a hermit now, and Father Abbot carefully guarded his privacy. "I understand," I told the monk. "I knew that would be the case. I came on retreat to speak to God, not to speak to Father Louis."

I began to unwind in the total silence. As I was settling in, there was a knock. The guestmaster, I thought; but, when I opened the door, I was astonished to be facing Chuck Cummings! Chuck had been a year behind me in the minor seminary at Crosier; now he was a Cistercian (Trappist) monk here. He had heard that I had come for retreat and was delighted to see me. His mother had mailed him all the newspaper clippings about my notoriety over war resistance, and he had passed these on to the Abbot. Chuck had permission to interrupt the strict rule of silence to visit with me and to take me for a long walk around the grounds and out onto the paths in the woods. He was very animated and chatty for a man who lives wordless. The next day, a knock at my door. This time it *was* the guestmaster, with a puzzled expression on his face: "Father Abbot asked me to tell you that you may meet with Father Louis for an hour this afternoon just before Vespers. I will come to get you and show you where to go." He hesitated, then added, " I am very surprised."

I found myself waiting at the bottom of a flight of stairs in a hallway of the cloister. I had imagined a silent figure in long, white habit and black cowl sliding out of the shadows. But here, briskly trotting down the steps in work clothes was a guy who looked like a fishing guide from the Iron Range. He stuck out his hand.

"Hi, I'm Father Louis. Come on in here we'll find a place to sit a while."

The rest was that ordinary. He had read the newspaper articles and was most concerned about whether I had a circle of support around me. I assured him I did. We talked a lot about nonviolence, and he suggested I go out to California to check out the school in nonviolence Joan Baez was starting. See what Joan has got going, he said. I wanted to know how he could know in such detail about the race riots and the antiwar movement and everything else he wrote about.

"I even read a monograph in private circulation you wrote about the native peoples of Yucatan. How do you keep up on all that from a hermitage?"

"Oh, lots of people stop by here. They keep me posted. I write a lot of letters and get a lot."

I told him I was writing up a proposal to my bishop requesting that he assign me to the work of forming a community in Duluth focused on service to the poor and nonviolent resistance. It would be a mixed community, people of different faiths and none at all, men and women, families and celibates. He replied that he thought this sort of thing was the way of the future. He spoke of the need for monastic communities of men and women together. It was a chat, serious topics, but just a chat.

" Oh," he added, just as we were about to end, " I'm going out to Asia in the fall."

"To Asia? I thought you were a hermit now."

"I am, but the abbot has given me the green light to go to Thailand and some other countries to talk to the monks there. Catholic monks talking to Buddhist monks, we have a lot to learn from each other. We sure have a lot in common."

I went back to my retreat.

On October 15, Father Louis–Thomas Merton–would leave to travel through India, Sri Lanka and Thailand on a pilgrimage of monastic dialogue. In December, he would be electrocuted at touching a floor fan with faulty wiring in his small cottage room in Bangkok. Chuck Cummings would write me a mournful description of the return of Father Louis's body for burial in the cemetery at Gethsemani. I have read that some of the Asian monks observed signs after his death confirming their suspicion that he had been a reincarnated buddha.

After I returned to Duluth, life slowly began to return to near normal. It took about two months. I had not been contacted by the FBI. I was less frequently in the papers. I spent most of my time being a parish priest again. I was able to do some normal extracurricular things, such as attending a weekend seminar at the Welch Center in West Duluth. This seminar was a diocesan experiment with then popular T-groups. They were also called "sensitivity groups," a social psychology project which had been pioneered by the National Training Laboratory during the preceding twenty years. T-groups were a small-group format encouraging feelings-awareness, sharing of innermost thoughts, disclosure of vulnerabilities, giving and accepting confrontation, reconciliation and bonding. It was a welcome opportunity for me to drop my public persona and simply be Phil with people once again.

I was happy with my work in the parish; however, in May I presented Bishop Schenk with a thirteen-page proposal that I be released from parish duty and assigned to the study of creative nonviolence and the formation of "a new community." As I met with him, I could see him shaking his head, this kind man, thinking, What am I to do with this fellow?

"Father, these things have been tried before. They don't last. Father, you have really put me in a bind. Do you know I will not be able to assign you to any of the parishes on the Iron Range? They have told me they won't have you!"

"Yes, I suppose not, Bishop. But all the more reason this proposal..."

"No, Father. No. Give this plan of yours a year. Come back and talk to me about it in a year."

"All right, Bishop."

It is striking that he was so patient with me, so respectful with a young priest out of control. Clearly he had been indignant at my bomb-shell approach to protesting the war; and here I was suggesting my own assignment in something vague and outlandish. However I suspect that he may have actually been ambivalent about what I was doing. His official statement after the pamphlet affair actually defended me. And a printed interview with him at the very time I was proposing my own assignment left me suspecting that my public statements were not that far from his own thinking and that he understood that things need to be said in strong ways when it appears no one is listening. The May 19, 1968 issue of the *Minneapolis Tribune* reported an interview with him:

"Father Philip Solem is a good priest," said the bishop. " I had to react positively. I got angry letters, some pressure. I didn't think much of the method he used–sending copies of his antidraft pamphlet into the homes of students by mail. Some of these parents had sons in service.

"If you have an audience that wants to hear you, okay. Nevertheless I think some of these things need to be said. We have a world of violence and sometimes you think people aren't paying much attention to it. If we believe we are God's people, we ought to act that way."

But there were limits. On August 2 he called me in on hearing of a planned major draft resistance rally in Minneapolis scheduled for August 6, anniversary of the bombing of Hiroshima. I was to be the main speaker. He forbad me to attend. I argued with him that I had to go; the publicity was already out; everything was set. That was not his problem; I could not go. I pleaded and negotiated; and finally he relented, on the strict condition that I would not urge anyone to break the law.

"Bernie, come in here!" he called to Father Popesh in the next office. "Bernie, I want you to witness this! I want you to hear me telling Father Solem that he is not to urge anyone to break the law. That's a direct order, Father!"

I went to the rally and gave the main address. I told them right away that they would be disappointed in my message, explaining that I chose to obey my bishop and stay united to him. I would urge no one to break the law that day. I then went on to give a more general advocacy of resistance to evil in all its forms. That evening nine Catholic priests turned in their draft cards. One of them was Joe Selvaggio, whom I met there for the first time and who would marry Jackie and me two years later. The Twin Cities Draft Information Center had prepared a letter to be used in mailings to men classified I-A and in high school programs. One hundred seventy-five people signed it. It said: "To Men of Draft Age. We urge you to disobey the conscription law; we urge you to resist the draft and to refuse induction; we urge you not to fight in Vietnam. Although as adults we are not eligible for conscription, we are disobeying the law by urging you to resist. We join with over three thousand men of your age who have already refused induction."

On it continued, month after month. I am weary telling it. These were the days of the Tet Offensive in Vietnam, which marked the turning point of the war. American support was beginning to slip. Walter Cronkite in a special report on Tet opined that we were "mired in a stalemate" and called for a negotiated end to the war.

In September the Milwaukee Fourteen burned draft files, and I wrote to my good friend, Trenk: "You remember Fred Ojile? The small guy who gave the talk before I did (at the August 6 rally)? Now he is in jail in Milwaukee, being one of the fourteen. And so is my very good friend, Larry Rosebaugh, an Oblate priest with whom I taught two years at Duluth Cathedral High School and whom I visited (at the Catholic Worker House) in Chicago last summer. And so is Mike Cullen, the former head of the Catholic Worker House in Milwaukee...(where) we went to stay last June. And so is Brother Basil O'Leary whom I met at a Vietnam talk I gave in Winona last spring. All in jail, damn it. All excellent men. And I feel a little sick."

I went on in that private letter to explain that, although I refused to do these men the indignity of critiquing publicly this kind of direct action, I myself had grave reservations about it. I believed in the nonviolence of communicating with what was best in the heart of one's opponent and felt that adding the element of sabotage, breaking and entering, destruction of property, muddied the message and threatened those with whom one wished to speak. Moreover, a strategy of attack on government and corporate properties could eventually lead to attacks on people.

I had a chance to test this position a few months later when I myself was invited to participate in a top-secret, two-day planning session in a rural Wisconsin farmhouse organized by Phil Berrigan. Phil explained that the resistance movement's strategy was to steadily increase the numbers of people involved in these "actions" of destroying federal and corporate assets while staying to accept arrest. He himself had been part of the Baltimore Four, which had been followed by the Catonsville Nine and now the Milwaukee Fourteen. Next would come perhaps a twenty-one, then a thirty-eight, and so on. There were about two dozen people at this meeting.

I listened carefully and made my objections to this approach. At the end of the second day, it was decided that "another action" would go forward. Those who were "in" went to one room of the farmhouse to plan the next stage, while those who were "not in" were directed to withdraw to another room. As radical and urgent as I felt about the war, this was not my way, and I went to the second room. We were given no further information on the plan.

I went home and watched the newspapers day after day. Eventually it came: a simultaneous dual-break-in at Washington, D.C.–one at a Selective Service office, one at the offices of Dow Chemical, maker of napalm. One of them was botched. The brief newspaper account was carried without followup on page seven. There were arrests. I heard or read nothing more about it. There was no light at the end of this tunnel.

....

But we were not really in a tunnel. Life was spread out all around us, and there was more to it than war and draft. Shortly after New Years, 1969, Sister Gladys from a Franciscan convent in Superior, Wisconsin, just across the bay from Duluth, called me. She wanted to know if I had received the mailing inviting people who had participated in past Welch Center T-group seminars to apply for a followup marathon in February. Yes, I had seen it. Was I going to apply? She had been in my small-group when I had made the weekend several months back. No, I didn't think so, I said. I thought I had better be sticking to business a bit more for a while.

"Oh, come on," she begged, "Apply! *I* have applied. I was really hoping you would. I would really like to talk to you again. We made such a good connection on our weekend!"

"I don't know. Maybe, maybe not. I'll think about it."

"It's just a five-hour session–they're calling it 'a marathon.' One evening. You can get away that long. Come on."

"I'll see."

She must have talked me into it, because I sent in the form. A week or two later I got a notice from the Welch Center. I had been selected to participate. They had received many applications, but this initial marathon would be only one small-group: three married couples, a single layman, a single laywoman, one priest, one sister, led by Iver Bogen from the UMD Psychology Department. Sister Gladys was not on the list. Sister Jacqueline Vesel, O.S.B. was.

FIVE

Falling in Love

We gathered in a small, comfortable upper room of the Welch Center and sat on floor cushions. I knew all these people. One couple had been on the weekend seminar I had made here earlier. One was Welch Center staff. I knew Iver from UMD, and Don and Bev were in my parish. Matt and I had gotten to know each other somewhere or other. And, of course, I had met Sister Jacqueline a number of times at Sister Ambrose's philosophy discussion seminars at the Villa Saint Scholastica.

It was to be a five-hour, intensive, personal encounter ending at midnight. Iver structured group activities to facilitate a trusting give-and-take about feelings rather than ideas. At one point he directed us to pair off and instructed us to look into a partner's eyes without words for a full two minutes. What Jacqueline remembers that she saw in my eyes during that two-minute eternity was "Love. Just gentle, tender, love." I saw that her eyes were green, fluid, shimmering like the play of sunlight through leaves in breeze, now mirth, now grave intensity. We did not fall in love in that moment, but we became keenly aware of one another.

....

What was it that powered our movement away from the structures of chosen religious commitments toward behaviors which threatened them and gradually ushered us toward a decision, a year and a half later, to leave them? It was no one thing, certainly not the intimacy of looking deeply into one another's eyes. We were both well grounded and had put in years of heartfelt labor to be what we were–nun, priest. Neither of us were dissatisfied with our vocations, nor were we considering leaving them. However, like everyone else, we were being swept along in the fast-moving river of time, and the times indeed were a' changing. It was a period of unusual transition for the churches, for society in general. The reformation taking place within our home church was not primarily about the cut of nuns' habits or the retirement of Latin or the debate on birth control. Deep transformation was taking place at the less visible level of philosophy, a wholesale reevaluation of meanings. We had been taught religion at a time when the church scarcely seemed to flow with the river of time, seemed instead to stand like a rock amidst the agitations of the world eddying round it. Our church was One, Holy, Catholic, Apostolic. We learned to be proud of its stability and uniformity. We were proud of its flocks of nuns, effaced individuals, as indistinguishable from one another as penguins. Proud of its stately processions of priests and mitered bishops vested in glinting garments of bygone ages, passing between the drawn-sword salute of Knights of Columbus. Men who chose to become professionals became acquainted with the mystic language of the church and could read the *Enchiridion Symbolorum* (a compilation of centuries of dogmatic decrees and definitions) and the volumes of A. Tanquerey, the professional's codification of dogma. Definitive answers were given, sometimes cloaked in mystery, but always answers beyond challenge.

By the time each of us entered formal training, Jacqueline in the convent, I in the seminary at Louvain, the official church was showing clear signs of movement and flow. The Second Vatican Council spoke of the solidarity of the church with the whole human family and acknowledged deep-seated changes in the social order, in attitudes, morals, and religion. Sister Jacqueline made her final vows at a time when the meaning of the vows of poverty, chastity, obedience, were being reexamined, not only at the upper tiers of Catholic authority but at mid-level among theologians and at the grassroots among those living the vows. The language used in this rediscovery was strikingly different from what it once was and carried the influences of current secular philosophies.

Jackie recently showed me a spiral notebook that she had used to take notes on lectures she had heard in 1967-68 at the priory and during her posting in Minneapolis. There is a summary of Sister Elodie's instruction on the vows which opened with a quote from the great Cardinal Newman to the effect that "renewal (is) the normal state of (religious) community...identity of community is perpetuated by change." This was followed with a development of themes of freedom, personal responsibility, and "openness–limpidity of the whole person." Her discussion of human sexuality, seldom addressed as such in former times, did not focus on sin, shame, and reproduction, but on a recognition of its place in the physiology and psychology of the whole human person.

In another place, Jacqueline's notes report on a 1968 two-day conference at the St. Paul Auditorium called "Institute of Man." Chicago Cardinal Cody opened it with a keynote on human rights, including "religious freedom, the right to act according to conscience without force." She had many pages of notes from talks by some of the best theologians of the day speaking on sexuality, ecumenism, religious vows, and the inner dynamics of religious life. These lecture notes reflect energy and momentum, relational language with overtones of European existentialism: "being present to...," "standing as an authentic person in accepting responsibility for...," "dialectical availability." They speak of growth, development, "dynamic views of sexuality."

It was a new intellectual climate. At the same time, role constraints were relaxing. Developing warm personal friendships in and outside the convent was becoming normal. The Welch Center encounter groups and followup marathon were church-sponsored; and in these intense experiences, Jacqueline found recognition that her affective world and sensitive inner life was acceptable. She had always feared that feeling so intensely was suspect. It had certainly seemed so as she was growing up and was never encouraged during her early years in the convent. Now the whole meaning of relationship in her life was being affirmed and especially her relationship with God. For her, God had never been someone "out there," but always a strong presence within. She had once been fearful of talking this way, fearful that this sounded questionable and suspicious to other people, at worst, heretical. She had intuitively known that a pious goal of "dying to one's self" should not mean extinguishing feelings. Until now, however, she had not known how to move out of this toward health. At last there was clear validation of her strong emotional life and need for personal relationship.

For my part, my very zeal for the priestly life as I saw it was carrying me away from the structures that supported it. I spoke publicly of my love for the priesthood and my scorn of clerical status, which I described as a condition of privilege and separation from the people, a domestication of men called to proclaim and live the radical gospel of Jesus. Having recently run a fearful gauntlet of public notoriety, in which cameras and reporters exposed my innermost beliefs, feelings, and motivations for all to see, I was in a daring mood, unafraid of emotional turmoil and unpredictable relationships. In fact, just days before the five-hour marathon, I had given the new co-adjutor bishop, who would soon succeed the ailing Bishop Schenk, an outline of the new priestly lifestyle I intended to take up. It was no longer a request but an ultimatum that I be released from parish duty for full-time work on nonviolence research and community founding. It announced that I would begin by summer, in effect, reassigning myself. I had made a less audacious proposal to Bishop Schenk the previous year, and he had asked me to let it lie for a year. Now in February, 1969, he directed me to take the matter up with his assistant, Bishop Paul Anderson. This new bishop was a sincere, humble, honest man who, only a few months earlier, had been a parish priest in South Dakota. I doubt he ever wanted to be a bishop. He was always friendly and respectful with me and would eventually become a good friend. However, he must have been dismayed at the scope and tone of the eleven-page document I handed him declaring my plans. It was not new material–I had been proposing these ideas for well over a year–but it was sharply chiseled now and very unconventional. It began with a thought that I had once written down in my personal journal:

> *The very things which our elders and our teachers taught us to believe and to do will cause them to take scandal on account of us and to oppose us, if we do them. We should be patient with them and kind, trying to understand that never in all the world did they think that we would take them seriously.*

I would no longer live in a rectory nor serve as parish priest at St. Anthony's. I would live in a rented apartment in voluntary poverty and not look to the diocese for financial support. I would remain celibate and serve as a street-priest, earning a living. I would study nonviolence and work to form small communities of nonviolent activists. I would continue as a diocesan priest, celebrating the liturgy regularly and available to parishes and chaplaincies as a substitute where needed. I intended "to read, study, pray, and plan exploratory workshops and seminars; to continue draft counseling; to expose myself to the realities of lay life and the day-to-day difficulties of survival and to put myself in the position of vulnerability to learning much of what the clerical culture has protected me from...."

What did Bishop Anderson think of this? I can only guess he was not unsympathetic and even appreciated the idealism driving it. However, he must have wondered if this was the beginning of the end for me. In any case, he did not say no. He delayed a response. Unwilling to be put off, I followed with a letter in April formally resigning from my current assignments and pledging continued loyalty to the church.

....

On the March 8th page of her appointment book, Jacqueline jotted her feelings about the Welch Center evening:

How tremendous! Our marathon was a total success as far as I was concerned... I feel very loved, very 'on-the-way' and I believe God is working very strongly in my vulnerability, preparing me to accept greater & greater love–how I ache with it.... I thank God for great happenings. I could go on and on–I'm beat!

The rest of us felt similar elation, and at the end of the evening most wanted to continue meeting. Tony and Marge offered their living room. We agreed to get together once or twice a month on Thursdays for an improvised continuation of "our encounter group." We did meet three or four times until summer; and each time I hastened to offer Sister Jacqueline a ride, since she had no car. We were eager to get to know one another. I think I drove slowly–to make the ride last.

The morning after our final gathering–it was a glorious May morning exactly two months after we had first really met–she and I spoke on the phone, a long, unhurried conversation, with lingering silences...speaking of the previous evening's sharing and also of the depth of feeling we had for each other in our surprising new friendship. We also spoke of our hope and belief that this kind of depth could be sustained by men and women committed to the unmarried life for the sake of the ministry. We were in clear agreement that the special love growing between us should warm and energize the service we would give to the people of God and that we would remain separate in our consecrated states of life.

When she hung up the phone, Jacqueline noticed that all this while she had been absent-mindedly sketching on a message pad the image of two flowers side-by-side, one slightly larger than the other.

When I hung up the phone, I went up to the empty church and began to pace the aisles with emotion rising like a tide. "My God!" I said aloud to the master of that house. "I am falling in love! Can this be? I am in love with this woman!" I said it with a sense of shock at first, then said it again and again in joy and amazement. I knew it was good. I knew it was trouble. I knew we would be all right. And I continued to pace and pace and laugh and talk in that church.

....

Bishop Anderson asked me to defer my departure from St. Anthony's until the fall, since the new pastor there, who had just replaced Father Partika, would be out of commission all summer from double hip-replacement surgery at the hospital in Rochester, Minnesota. My third pastor in four years was Fr. Jim Crossman, a pious, warm-hearted man, meek and humble, a good priest. He was twenty years senior, but we quickly became good friends. I agreed that I would stay on at the parish until he healed from surgery and was ready to return to work. This made me, in effect, the pastor of this parish without the title. I was suddenly in charge, a strange irony. As unpredictable and troublesome as I had been in the diocese for the past four years, I had also been a stable presence in the parish during the transitions of three head-pastors. I had come a long way from my arrival day, fresh from the seminary, when the first pastor had designated all the rooms of the rectory, including the kitchen, that were off-limits to me. During this summer when I had just fallen in love with Jacqueline, I took on the full responsibility, pastoral and administrative. I became familiar with the financial books, raised extra donations from parishioners to have the interior of the church painted for the first time in fifty years, and had new carpet laid on the shabby, scuffed wooden flooring. At the same time I continued war resistance activities and community work, regularly hanging out at 25 West Fourth, a local commune, with hippies, flower children, draft resisters and alienated young men passing through on their way to Canada.

When the school year ended, Sister Jacqueline went to Tower to teach summer catechism to children. She lived with her parents at home in Soudan. At the end of her teaching session she invited me to visit and meet her family. She introduced me as her friend; and, whatever misgivings they might have had about their controversial visitor, they received me with easy friendliness. Her dad, Matt, took the two of us out fishing in his boat on Lake Vermilion, and I was even invited to stay overnight at their friends' home. Jacqueline and I thought all had gone well. However, her mother told us later that, as soon as I had left, Matt had turned to her and said: "Honey, those two aren't just friends! They're in love!"

....

True, but at this point Sister Jacqueline fully intended to continue living her vows, and I intended to remain a priest. Midsummer I gave the bishop a three-page description of my plans. After restating my commitment to the priesthood, it outlined a program of research, establishment of a peace center, founding of a community house, and a schedule of devotional routines and pastoral service. For over a year I had been working out these ideas with my friend, Sister Ambrose. For a time we thought this might be a joint venture. She also was pressing to develop new forms of community in the Benedictine tradition: men and women, families and singles living together in contemplative prayer and radical reform of life. Our shared vision blended the contemplative life with social engagement. We thought to co-found a "house of peace;" however, we did not agree on its location. Ambrose wanted a renewal of monasticism and saw the house in a place withdrawn, a light on a hill, which would attract and inspire. At a time when all her peers had put aside traditional nuns' clothing and deportment, she continued to wear the full habit, black veil and black gown down to her black shoe tips. She wanted to call people to a forest retreat house. I was determined that our work be in the heart of the city where the people were. Ambrose and I remained close friends but took diverging paths. That summer she and two other sisters opened The House of Peace as a contemplative monastery and

retreat center in an abandoned hospital in the tiny, end-of-the-road community of Winton, three miles beyond her hometown, Ely.

Sister Jacqueline continued to live at St. James Convent in West Duluth and returned to St. Rose School for a second year that fall. She and I
would often meet at charismatic prayer gatherings, which were newly in
vogue among Catholics. These sessions of song, tongue-speaking, listening to the Spirit, prophecy, and Bible prayer took place in family living
rooms and convent houses. Sometimes I would be asked to celebrate the
Eucharist. Sometimes we would join in unlikely fellowship at the Duluth
Gospel Tabernacle where Pentecostal praise and exuberant witnessing
had always been the norm. We and our friends would "pray for a passage," then randomly open the Bible, hoping it would not fall open at
Leviticus, and devoutly read what lay before our eyes, listening for a personal message. It alarmed Jacqueline and me when, more than once, we
got something like this from an Epistle of Paul: "Everyone should stay
in whatever state he was in when he was called" (I Cor. 7). We had been
thinking that almost anything might be possible in our church-in-transi-
tion in days to come. No doubt, as our love grew hotter, we hoped there
might be a chance for us to be together somehow. These passages worried us. Was the Apostle mystically warning us off?

On August 22, Bishop Anderson wrote me a letter of authorization to
begin the exploratory style of ministry I had proposed. My good friend,
Brooks Anderson, a Lutheran campus chaplain, had offered me rent-free
space in the basement of the Lutheran Student Center , an old mansion on
Superior Street . He helped me clean out a dingy junk room, which had
once been the coal bin, and whitewash its stone walls. In keeping with
my aspirations to live in poverty, I had given away all my possessions
and only brought in a few books, a wooden kneeler for prayer, a bed, and
my clothes. On the wall, only two pictures: Mohandas Gandhi, Thomas
Merton. I had access to the basement kitchen and telephone, shared with
a dozen or so male and female students who lived on the second and
third floors. We began to live a mild form of community there, eating together, recreating together, having periodic house meetings to work out
practical matters. I began my nonviolence study, began writing essays.

Bishop Schenk died that fall. I continued to go up to St. Anthony's
to help out with the weekend Masses. I was now living only two blocks
from Bishop Anderson's house, so I concelebrated weekday Masses with

him in his chapel and joined him for breakfast afterwards. A number of liberal Catholic families had approached me and asked me to start "a floating parish" with them, an experiment being tried in other parts of the country. The bishop okayed this and even offered the use of his chapel and sitting rooms.

I was easily able to keep him posted on the progress of my activities, but not on the yearning of my heart. Hovering about all my energetic undertakings, never absent from my thought and feeling, was this woman. She was with me constantly, and now my anguished prayers were that we could one day, somehow, be together. Surely the church rules would change, surely priests would soon be allowed to marry. It was only a matter of time, that seemed clear. I do not think that she was thinking this way at that time. For her to be with me would mean leaving her vows. Not so simple for her. I could begin to think about being a married priest; she could never be a married nun. She did not want to hear the word "marriage."

....

A quiet, clear evening. Autumn. I was fishing with a friend — I don't remember whom — not someone I could freely talk to, probably a guy from my parish. We were in a boat, hunched over our poles, silent together, waiting for a bite. The swifts were darting and swooping all about us, dipping and turning, flycatching inches above the water. These words rose through me as though up from the water:

Les oiseaux volent sur les vagues,
Leurs ailes touchantes l'eau douce et bonne.
Et le soir sonne la fin du jour:
Jacqueline. Jacqueline.
(The birds fly over the waves, their wings touching the water, sweet and good. And the evening tolls the end of the day. Jacqueline. Jacqueline.)

....

Her father was in Minneapolis for more radiation treatment that fall, her mother with him, staying with Aunt Julie. Jacqueline spent a weekend with them in November, and I also went there to visit them. Matt was gaunt, thin, not the man I had seen casting from a boat into Lake

Vermilion in July. The family appeared to take my attentions as something normal. Their attention was on him, not on us.

....

From Jacqueline's appointment calendar:

Jan. 3, 1970...dinner at 5:00 with Sr. Jean Paul – Rev. Jim Price & wife at seminar after dinner till 12:00 – Mass – Jean Paul, Phil & I talked till.... (trails off). Then: Jan. 4 (Sunday): services at Calvary Baptist, Jim Price's church – very good.

We clearly were moving toward a time of decision. It had now been a year since we had begun falling in love. Jim Price was a counselor at the university and pastor of the only black Baptist congregation in northern Minnesota. It must have been an interesting novelty for these folks to have white Catholic nuns showing up for rousing, swaying, hand-raising singing and hot preaching on Sunday mornings.

Jim was our good friend, and a group of us had begun to meet with him frequently for long, soul-searching discussions. All of us were in transition, seriously considering leaving the religious life. This was the only venue where Jacqueline and I could be open about our love and our struggles of vocational discernment. Jim offered us private counseling, and we began to meet with him regularly at his and Marylina's home. Usually we would come together; but sometimes he would see us individually. We must have clocked at least fifty hours of counseling with him in group, couple, and individual sessions over those first months of the year. By February Jacqueline had decided she would apply to the Vatican for a dispensation from vows. She had not yet decided to marry. Around that time I knew I would have to talk to the bishop about this and request a leave of absence.

Jacqueline spoke to the house superior at St. James Convent where she lived. The sister was very upset and, without much discussion, insisted: "You have to leave at once!"

"I'm not leaving now!" Sister Jacqueline retorted. "I have to finish the school year. I am going to see the bishop!"

She did go to see him. He was kind to her and "...talked about everything *but* what I was there for. It was a very strange conversation. He was very good to me."

I had a similar experience. Bishop Anderson and I had concelebrated weekday Mass together in his chapel as usual that morning. We were sitting in the sunshine at breakfast at his kitchen table. I told him about my relationship with Sister Jacqueline, told him that it was getting very serious and...

"Well, Phil, these things do happen. And sometimes they can be good. They happen...pass me the salt, please."

That was it. A week later I told him explicitly that I wanted to take a leave from the diocese. I told him Jacqueline and I did not have definite plans to marry but that it seemed to be the direction we were heading. He was less offhand, but made no effort to dissuade me. I was surprised but realize now that he had been expecting this conversation for a long time and knew from experience that I was not one to be talked out of things. He simply asked me to talk to Bernie Popesh about applying for laicization from the Vatican.

"No, Bishop," I said. "I do not intend to apply. I am a priest and want to continue to work as a priest, even if it is in violation of canon law. I am not asking for permission to become a layman. I am wanting to marry her, that is the only reason I am doing this–not because I want to leave the priesthood."

He understood me. In the Catholic system, once a priest, always a priest. I had taken no vows but at ordination had accepted the church law forbidding marriage. Now I would violate that law and continue the valid exercise of priestly ministry–Mass, absolution of sin, marriages, all of it–without authorization.

"I really wish you would get laicized, Phil. But, if not, I'd ask you to be discreet and not make unnecessary trouble. Don't go saying home Masses up there in Dan McEnery's parish (a fierce Irish pastor up on the hill)."

I promised to be careful.

On March 6, Sister had a formal meeting with Mother Martina at the Villa. Papers were signed. On March 9, the bishop wrote granting me a "six-month leave of absence." He thanked me for my years of service... in effect, a goodbye letter. I must have taken umbrage at the way he had represented my leave in a notification sent out to my fellow clergy in the diocese, for a week later he wrote me again:

Dear Phil...I would like to say I am sorry if I in any way embarrassed you or misrepresented your true aims in the letter that was sent to the priests. It perhaps did seem funereal in tone, but this last week I have prepared three sets of papers for priests who want to be laicized and then you asked to be relieved of your duties at St. Anthony's...I have always made the effort to be kind to you and to listen to you, although it has been difficult for me to understand completely what it is that you are trying to do. I feel that even you do not know. When I said that I truly appreciated what you had done for people and the diocese, I meant this most sincerely, and I still mean it. God be with you.

Although much time would pass, we would meet again, heart-to-heart; and I would be afforded the opportunity to heal and be healed from the hurt that I was doing to this lovely man.

....

Jacqueline continued teaching at St. Rose School into the spring until June. I had offered to stay on at St. Anthony's through Holy Week and Easter to assist while the work of the liturgy would be most demanding; but the bishop had said, no, now that I had decided, I should go. So I gave a final homily at all the Masses one Sunday letting the people know I was leaving, then went to my coal bin room at the Lutheran Student Center and put aside my Roman collar and black suit for the last time. Holy Week was beginning. I was unemployed.

A family in the parish who owned a small floral shop hired me to deliver Easter baskets and bouquets during the Holy Week rush. Then a boyhood pal gave me five weeks of work in Minneapolis/St. Paul as a temp with a grocery chain distributor. My work was to ride along with salesmen on their supermarket rounds and apply stick-on correction labels to Kool-Aid cartons which had been misprinted. The last week I was given a rental truck loaded with Kool-Aid racks which I was to deliver and assemble in store aisles from town to town upstate, on into territory where I had recently been the parish priest. The job was humbling, the pay good, the work mindless. I was grateful for all three.

On May 1st I was back in Duluth and joined Jacqueline for our final gathering with Jim Price and our discernment group. This session lasted well past midnight, on into the early hours of the morning. At the end she and I wearily sat alone for a few moments in the kitchen. We had been talking all evening about uncertain days ahead. Most of the sisters in the group had already petitioned for release from vows. Summer was coming. I wanted to marry. Jacqueline had been fearful and uncertain, not ready. I had never directly asked her for a decision. Now I did. I recall her exact words:

"Oh, I don't know, Phil. I guess so."

....

Two weeks later the rescript from the Vatican arrived dispensing her from her vows. We were now both free to be together openly but resolved to take some time before moving toward marriage, personal time to find our identities outside of religious life and time to find work. Time, also, to get reacquainted. When the school year ended, she moved to Minneapolis to live with the Dale family and work in a summer youth program at Augustana Lutheran Church. Mornings she worked the day-camp with low-income, inner-city kids; afternoons she made home visits to their families.

I stayed in Duluth and opened a storefront draft counseling office on First Street called the Duluth Area Peace Center. Our local peace committee set it up as a field office of the American Friends Service Committee and funneled donations through their nonprofit tax-exempt books. For the next year-and-a-half this national Quaker service organization would be my employer and bring me at times to Des Moines and Philadelphia for supervision and training. I was already thoroughly trained in Selective Service law and owned a set of the government regulations manuals. I knew the legal draft exemptions, deferments, appeals and conscientious objector procedures as thoroughly as any draft board clerk. My salary was one hundred dollars a month—less than my mother earned when she went to her teaching job in Ely in 1927.

Jackie did much better. The Human Development Center in Duluth contacted her midsummer. They had heard of her changed vocational status and wondered if she would be interested in a position on their Child Team as a group worker in their Day Treatment Program for children. Connie Burdick would be leaving her position there soon and had recommended Jackie as an ideal replacement. When Connie had gone out as a consultant to Sister Jacqueline's classroom at St. Rose School, she had been impressed at how naturally and successfully Jacqueline had taken to the group process methods she had advised. At the time, neither of them could have suspected that this collaboration would constitute a preliminary job interview. Now, in the summer of 1970, Jackie had an excellent job waiting for her with good pay, good training opportunities, and the beginning of a lifelong career as a psychotherapist. She would start work as soon as we returned from our honeymoon.

....

The answer to how we would live was taken care of. Now, where would we live? There was not a great deal of uncertainty about this, for the draft counseling and the Peace Center were a continuation of the work which I had originally proposed to two bishops. Jackie had agreed to join me in the project of founding a communal household as the center for an extended community of service. While she was working at Augustana Lutheran in Minneapolis, I was meeting weekly with a group of thirty or so people in Duluth who were interested in establishing an intentional service community to sustain a variety of alternative projects: free school, newspaper, food co-op, runaway shelter, underground railroad, war resistance. All this planning took place during potluck suppers at the Lutheran Student Center where I was living.

At the end of July, Jackie finished her job in Minneapolis and went home to Soudan for several weeks to be with her family and sew her wedding dress. During that time she came down to Duluth several times to join the final stages of planning the new community and take part in house hunting.

Six of us from the larger planning group decided to move together into a communal household to provide a base and meeting house large enough for the undertaking. We would pool our money to buy one of the large older homes in east Duluth. There were many of these, relics of the city's glory days in timber and mining early in the century, affordable now because they were too overbuilt for the current typical family market. Few of us had much money to pool. However, Mary and Ed Fleege,

St. Anthony's parishioners, offered to loan two thousand dollars without interest for a house down payment.

Equipped now to begin house hunting in earnest, the six of us soon made a number of tours and quickly settled on a homely three-storey house with a rather charming circular turret facing Chester Creek and a solid stonewall basement, concealing a second sub-basement below that. It had a large kitchen, a beautifully wood-paneled dining room, two living rooms, two staircases, and many bedrooms on the second and third floors. It was perfect.

The six of us who scheduled a sit-down negotiation session with Mr. Irwin, the owner, were Matt Doyle, Bob and Patsy Sun with their infant, Kiya, Jackie Vesel and Phil Solem. We had prepared our bargaining strategy carefully. Matt, from a family of business people, had the most experience and business sense. He would be our spokesman. The asking price was $26,000. We could casually tour the house one more time, asking a lot of questions, then open with our offer of $21,000. From there, we would allow ourselves to be bargained upward to a ceiling of $25,000. If Irwin would not accept that, we would look elsewhere.

A few days after our first walk-through, we sat down with the owner at the end of our second inspection, during which we had affected mild, detached interest. Not entirely certain of our dance, we chatted for a bit about other things, circling. Then Matt brought up the question of price.

"Well," Mr. Irwin came back suddenly and firmly, "this is a good house and I am not willing to give it away. I am going to have to get no less than $19,500 for it!"

We sat speechless, glancing from one to the other. I hope our mouths were not hanging open. Matt had the presence of mind to request politely that we be excused for a moment to talk this over privately.

"Of course," said Mr. Irwin.

We caucused in an adjoining room. Very briefly.

"Now what? He underbid us!"

"There goes our strategy."

"Strategy," grinned Matt. "I guess this is the point where we agreed we would counter-offer $21,000. But maybe—maybe we should just—cave in!"

SIX
....

"However, when you stand over here..."

A boat lay half-pulled-up on shore in the weeds where Mike and Jo had left it for us. By the light of a golden rising moon we stumbled and groped our gear and food down from the car and were soon motoring across shining black water toward their island. Our honeymoon cabin for the next two weeks would be a basic mobile home which had been dragged across winter ice onto two acres in Big Sandy. We would wake beside each other in the mornings, astonished at what we had just done, wondering what we were doing here. Moments later, I would be telling her outrageous tall tales and getting her laughing. We spent the days exploring the tiny island, reading in the sunshine, pouring over handbooks on Minnesota birds and flowers, swimming and boating. We took shovels over to Battle Island, just across from ours, to excavate in vain for flint arrowheads where a major fight between Chippewa and Sioux had once taken place. Each morning we meditated and prayed, then celebrated the Eucharist at the kitchen table. Awkwardly we learned the movements of love. In preparation for marriage that summer, each of us had been reading what we could find about the joy of sex, arousal response, growth in relationship. Probably Jackie had been getting some education from women friends, and she had passed on to me what she had been learning. I can't say I was talking to guys about this. On our island, making love did not come as the most natural thing in the world; but we were learning and were laughing a lot.

A lot of people had advised us to take time for each other and not move into a community house at once. Our view was that we would need the presence of friends and supporters at the start of a highly visible and controversial marriage. I think our decision was correct: life in Chester Creek House during the next four years was rich and wholesome.

Reentry from honeymoon in the first week of September was immediately intense. The first morning back in Duluth, Jackie and I struggled out of bed well before dawn and went down to the Civic Center to help serve cocoa, donuts, and leaflets to drafted young men gathering to be loaded onto buses headed for the Armed Forces Examination and Entrance Station in Minneapolis. This had been a monthly part of my work at the Peace Center. For Jackie it was the first time she had taken part in resistance activity. Along with her steady, clear gaze and the cup of cocoa she handed each young man, was a leaflet informing him of alternatives to accepting induction a few hours away. What we were doing was legal; but now she was sharing with me the familiar atmosphere of hostile tension, the subdued mood of dread and resentment from young men and their parents who had come to say goodbye at this miserable hour of the morning. Later that week we went to the movie "Z" about the resistance to the Greek dictatorship of the 1960s ending in repression and assassination of the leftist democratic leader. That night in bed, she clung to me and wept, fearing she would lose me.

That same day, the first back from honeymoon, I received a phone call from a St.Louis County social worker asking if Jackie and I could temporarily house a young mentally ill black woman. In those days there were few community resources. Our community house was not yet available, and we were living for a week or so on the third floor of the Lutheran Student Center. We said yes. I think her name might have been Sharon, perhaps eighteen or nineteen years old, I don't remember. She was attractive, spacey, delusional, and given to hallucinations but not threatening. At that time Jackie and I did not know anything about schizophrenia. She had been released from the state hospital too early and was not doing well in the community. Perhaps with a little more time...? She slept in the room across the hall, ate with us, hung out with us in the evenings. We took her along whenever we went out, just looked

after her. After a week, it was not working. She was becoming more un-
raveled, and I had to call the social worker back. A day later Sharon (I
think) went back to the Anoka State Hospital.

Just in time for us to move into Chester Creek House. This would be
home for the next four years. It was, by indirection, a fulfillment of the
proposal I had made to two bishops. Jackie and I saw it as a continuation
of our shared spiritual life and the place from which to live our marriage
of service. It would eventually become transition to a life we were not
anticipating. Although we were founders and leaders of this experiment,
the community venture, full of surprises, would shape us as much as
we shaped it. A year and a half after we moved in, I wrote a book about
the community's formation and first year, presenting even-handed reflections on it as an experiment in nonviolence and alternative lifestyle.
However, the book ended just as some of the most significant changes
in our lives were about to begin. Much of the description in the next few
pages come from that manuscript (1972):

> *They ranged through the giant house to stake out rooms like settlers on a*
> *vast, open frontier. Only three bedroom areas were needed now: for Matt,*
> *for Jackie-Phil, and for Patsy-Bob-Kiya. Plenty of guest rooms.*
>
> *It had been a showpiece home, built before the turn of the century by*
> *a wealthy family that eventually went bankrupt. There had been servants,*
> *as was clear from the two staircases, side-by-side, one broad, open and car-*
> *peted to the second floor, the other narrow and plain to the third. There had*
> *been a cloakroom by the front door, two parlors, three fireplaces, and an*
> *elegant dining room with dark oak wainscoting, paneled ceiling, parquet*
> *floor, cupboards with cut-glass doors, and many mirrors....Climbing from*
> *a third-floor bedroom rose a round turret with windows facing north to*
> *the city banking up the hillside, west toward the creek, south toward Lake*
> *Superior which opened like an ocean in the brilliant autumn sun, three*
> *blocks away.*

Matt Doyle was an elementary school teacher. He had grown up in a
close Irish Catholic family of business people. He had a quiet, playfully
ironic manner. It was hard to know what he was thinking. His interest in
the community was stable and practical. Bob and Patsy Sun were from
California. They were noble and compelling personalities, committed to
respect for the environment and egalitarian ideals. They had lived com-

munally for years–at Tolstoy Farm in Washington State, at the Community for Nonviolent Action in Connecticut, and in the Freefolk commune near Bemidji, Minnesota. Their son, Kiya, was six months old when they moved into Chester Creek House in Duluth.

Patsy and Bob suggested the community's first service project even before moving day. They had been working with a group of people on plans for a new Whole Foods Co-op and wanted to offer the ample basement of the Chester Creek House as a startup location. Matt, Jackie, and Phil readily agreed.

From the 1972 manuscript:

Monday evening. The house was quieting. Jackie and Phil still puttered and shuffled boxes and furniture in the hall and living room. Arranging rooms gave Jackie the feeling that this was becoming home.

People began to arrive for the co-op meeting. At first Jackie would go to the door; but they entered without knocking, walked past and up the stairs, as though the way were familiar. Long hair, bushy beards, wire-rimmed glasses, "Hi, where's the meeting?" beads, bushy hair, frazzled hair, scrawny mustaches, frayed army jackets, boots, bare feet, tattered denim, "Patsy and Bob upstairs?" patches over patches, wrinkled shirts.
She came back to Philip tense and shaken.

"My God! I feel like this isn't my home!"

"What's the matter?"

"I'm afraid this is going to become some kind of hangout for those people. They give me a feeling that they live here just as much as I do!"

To Jackie the meaning of alternate lifestyle was coming home abruptly. "Those people"sat about on the floor upstairs talking about ideas that were foreign to her, using vocabulary that was strange or rude for her. They might have been a picture from National Geographic....Phil, although short-haired, clean-shaven, and until recently always dressed impeccably in ecclesiastical black, had established deep friendships with people from the hip culture; he felt close to them. But Jackie, who came from a more conservative background, was profoundly threatened.

Perhaps it was difficult for her to appreciate that Patsy and Bob were also threatened. For seven years they had lived together and struggled for a simpler lifestyle. They both lived under a severely exacting moral code, and their consciences demanded that they withdraw from the soft life which

America cherishes. They were painfully aware that most of the world does not have enough food...is ill-housed, that comfortable Americans are masters of war-making. The comfort and wealth they were now moving into (only for the winter!) was a bawdy temptation. The huge house was a caricature of bourgeois elegance....They, too, were afraid. Afraid that they would relax into old ways, reverse the costly struggle, relapse into the old culture.

From the outset the house had taken a different character from what had been envisioned during the summer planning meetings. The original idea had been to form a dispersed community of people bonded by commitment to social action with headquarters in a neighborhood house. Forty to fifty people worked on this, nearly all middle-class home owners, most of them church-connected. At one point in the summer, nineteen people had declared their intention to move into the communal house; but that number dropped to six by moving day. Three of us, Bob, Patsy, and Kiya, were from the counter-culture; three, Matt, Jackie, and Phil, from conventional society. Immediately, all energy went into forming and consolidating the household, and the outer community withered for lack of leadership and attention. Nevertheless, projects of the original large group were taken over by a quickly growing household, and Chester Creek House became the sponsor or initiator of a range of service activities: Saturday Free School, an underground newspaper, the Whole Foods Co-op, shelter for runaways, hospitality for transients, the Duluth Area Peace Center, sanctuary and way-station on the underground railroad to Canada, and a weekly potluck supper open to all visitors.

Almost at once new people began asking to join us. As long as we had been only five adults, decisions had been made quickly and easily, but growth required policies and procedures. First a shaky young couple moved in, stayed a month and left. Then Lena (Lynn) came, then Kris, two intelligent, strong, young women. Then two young people uncertainly searching for direction, first Linda, then "Mouse," whom we promptly renamed "Blue." Next Arno and Mary, charismatic and beautiful, who came to visit "for a few days" and stayed. Meanwhile we waited for Don and Bev, founding members of the community, to return with their four children, Chris, Nick, Marty, and Amy, from a two-year social work program in Ann Arbor. Then Sue came, a former nun who had also been part of the original planning group, then Mike who just drifted by, then Cassandra, a friend of Kris. Some of those stayed for a while and moved on; but at the end of the first nine months we were eighteen in the house.

It would have been chaos without weekly house meetings. All decisions were made by consensus; no vote was ever taken. Money and personal possessions were not held in common. Each person or family group proposed an affordable financial contribution toward household expenses. No standard rate was set; all was negotiated, even contribution of work or food in lieu of cash. Household chores were rotated and posted on a kitchen door. Slackers were hounded, as in any family. No street drugs were allowed in the house. None of us were willing to risk arrest because someone wanted to smoke some grass; however, we did agree to legal exposure for housing fugitives from the military. Crashers, our term for transients, could stay for three days and would be expected to help with housework. We developed a careful procedure for accepting and rejecting new requests for membership in the community.

All these practical matters were agreed on easily and maintained with reasonable smoothness. They were not the hard part of communal living. Relationships were. It was Patsy who brought home from work the idea that we invite professional consultation on our group process. She had been a group worker in the children's program at the Human Development Center, which was located only a block away from Chester Creek House. Two group and family therapists, Ed McParlan and Marsh Ward, had offered to do some pro bono work with our household, a kind of study project for them and a benefit for us in developing healthy communication. My manuscript described them:

> When they came for the first meeting at the end of January, Ed and Marsh made it clear that this was new to them, too. They suggested meeting only five times and then discussing whether they and the group wanted to continue or whether it had been enough–or maybe too much. They worked beautifully as a team: Ed perched or sprawled in an easy chair, occasionally initiating discussion, occasionally interrupting, recapitulating, offering feedback, keeping silence for long periods, shifting position in the chair. Marsh leaned back on the sofa remote and immobile as a fixture, slowly moving his head like a TV camera to follow the conversation. After a few sessions their style became apparent: Ed stayed with the conversation line

as it darted from Patsy to Matt to Jackie to Lena to Bob to Patsy to Kris;
Marsh tuned it out and attended to voice tone, gestures, facial movement,
body posture; at times their eyes and lips would flick significant, inscru-
table messages to one another.

It was not clear where all this was going, but the members of the house
began to talk to each other about their feelings toward one another, about
the expectations and fears and uncertainties they felt. "You people don't
feel very comfortable expressing your angry feelings to each other, do you?"
Marsh observed. The three-hour sessions every other week were beginning
to lay a bed of emotional trust....

After the first time, Bob was still cautious. He wrote in the (household)
journal: "Last night we saw each other in a new way. With the help of Ed
and Marsh from the Human Development Center we spent three hours
sharing feelings. I was struck several times how the tone of what went on
was very different. It is not the only way of seeing each other but it is a use-
ful one. My only fear is that once the distance between us starts to crumble
the well-oiled efficiency (joke) of this house will be threatened."

Two weeks later his journal entry revealed a slight shift of attitude:
"Last night we met together with Ed & Marsh again. We spent a lot of
time tuning into our relations with Matt. It was very different than the
tear-filled session before, but I felt it was valuable. I want to work on giv-
ing Matt feedback when he leaves me confused. Also I want to think about
what I feel I can demand-expect of people I live with. I hear Ed saying your
feelings are valid: you can demand anything you can get away with. I feel
myself alive. Bob."

More than any other single influence, the regular meetings with Ed
and Marsh have moved Chester Creek Community beyond an organiza-
tional living arrangement to become a personal, living community.

....

Three months after we moved into Chester Creek House, Jackie's
dad died. We had gone to my parents' home in Chisholm for Christmas
Eve and planned to go on to Soudan the next day. On Christmas morning
the call came. As we drove along the towns of the Iron Range that clear,
sky-blue, sub-zero morning to be with her family, I kept glancing across
at her in the car seat next to me, trying to read her emotions, trying to see
if she was distraught at having been so close but not there when her fa-

ther died, wondering if she regretted that we had not planned to go first to her home and then to mine. But that was not it at all. She was calm, quiet, and told me she was glad she was not there. Not yet knowing her well, I was mystified. Later she helped me understand that, for a long time, she had been separating from him, from the control he had on her life, as she struggled to become an adult and form an independent sense of self. She had been standing up to him more and more, even as his own powers were fading with advancing illness. Her marriage to me, only four months earlier, had been her strongest declaration of independence. However unplanned, not being at his deathbed marked transition to a new stage in her life. Completing this crossing would take years; and, in days ahead, she would often take the fight into our own quarrels, resisting and confronting me, defying my assertion of certainty and correctness, pushing back hard against my efforts, calling me *"controlling*–just like my father!"

Her new job at the Human Development Center helped with her transition. It was, she says, "a time of coming into my creativity." She began by working in the Center School with troubled children not manageable in the regular school system and soon began to develop innovative outreach programing by going into the schools to do consultation and teacher training based on what she had learned from Connie Burdick who had come to help in her own classroom while she was still a nun. In those days, kids' feelings were not understood or addressed in education, and troubling behavior was met with increased control. Her work in the Center School classroom served as a lab producing material for training parents and teachers. She helped them recognize the feelings and energies behind the problem behaviors of their children, helped them understand that perhaps eighty-five percent of behavior comes from the "child-part," the hopes and dreams of any person, herself included.

She was doing this work in her own life, as were her colleagues, including the other therapists working with adults. The Center's administration authorized free-ranging exploration into an effervescent surge of new therapy modalities and allocated generous funding to bring in some of the best minds and practitioners in the country as trainers. Staff were encouraged to innovate. Jackie moved her office, from the basement classroom area, upstairs among the psychotherapists. While she was developing a program of community workshops as a member of the Child Team, she also was participating in training available to Adult Team therapists. The Human Development Center in those days was run democratically almost like a co-op. Whoever had a good idea and energy to implement was rewarded for making it happen. Eventually this liberal era would pass, to be replaced by an inevitable preoccupation with documentation, accountability, and the bottom line. However, the groundwork for professional excellence and solid programing was laid during this earlier creative period when Jackie began to work there.

Meanwhile, I was working at the Duluth Area Peace Center, a hole-in-the-wall storefront office downtown. Every day young men would come through the door looking for information and advice on the draft. Most wanted to know about exemptions and deferments and conscientious objection. I ran each of them through a survey of options during an initial interview to be sure he had the full picture–all the way from student deferment to emigration from the United States. There was one fascinating case where the young man stopped me in my recitation of options at an obscure exemption concerning a son's immunity from the draft when a parent had received a disabling wound in combat. The conversation went something like this.

"My father was wounded when he was in the army. Shot in the legs getting down from a tank. Way before I was born. I don't know if that counts."

"Really? When did that happen?"

"World War II."

"Really! Do you think you can document this? Do you know where this happened?"

"Poland. At the beginning of the war. He was in the German army."

"Uhh...." We moved on.

Sometimes the man coming through the door was AWOL. The book on community that I wrote in 1972 tells one story:

"Everett" was obviously an alias. His Hawaiian ancestry made him look Indian, which would be an asset when he came to cross the border north of Duluth. Phil explained the sensitivity of various crossing stations, the point system at immigration for becoming a permanent resident of Canada, and the need for a minimum of cash in order to get in. That last item was a problem. Everett was broke. What he needed now more than informa-

tion was a place to lay low and a job for a month. Phil took him home that evening and introduced him to the people at Chester Creek. He was given a room and a place at the community table; and in a few days he was working night-shift at a factory. To outsiders he was just a guy who stopped by needing a place and a job for a while. Then one night Everett wandered out for a walk. Police picked him up as a burglary suspect, took him to the station, grilled him, ran a check through the computer, and released him. The next day a badly frightened Everett hit the road for the Canadian border without waiting for a paycheck. The last word from him was that he had been turned back at the crossing for lack of funds and was working with some loggers in the backwoods in order to gather enough for a second run.

In addition to the draft and military counseling, I put out a monthly newsletter called *Peacework,* ran nonviolence training workshops, and even taught a continuing education course in nonviolence at the university. This was the work for which I had petitioned leave from the bishop a year earlier.

....

It was a community tradition that the person who cooked supper for the group that evening was excused from cleanup but had to write in the house journal while the others were doing dishes. A selection of these entries gives a feeling of daily life:

Jackie, January 6: It was so good to come home tonight to a friendly gathering in the kitchen–home folk and friends just chatting. I get a bit anxious about cooking by myself because of the time element and my lack of skill as a cook (for a large group). Expressing my feeling was all it took to get two contributors to the meal and two errand runners to the store. Kris set about making pudding, Matt made cornbread. Blue followed on Lynn's heels to the store after I forgot to have her get mayonnaise...Our house has grown in so many ways–in size, surely in warmth and unity, and in understanding. I feel a real effort within our group to accept each other for what we are, tho we have different ways of living out our lives....

Patsy, January 10: Kiya cries upstairs. Linda goes to get him before I even look up. It is such a good thing for all of us to share the care of Kiya. Bob, Kris, and Lena have just returned from the free school retreat....

Matt, January 11: No house meeting tonight. Supper was a little late. Bob was going to an S.E.D. meeting, Linda went with him, so we called off the meeting. Patsy, Lena, Matt, and Kris had a chat for about an hour anyway. Blue stayed, too, but didn't say much. Now dishes. Kris needs a ride to Two Harbors. Blue needs driving lessons. Patsy wants more community. Lena needs closer friends here. I need to say no (and I do it)....

Patsy, February 10: Monday's meeting was a real bummer for me. It is the first really hurting, bruising group thing that has happened to me here. It started with a discussion on Linda and Bob's coming trip to Cuba. I was surprised–and I guess pretty indignant–with people's expressions of their fears about it...it made me angry that people were so scared of what other people would think of us for that...I felt so alone. It was not their fault. They never said they would walk through hell with me to the new world... Kris was very hurt because I said she lacked courage. I really came down on Phil because I believed in him most. Both Jackie and Kris reached out to me...I felt their hands holding mine. Saw Kris's tears and still felt alone...I carried that unresolved feeling to my work. It is the first time I have been so involved with people here to carry really distracting feelings away. Unlike Jackie I felt not renewed trust but broken trust. Phil walks around looking sad today. I wonder where he's at but am unable to ask him. A community can do two things. It can help you be stronger. It can give you the strength to be weaker. I don't know what this community can do for me.

Kris, February 18: Happy voices in the kitchen doing dishes and fooling around. Lena went to visit her parents...Linda has gone to an SCC meeting...Bob and Patsy and Kiya will go to Sue's for dinner...Matt will go to his uncle's...Blue is going cycling....Only Phil, Jackie, and I will be left home. I felt really troubled today as I left the house, but the activity of the day cheered me up and I enjoyed making dinner tonight. I feel burdened by the meaninglessness of things I am doing and am sad that my unhappiness burdens others as well. I saw Jackie as I left for school. She was walking with her kids. I am really thankful for her cheerfulness and enthusiasm. You really brighten me up, Jackie! Love, Kris.

In the midst of this, but privately, Jackie and I were working out the tensions of our own relationship. What had attracted her to me now began to chafe: my self-confidence and certitude. Given the affirmation I had from my parents, successes in the seminary, frequent leadership positions, advanced education in Europe, and public opposition to church and state authority, I trusted the compelling conclusions of my intellect. Jackie had acceded to my urging that we marry, had followed me into this communal experiment, and had joined me in actively resisting the war. She soon saw that she had to make her own place in this marriage. This meant not allowing me to define everything.

Jackie is intelligent and strong willed. Her mother used to complain to little Gerry: "You are *so* persistent!" I found her so, and she reminds me that I had a hard time accepting correction. Even before we were married, she began to fight me.

Our very first quarrel took place over the phone when we were in the full flush of rosy love and envisioning a life together. I had spoken of her getting a dispensation from her vows and my continuing to exercise priesthood after our marriage. She was furious at the unfairness of that bargain and railed at my blithe assumption that she would easily give up her nine years of religious life while I would carry on and give up nothing! I thought she was being unreasonable and said so, a major mistake. A nun was, by definition, unmarried; and a priest was in a permanent condition–"once a priest, always a priest." My impeccable logic was gasoline on the flame. I hung up the phone that evening dazed and shaken. I had no idea what had just happened. I had a lot to learn.

I started our second quarrel. I was to meet her at a specified time just outside the Augustana Lutheran Church, where she was working that summer we were to be married. I suppose I was trying to figure out how to be married. The syllogism in my head went something like this: "All couples quarrel. We will be a couple. Therefore, we will quarrel." The how-to part was looping through my memory like this:

"Mil, hurry up, come on!"

"Art, don't rush me. I don't want to get there an hour ahead of everyone else."

"Goddamit, Mil! I don't want to be late! Jesus Christ!"

So when Jackie did not show up exactly on the dot and I had plenty of time to pace the street furiously in front of the church, I was pleased with the opportunity to practice being a husband. We had a perfectly miserable evening, of course.

In the first years of marriage we staked out positions. Jackie's was: "You are out of touch with your feelings." Mine was: "Feelings aren't the most important thing in the world!" From our very first quarrel, she had found a way to confront my control. I loved her and took her seriously. She brought home from Center School a wristband golf-score counter used for behavior modification with the kids to reinforce positive behavior. I strapped it on and wore it day after day, clicking the button each time I made a "feeling" statement. At the end of the first day I had logged five! (including a questionable "I feel hungry"). At the end of the week I was up to twelve or so. I was beginning to learn the world of feelings. I began to learn that, with Jackie, presentation was everything. With her, food is not just nourishment; it has to be presented in balanced color and arrangement on the plate to be a meal. We could contend, disagree, even dispute with each other as long as presentation was respected. Feelings were as important as ideas. No domination, no disparagement, no more strait-jacketing. In fits and starts, we began to work out this dance of seeing things from one another's position. As though, she said to me or I to her: "Yes, I see that it seems obvious to you. However, when you stand over here...."

Living at Chester Creek House was having a similar effect on us all. For example, during that first year, stable, sensible Matt sold his car and bought a bicycle, quit his teaching job, began to travel and started writing a novel. And I wrote in the house journal on February 16:

> *I made my first vegetarian supper tonight. What is more, it was an origi-*
> *nal creation, a hotdish of barley, rice, lentils, raisins, eggs, and mushroom*
> *soup. Not bad. Called it 'Sneaky Raisin"...I find myself struggling with*
> *new experiments in things I used to consider fadish. Jackie and I are in this*
> *together, exploring new ways of living. It is hard to say where it began,*
> *probably with the move into Chester Creek House...Sunday Jackie and I*
> *hitched to Park Point to visit Fran and Jo. We left the car at home. Gradu-*
> *ally we hope to wean ourselves from it completely...The other day we were*
> *all talking about making an effort to eat more simply and to live no higher*
> *than what would be the food allowance in a welfare budget. We checked that*
> *out and found that we were already living below a welfare budget....*

Jackie and I had entered this community as a continuation of our religious life, but we were not in control of the venture and gradually moved to new points of view and new values. The very issue of religion was ambiguous in the community. In the 1972 book I wrote:

(People from outside) continued to relate to Chester Creek in anticipation that out of it might grow a broadly defined community of faith in which their own religious searching might find oasis. Much of this centered on Phil who was still viewed as a strong religious figure, even in his exiled Catholicism; and he himself was only half-aware of his hopes that the house might become a kind of secular church in which his priesthood could find expression. There was in fact a subgroup, almost completely Roman Catholic, which gathered there regularly for prayer and the celebration of Eucharist. But Phil provided hesitating leadership....

Jackie and I were both moving into a period of searching and uncertainty about our faith. We had bravely stepped outside the church, while insisting we were still in it; yet most of our friends and activities were now from a different world. We were seeing many things from a new point of view. It is difficult thirty-five years later to recall how these subtle shifts in our inner lives were happening; but there are hints in a travel journal we kept when we hitchhiked around Europe the following summer.

Before we married, I had playfully said to her, "Stick with me and we'll travel." We have traveled–most of our life together–with very little money. One Saturday morning, seven months after our wedding, we lay awake in bed chatting about whatever, including my student days in Louvain. Jackie said she would love to go to Europe some day. By evening it was a decision and a plan: We would hitchhike to New York, backpack and tent all the way, find the cheapest flight across, hitchhike up to Norway (she wanted to see fjords) and down to Bavaria and back up to Paris, five weeks. We would scrape together a thousand dollars from the next six months of Jackie's paychecks. I began to study Norwegian. The following July we were ready to go, with fresh passports and tickets on Icelandic Air. A week before departure, we visited our good friends, Eric and Vernal, on the Iron Range. They are great world travelers and had lived and worked in Ghana.

We were sitting in their kitchen (it is our travel journal speaking now)
drinking lemonade and looking over Michelin maps Eric was going to lend
us. I picked up one of Africa out of idle curiosity. Eric said: "You know, you
should go down to Marseilles and take a boat across to North Africa." Jackie
said, "Hey, let's!" I said, "I don't know...."

So we got cholera shots for North Africa and dropped Norway.

It has not been easy finding out how to get to Algiers or Tunis. Seems
that no one around Duluth ever thought of it before. For example, I stopped
in at the travel agency yesterday to ask about boats on the Mediterranean.
The woman was stumped by that one–but she finally found a freighter that
carries a few people every other Saturday on a round trip that takes ten
days. I said that this was not much good for us; and since Marseilles was
one of the most active ports in Europe, weren't there other options? She was
quite sure this was the only boat. I then said we might have to take a plane. I
could hardly believe her next words: "Or maybe you could take a train?"

Two days later our Chester Creek friends dropped us off on Highway 2 in Wisconsin, just outside of Duluth. In those days hitchhiking
was not perfectly safe, but it was very common. Young people were cris-
crossing the nation on their thumbs all the time. At some stops we had
to go to the end of the line beyond those who had arrived ahead of us. In
Flint, Michigan, we camped behind a police station. In Buffalo we stayed
with my priest-friend from Louvain days. After four days we were on
Manhattan. With stops in Iceland and Luxembourg, we went on to stay
with Jackie's friends at a U.S. Air Force base near Frankfurt and with my
friends in the Bavarian village of Seeshaupt.

Hitchhiking was easy in Germany. Rides were frequent, friendly,
and fast–very fast because of the no-speed-limit *Autobahn*. Twice on the
trip, once in Germany, once in Switzerland, vehicles that picked us up
suffered overheating engine-seizure. *"Motor ganz kaput!"* We felt guilty
about leaving the stranded drivers with ruined cars alongside the road,
as we simply put out our thumbs and continued on.

We put up our tiny, canvas pup tent by the Bodensee in Austria, by
the Aare River in Switzerland, and turned south at Geneva heading for
the port of Marseilles. We arrived in the dark, camped on hardpan, rose
to a merciless sun, and struggled to the *Gare Maritime* to learn that the
only ship this day was to Algeria, which we could not board without a

visa. The ship to Tunisia, leaving in two days, was full. A compassionate Algerian family, sitting on the floor in the waiting room eating their lunch, consoled us with salty black olives from a bag and a chunk of flatbread.

We broke our budget and took a room, four dollars a night, at the Hotel Neuilly on the rue Theâtre française. The next day was our first wedding anniversary, and we decided to be happy and have fun. Meandering about Marseilles took us to a travel agency whose address we had left with friends and family. At the American Express window a letter from my mom and dad was waiting for us. At the next window, I overheard a conversation in French between a customer and a ticket agent: "No, that ship to Tunis is full, no tickets at all, no, none...wait... wait a minute; there is a message coming in...yes, yes, there are openings now. You can get a ticket." I crossed to that line, waited my turn, then spoke to the agent: "Did I understand that there are now tickets for the ship to Tunis?"

The next day Jackie and I were on the Mediterranean. An English woman named Philomena, who was traveling alone on vacation from her job as an advice columnist at a London paper, attached herself to us; and the three of us took a room in Tunis across the street from the Old City. We explored the souk, a warren of narrow streets and tiny shops. We piled into a van with the locals to ride down the coast to Sousse; and, after a delightful day at the beach and exploring the old fort, we sat, hot and weary, waiting for the last train back to Tunis.

Our journal remembers the joke that happened next:

We sat together on a luggage rack peering around in silence, anxious to get a seat on the train in order to be able to fall asleep (2 ½ hour ride). I looked up at the large clock above the doorway to see how much longer we had to wait. My eyes strayed to the left; and there, in beautiful blue and white Kodak color was a travel poster of snow and skis that said: "NORWAY."

The rest of the week we visited Sidi-bou-Said and Carthage, ate one last meal of couscous in the restaurant, where the goat carcasses hung all day from hooks in the display widows, and got dysentery just in time to board the ship back to France. Poor Jackie. We were both miserably sick lying on sleeping bags among hundreds of Tunisians on the floor of the open bay. There were about 490 men, all guest workers heading for jobs in France, about 10 women. Each time Jackie desperately fumbled through the tangle of sleepers during the night, heading for the women's bathroom, she found it full of men. Her wild gesturing toward the men's room and explosive fragments of Marquette School French only brought laughter.

We lived to get ourselves onto a train north toward Taizé, the ecumenical Protestant monastery which I had visited during my seminary days in 1962. I wrote in our journal:

> *Taizé has changed. So have I. I returned with a wife; and, as we approached the village, I recognized sights that I had seen nine years ago. The ancient Roman village church was the same. The workshop was still there. But, as we came up to the brow of the hill, everything but the large Church of the Reconciliation was different. Hundreds of young people milled about. There were dozens of tents everywhere. As we stayed these days, the sense of contrast increased: throughout the summer there are 1500 to 2000 young people here weekly. Many come and go every day. The word has spread throughout the world—as far as India and Venezuela—that this is a center where young people are grouping and regrouping to search, to find meaning, to formulate the social and political action with which they will impact their world. Three times a day the cluster of white-robed brothers gather in the church for the Divine Office, as they have since 1940. But now they are surrounded by 1800 young people, who sit on the floor and participate fully in the prayer. At Easter there were from 6000 to 8000 here, and the church was too small. So the brothers had the front wall of the church knocked down and huge tents attached in order to accommodate all who came....*

We, too, were searching for meaning. We met several times a day in organized discussion groups with young people from all parts of Europe, nomads, (our journal continues) *like ourselves, who were seeking a bit more light and truth in a place where men had not refused to grow in the Church...all of us here in the name of Christianity, but half of us not sure we really believed in it....*

The preceding April, one of the Taizé brothers had come from Chicago to stay at Chester Creek House. Now we met Brother Frank again back here in France and were able to disclose our own spiritual uncertainties to someone closer to our age and background. My journal entry:

I was particularly eager to talk with him about my own religious questions and searchings, which go deeply to the basic question of Christ and God's presence....I think Jackie and I feel a great deal of identity with these young people who come here...a desperate sense of search for truth, true living, and ultimate answers. We are in the dark, in confusion, and we are hungering....

Jackie added her reflections about her small group discussions:

The faith-sharing (or might I say "doubt-sharing") has been of the most intense kind–recognizing that some of us find ourselves in no light of faith very often, but with serious doubts concerning Christianity's claim to be one which saves the world. I have, in fact, searched more deeply than ever into my own faith, my lack of honesty in dealing with my own doubts because of the fear of having no comfort or security to hang onto. Fortunately, Philip's mind and spirit are too rational to allow easy answers to lonely problems and together we delve into our own spiritual life with a zest that is both painful and cleansing. In our talk with Brother Frank yesterday, he assured Philip that he must search these things to the depths and bear the pain of it.... With our small group once again today we...came to grips with the pain of not knowing and the risk one takes to believe.... It is not easy to accept Christianity these days. There are, as Phil said, so few credible Christians, but to see a man like Brother Frank, whose life, without words, speaks of a life deeply lived, you must see or refuse to see. My faith has undergone many changes. I no longer look to laws or structures to define it for me, but for a relationship with an inner power which confuses and confronts me. This is not, of course, my first experience with doubt or confusion, but it is a much deeper one, in which I find myself, because of my inner life, answering yes, when I don't even know what is being asked. Over the years I have defined this as Christ; now, if that be him, I can only say, "I believe, help my unbelief."

We stayed nearly a week at Taizé, then bummed a ride with someone driving to Paris in a tinny *deux cheveaux* and took a train onward to Luxembourg to catch the flight back to Kennedy. The original plan had been for us to hitchhike home from New York, but we phoned ahead to say we were exhausted and broke and would arrive on the afternoon flight.

Now, one last journal entry from the two black notebooks:

Saturday, September 4, 1971. The flight was fine except for a little turbu-
lence over Wisconsin. Brief touch-downs in Milwaukee and Green Bay. The
turbulence within us increased as we approached Duluth. We were getting
so excited. Finally, there it was below–the South Shore of Wisconsin, Lake
Superior, tiny sailboats, the North Shore, Lakeside, Woodland, the airport.
We strained hard against the window, trying to see familiar forms in the
windows of the air terminal as our plane rolled in on the runway. Sud-
denly, Jackie squealed, "Look, there they are!...Is that them? Oh, no! Look,
Phillie!" Down the runway they were marching–a marching band, Bob in
the lead like a drum major banging kettle-covers, Patsy, Kiya, Sue, Cassan-
dra, Kris, and Lena–all playing tin funnels or pots or some other kitchen
musical instrument. They stood, marching in place, playing and singing a
"song," as we rushed from the plane. No key to the city was awarded and
no welcome speeches given–all dignity broke as we hugged and laughed
and talked at once and hugged again on the landing strip. It was so good to
be home! They wore signs pinned to their chests saying "Welcome home,
world travelers" and "Welcome back, Jackie and Phil" and "Happy Sun."
At that moment, after traveling thousands of miles, and after 5 ½ weeks
in wisconsin, michigan, canada, new york, iceland, luxembourg, germany,
austria, switzerland, france, and north africa–at that moment...we knew...
that this... was the best part of the TRIP!

....

That fall my dad was diagnosed with terminal cancer. I knew I had
some things to say to him in the days ahead. Jackie's and Patsy's work
at the Human Development Center and the Ed and Marsh meetings, had
inclined us all toward a more psychological view of life and relationship. I began to think of "finishing unfinished business" with my dad.
I thought it better to say goodbye to him still living rather than to work
out unexpressed hurts and resentments later in therapy with a dead man.
Whenever Jackie and I went to Chisholm to visit my parents, I found occasion to talk to my father about the estrangement I had felt because of
his alcoholism and about a variety of other complaints which I can't even
recall now. It was strong stuff for a guy who did not put much stock in
psychology, and I saw my directness baffled and pained him. During
my seminary days he had often told me how glad he was that I didn't
cause him any problems, meaning, of course, adolescence problems. As

an adult, however, I gave him plenty of grief: my antiwar notoriety, my marriage in defiance of the church, our living in a commune, and even my insistence on hitchhiking to Europe when he begged us not to, pleaded with us to let him buy us bus tickets to New York. I don't know our talks did him any good. I doubt I ever apologized for my part. I asked Marsh Ward to see me in therapy during this period of saying goodbye to my dad. For four to six sessions I sat in his office at HDC, preparing what I needed to say to Dad, reporting on how it went, telling Marsh a dream I had. This one: I am sitting across a table from my dad talking to him. I turn my head slowly to the right and I am looking into the face of Bishop Anderson. Doesn't take Sigmund Freud to figure that one out.

Mom called the afternoon of November 6, my birthday. "Phil, Dad's gone."

My very first thought: Damn, they're planning a birthday party for me here at supper. "Oh, Mom! How are you doing? I'll be right home." I walk into my bedroom, get out the suitcase, and begin to pack, feeling nothing. Suddenly I collapse onto the suitcase sobbing.

....

A week after the funeral, Jackie and I took part in a workshop introduction to a new mode of therapy called Transactional Analysis. The first session was on the human need for "strokes," physical and emotional contact between people. It led off with a ten-minute film documentary about "Susan," an infant suffering from marasmus, "a condition of progressive emaciation, esp. in infants, as from inability to assimilate food." Susan had been born to parents of average education who had not wanted the pregnancy and were repelled by its result. The mother felt nothing but squeamishness and complained, "Babies are a poor excuse for human beings." Neither parent picked her up or cuddled her. When Susan was brought to the hospital at twenty-two months, she had the weight of a five-month-old and height normal for a ten-month-old. She had no motor skills, could not crawl, speak, or babble. She would not tolerate touch. Medical intervention did not succeed in helping her thrive. She was withering. A new program was tried. Volunteer grandmothers came in shifts throughout the day and night and held Susan tightly, despite her angry thrashing, spoke to her, cuddled and rocked her. After weeks she began to quiet and take food. After two months of attention and physical touch, she had developed affectional response, gained six pounds and grown two inches. She had begun to crawl . At the end of the film, we watched an undersized Susan taking her first steps with support.

After the workshop, Jackie and I were sitting in the Pizza Hut with beers, waiting for our food.

"What did you like best today?" she asked.

"The film. About Susan." (A sip of beer.) "I thought as I watched, 'That's not a bad way to spend a life–caring for a child and loving it to full life.'"

Jackie just looked at me quietly.

"Jackie. I think I am ready to have a child."

"I, too, am ready, " she said.

Had we talked about it much before this? We must have–but everything else about us was so unconventional, and we were concerned about bringing children into such an uncertain world and about our own complex lifestyle. Whatever our thinking about our marriage, until this moment, we had not decided to have children. I added something else to that conversation. I said, "This may sound odd, but I have a clear image that my father has just stepped out of the way. Now I can be a father."

I was thirty-three, she thirty-two. Jackie insists, "It *took* on our very first try. I felt it! I know it!"

I think she is right. The first pregnancy test at the clinic said no. We did not believe it. A month later the second test said, "Now it reads positive. You are pregnant."

That same month I announced that I would resign from the Peace Center. The obvious reason was that the need for draft counseling was over. Although the Vietnam War would continue for two more years, conscription ended in 1973. The deeper reason was that I was experiencing a cascade of change in my inner life. Three years later (1976) the *Duluth News Tribune* would interview me about this period and report: "Solem, now a therapist at the Human Development Center, ended his involvement in the antiwar movement in January, 1973. 'I felt myself wanting to get out of there. I'd been there long enough, my impact was fading. I wanted personal change...I'm involved in different things, different work, different colleagues.'" Not a very elegantly stated departure, but succinct and true.

Jackie supported my taking time out to reevaluate my interests and commitments. She encouraged me not to feel pressured to find a job. Her due date was in September, and this was only February. Her job at HDC would support us. I was only giving up $200-a-month from the Peace Center, so I decided to replace it by baking bread. Kris gave me some long, black, commercial bread pans she had, and I began to develop a bread route. Every Monday, Wednesday, and Saturday I would arise at 4:00 A.M., go down to the large Chester Creek House kitchen and began measuring and mixing. I began by using my mother's Swedish Rye recipe and developed others later. I would take her recipe, triple it, and make it three times. By noon forty loaves were cooling, ready to be bagged and taken to the Whole Foods Co-op, which had recently moved from our basement to a store property, and to a natural foods store on London Road. Several group homes in the area also contracted for regular deliveries. I suppose I made a little over a hundred dollars a month, not much of a comedown. The days I did not make bread I wrote short stories and did maintenance jobs around the house–and went for walks along the creek, thinking.

My faith was going the way of my peacework dedication. I found questions of religion mildly irritating and no longer interesting. The rationale for pacifism had faded. Gradually I saw, to my own surprise, that I no longer believed. There was no sense of emptiness or lack of meaning, rather the refreshing feeling of clearing out cluttered storerooms and getting rid of stuff. Like retiring from a job, cleaning out the desk, sweeping the last dust and useless paperclips into a waste basket, and going home.

I was suddenly tired of being a professional religious man. Of being a controversial figure and an idealist. Of earning a hundred dollars or two a month. I wanted to be a father and to join my wife in a respected profession. A real job–I would need to get a real job soon, as the time of our child's birth approached. Jackie herself had made the transition more gracefully. She had been working in the mental health profession for two and a half years by this time and enjoyed the aura of prestige and competence it brought. She had a lively intellectual and social life with colleagues at HDC. I was invited to their staff dinners and parties, and the field of psychology and psychotherapy was now more interesting than religion.

My attitude did not just evolve, it swung. I soon had a chip on my

shoulder about belief and looked for opportunities to argue. I recall myself saying things like, "The Bible says we are made in the image and
likeness of God; but, really, we create God and make him into our own
image and likeness." I remember saying this in our kitchen to my young
friend, Mark MacDonald, when he came to visit one day. Mark had been
my disciple when I was running nonviolence training workshops a few
years earlier. Then he decided to enter the seminary and study to become
an Episcopal priest. I am afraid I might have been rude on that occasion.
Mark must have wondered what had happened to me, but I doubt if my
agnostic argument shook him. He is now the Bishop of the Episcopal
Diocese of Alaska.

With the waning of belief came spongy morality. The Broadway lyrics from *My Fair Lady* sang: "The Lord above made liquor for temptation–
to see if man could turn away from sin. But wi' a littl bit o'luck, wi' a littl
bit o'luck, when temptation comes, you'll give right in!" A wink at temptation, a smirk about sin, scraps of the old belief system. It was not just
liquor at parties, it was flirting and fantasy. This was the beginning of
some hard times between Jackie and me. We had been moving in tandem
from the religious world of our formative years toward more middle-
aged secular interests and values, but my changes were more excessive.
We had both moved out of the old structures and grown, keeping in touch
with each other and staying clear about how we affected each other. The
fading of my faith had not alarmed her, and even mirrored hers in a way;
but seeing me in action on a number of occasions now shocked her profoundly. She was pregnant with our child. Where do you think you are
going? she demanded. My response was indignant and willful, but she
did not waver. She had been following along with me these years, trusting me, she said; but now she was shocked and resentful, wondering if
she was going to have to take care of herself alone.

I came to my senses. I woke up and stopped my foolishness. Now it
was late spring, and we began going to Lamaze natural childbirth classes
together. I began looking for work in mental health and applied for a tech
position on a hospital psych unit. But Jackie came home from work one
day saying there was an opening at HDC for a group worker in the Harmony Club, a therapeutic social program for adults with chronic mental
illness. I applied and was hired.

Neither of us had clinical training when we started with the Human

Development Center, no relevant academic degrees. We were each hired on the strength of our personal gifts. She had several years' training and experience on me now, but we both decided to sign three-year contracts for training with the International Transactional Analysis Association in order to upgrade our skills and acquire credentials. These contracts required us to learn a growing body of TA theory, lead two ongoing therapy groups, submit audio recordings of that work to a clinical supervisor monthly, attend a schedule of training workshops, enter therapy ourselves, and pass written and oral exams.

This program and the arrival of our child would be our primary focus for the next several years. Chester Creek Community continued to be our home; the Church was home no longer. I delighted in the feeling of being just an ordinary guy: in love with my wife, expecting a baby, starting a new career, getting a regular salary ($9000 a year!), with a new circle of fascinating peers.

Jackie and I drove the scenic twenty-two miles along Lake Superior to our HMO clinic in Two Harbors every few weeks now for late pregnancy checks. Friends at Chester Creek rearranged rooms so we could have the baby's room next to ours. One day we brought some friends to show them the nursery and, on opening the door, ran into a blowback of "Surprise!" and a mass of bodies and beaming faces coming at us, dozens of friends pouring out of the nursery to sweep us into a rollicking baby shower.

At the beginning of May, we began to write letters to our unborn child in a large book. Jackie spoke first:

> *I begin this book about midway through my pregnancy...For a long time, 2 ½ years, we were not sure we would ever be parents...What a world, we thought, to bring a child into. Then, in one of our efforts to expand our experience and ideas, we attended a weekend workshop in Nov., 1972. It's impact changed your dad's mind and reaffirmed my belief that life can be passed on and enriched by loving and caring people. Maybe your dad can write about the experience which had such an impact on him.*

I took it up there and told the story of Susan. A month later I wrote:

> *I think I am beginning to love you . . . I wish I could call you by name, that would help. But we do not know yet whether you are boy or girl. At*

this point you are either Sara or Kalon to your mother and me...This is the last week before I begin a new job: at the Human Development Center. I resigned from my job with the Peace Center five months ago, and this intervening period has been one of major internal and external changes for me. In fact, during this time, I feel my life philosophy has changed deeply. My religious beliefs and feelings have overturned. I have withdrawn from community social action and political involvement. I feel as though my life has clicked into a new phase–I can hear the tumblers falling and a new combination being set...(and) I feel myself moving out of the idealism of the past 25 years and into a mood of here-and-now realism.

Midsummer, Jackie wrote:

This has been, by far, one of the most creative, intense, emotionally vibrant joyous, painful and challenging times of my life. When we began on this path there were many fears and anxieties about making sure you would have the greatest possible number of chances for a good beginning. I became preoccupied with the food I was eating, the amount of sleep I got, exercise, preparation by reading, and the right doctor...My emotions, normally very intense, have intensified even more which caused me to respond to all the changes in my body and my relationships very strongly. Your dad, Phil, and I were beginning to go through some scary times in our relationship, which made us have to look more closely at the strains that your life coming into ours was causing. We were experiencing different things. I needed more of a feeling of security than ever before...and your dad was more and more beset with insecurity about what was happening to his emotions, his discovery of new and exciting horizons in his relationships with others and wanting to reach out further with his life. Together we struggled intensely to find a deeper rootedness. Your dad's new job was providing us with a securer financial base but less time together. His struggle to adapt to all his new experiences was beautiful and scary to me: Beautiful because I love to watch him grow and become more handsome, stronger, more available to other people and scary because of these things and the threat they were to me when I seemed to want to become more dependent on him. Now, weeks of struggle leveling out, we find ourselves more in love, more trusting than before and with more room for others as well.

Then came a brief, hurried entry starting with *"September 19, 11:00*

P.M. This is it!...." It was the onset of labor. The journal was neglected for more urgent matters. It lay somewhere, silent, until after the birth. In early October, I took it up again to tell what had happened:

Dear Sara—at last I can talk to you and call you by name. At last I know who you are. For days now I have been studying your skin, feeling your warmth against my arms and my chest, smelling your most welcome smell as I enter your nursery room, looking deep into your eyes and fancying that you, with that peculiar, puzzled look which furrows your eyebrows and rounds your tiny mouth, were looking back into my eyes to discover who this man with the firm hands and deep voice is. Sara. At last!

We did not sleep much that night I last described. Around 2:00 A.M. Jackie woke me to say that the contractions had begun and were coming regularly. I began timing them—7 or 8 minutes apart. We kept timing and resting, and even, toward dawn, we both dozed fitfully. By 7:00 A.M. the contractions were close to five minutes apart. The doctor had told us that, when this happened, we were to go to the hospital. We got up, showered, packed, ate breakfast, and set off for Two Harbors, 25 miles away. Our friend, Bev, drove. She planned to wait out our labor in the waiting room and to film your birth in the delivery room.

Jackie checked into the hospital around 8:00, she and I settled into the labor room, and the long wait began. For a long time we were comfortable. We had our stereo along and a sackful of classical music records from the library. We talked, timed contractions, and waited for time to pass and her cervix to dilate. Jacqueline even danced a bit to a Mozart symphony; we have that on film. Periodically a nurse came in to check for cervix dilation. Not much happening. Hour after hour passed. We went for short walks. Beverly went downtown to buy a game and joined us with it in the labor room. We were having fun, stopping whatever we were doing every six or seven minutes to time contractions. There were no signs of increasing dilation.

Eventually the fun stopped. Jackie, Bev, and I were getting tired, and Jackie could no longer concentrate on games or talk or much else. The contractions were absorbing all her attention and energy. I had a constant, vague headache. It was suppertime. No dilation. Jackie began to get very discouraged and exhausted. She wanted to stay in bed. I kept trying to keep her active, but her balloon had burst; she looked so drained and far away.

Her eyes were closed all the time, trying to snatch rest between contractions. I was feeling a heavy weight deep in my head and about my shoulders–our lack of sleep the night before.

At every nurse check, no dilation. The doctor was referring to the contractions as "ineffective" and looking bewildered. The evening passed. It was night. Dr. Griesy came in, gave Jackie a shot, and prescribed a medication to reduce pain. She needed to sleep. I placed cushions from the hospital chairs on the floor and slept beside her bed. At 11:00 P.M. I awoke suddenly and my eyes were looking at the white heels of a nurse's shoes. She was leaning over Jackie, and I heard her say, "6 or 8 centimeters dilation." At last. I struggled up, feeling drugged and leaden. My head ached, pain in my back muscle, and I felt dumb and useless. But I finally found my place at Jackie's side, wiping her face with a damp cloth, talking encouragement to her. To my joy, I heard them say it was time to move to the delivery room! Bev and I were sure the birth would come in the next hour.

Jackie was wheeled from the labor room to the small, green delivery room a few steps down the hall. I donned hospital gown, cap, face-mask, and entered the room. The doctor arrived. It was midnight, the beginning of September 21ˢᵗ.

Then began the ordeal of Jackie's pushing and breath-holding. With all her might she would push, bear down, hold her breath, turn red in the face, and fall back exhausted as the contraction passed. Again and again she summoned stamina from some unsuspected reserve to do this, every three, four, five minutes. Until one o'clock, until two, until three. The doctor slept outside the room on a gurney. The nurses changed shifts. I stayed at Jackie's side, urging her to push harder, not to let her breath go yet, wiping her lips, fetching her ice, supporting her back as she lurched forward to push with the contraction. From time to time a nurse would suggest I slip out to have coffee with the night-shift nurses. I almost felt guilty doing it, for Jackie had no such respite. But I would return refreshed to help her further. There were times when I felt it took all my strength to help her through a contraction. As it subsided, I would collapse onto a metal stool beside the delivery table.

Suddenly, at four o'clock in the morning, Dr. Griesy came in again and said we should wait no longer. He would perform an episiotomy and use forceps. Jackie became worried at the mention of forceps. I felt a great deal of trust in Dr. Griesy, a genuine sense of confidence in the man, not

just in his medical judgment. I tried to convey this to Jackie, and she acqui-
esced. The delivery room began to bustle. Surgical gowns were put on, tools
brought forward, a shot given. Bev filmed. The contractions continued. At
4:30 A.M. Dr. Griesy moved in decisively. From my post at Jackie's head,
I could hear the snipping of the episiotomy. Then the forceps were in his
hands. One half inserted; it rested there by itself, then the second half of
the tool. Another contraction–he worked the tool, pulling gently toward
himself–it seems someone shouted, "Here's the head!"

I saw your head slide out, then, right away, your shoulders and arms.
There was a pause, a moment's delay; and I could not tell, as I strained
forward to look over the end of the table, whether you were Kalon or Sara.
Then you came out completely and lay on your back between the doctor's
hands. I sat down on the stool and said to Jackie, "It's a girl."

I want to try to tell you my feelings during those moments. This will
not be easy, because they were feelings I have never had before, and I don't
know what to call them.

First of all, I did not speak anymore after saying "It's a girl." There
was plenty of commotion in the room, and I simply sat on the edge of it
without anything to add. I could feel the tears streaming down my face,
Sara. I knew I was sobbing quietly beneath the tissue face mask. I looked
and looked and looked at you. I felt no transport of joy, of relief, of pride.
I felt astounded, struck, bewildered. There were no thoughts for a time,
only a sensation of astonishment. I shrank back within myself, kept silent,
held my hands close to my body. I was surprised at what a stranger you
seemed to me. I knew the facts: You came from me; you were part of my
body; we would live together for years; I would care for and hold you. But
that knowledge heightened the estrangement. As I looked at you, pinkish
purple on the cloth, the shiny, wet cord still tying you to Jackie's insides,
you were only a few feet away, but you seemed miles away. I pushed you
away because you amazed me so. It would not have been so if you had been
some other man's child; but, because you were mine, you were stranger to
me than a stranger. All this in the first few seconds.

And then there was something else, which I feel it is important I tell
you. My first feeling when the doctor turned you over on your back and
I saw you were female was disappointment. That was part of the astonishment, Sara. I suddenly felt great heaving and shifting going on inside
my consciousness, as though I were a land mass grinding and cracking,

mountains heaving and collapsing into valleys and trembling in realignment. I had not known how fixed my expectation had been that you would be Kalon. It was as though that were a known fact and we had lived with that knowledge for many months already. Of course, Jackie and I regularly reminded each other that you could be either girl or boy and we really had no preference. All we wanted was a healthy child, etc., etc. But, as I first saw your body, I was confounded, as though a known, demonstrated fact had been proven wrong. And I had already, long ago, begun to operate on the mistaken knowledge that you would be Kalon. My whole concept of what it would mean for me to be father centered on being father of a son. In that lay hope and fear. I know now that I expected to live out with you (male) a generational conflict I had not yet resolved. I needed to complete my own relationship with Art Solem by being father to Kalon. Suddenly all of that dreaming about the drama and power of what it would mean for Philip Solem to have a child was emptied. Because you were not a boy-child.

And as I looked down at your body, I reeled and groped for purchase. I was not prepared for you, Sara. Then I choked away the disappointment, swallowed it, and scrambled to adjust to the wriggling reality before me. I tried to think of your mother, Jacqueline, what a fine, powerful, honest, tender woman she is. You, too, daughter, could become as excellent a woman as she—and then I looked away from you to Jacqueline's face at my elbow, and again I was astounded. She, too, was a stranger to me. I thought, "Who is she?" I stared, and I knew all about her, remembered all we had shared; but I felt estranged, bound to her, but dimensions and eons away. I needed to get past these weird, unfamiliar feelings. I desperately wanted to feel conventionally fatherly. (All this passing through me, I remind you, in the first sixty seconds.) Finally I found footing: a sentimental memory of a glimpse I had caught one day when I was downtown on First Street—a man standing at a garage door with his little girl beside him in a pretty dress, holding his hand. I remember thinking: "What a fine sight. I would love to be the father of a little girl like that. I would be happy with a daughter standing beside me." (Sara, I have begun to cry as I write these lines. There has been so much power unleashed.)

That helped. That image. And I began to see you in a new way. It was a temporary measure to allow me to come close to you and to love you. I saw you were beautiful. Very beautiful, Sara. And, as they lay you on Jackie's chest and worked to get you nursing, I risked reaching out to touch you—the furry, matted hair of your head. Later a bit more. I still had said scarcely a word, and I still was crying; but eventually, before we left the delivery room, I held you in my own arms. I knew I had made the adjustment. I had begun to want a Sara and had begun to let go of Kalon.

In the maternity room, Jackie asked how I felt about you being a girl. I was tempted to conceal what I just told you, but I did not. I talked to her about it and said I thought it important to face the feelings and not push them underground. It was then I decided, Sara, that I would tell you what I have. As I talked to Jacqueline, I saw that I had been preparing Kalon for a part in my play, handing him a heavy role as he came from the womb. When it was not Kalon but you, Sara, the role, the script, the play had no meaning. It was a relief to know I could start clean with you, my daughter, begin to build a free and open relationship.

All I have now to say in closing is that I love you as you are. I feel no fragments left behind of wishing you were a boy. I want you to be Sara, whoever that may be!

SEVEN

....

Mid-life

Carl Jung wrote: *"Wholly unprepared, we embark upon the second half of life. We take this step into the afternoon of life with the false assumption that our truths and ideals will serve us as before. But we cannot live the afternoon of life according to the program of life's mornings; for what was great in the morning will be little at evening, and what in the morning was true will at evening become a lie."*

Jung might have written these words for us. Had we just looked back over the previous year, we might have seen ourselves, not as daring individuals forging into uncharted territory, but rather as truly ordinary people living a variation of the human template. We were in mid-life; and our eyes were fixed, not on the past, but on what was before us: a baby daughter, a home, a place in society, new careers, and money.

My old friend and colleague, Father Jim Crossman, came to Chester Creek House to baptize Sara. It was a final carryover from that earlier life, now that we were unchurched. Jim himself had been on leave from priestly duties for the previous year, living in another state, trying at advanced age to start life over as a layman. Now he was back, discouraged and resigned, nearly ready to don clerical black once again. He offered to record the baptism in the cathedral parish registry; but he must have forgotten to do so. Years later, when teenage Sara would need a baptismal certificate in order to be confirmed, no record would be found. I would have to provide as evidence photocopies from the family photo album showing Jim baptizing her in the living room that December day.

As soon as the year turned, Jackie and I began training in earnest to become psychotherapists. Following an intensive workshop in Gestalt Therapy led by Erv Polster, we flew to California for a month of work in Transactional Analysis. The Western Institute for Group and Family Therapy, led by Bob and Mary Goulding, specialized in combining these two therapy approaches with the belief that clients would "get well" faster in group sessions rather than in individual therapy. TA had been popularized in those days by books such as *I'm Okay, You're Okay* and *Games People Play*. It proposed resolving psychological distress by analyzing communication between people, untangling confusing "messages," bringing to light covert, damaging insinuations, revealing damaged self-images formed in childhood. It used everyday language and clear diagrams, making it very accessible; yet TA was far from a pop psychology and had established itself as a subtle and sophisticated treatment modality. It was primarily a cognitive approach and partnered well with the more intuitive style of Gestalt, which entered the psychic depths by way of experience rather than concept.

The Western Institute was located on Mount Madonna, a former Catholic retreat property, accommodating a couple dozen trainees each month. Four-month-old Sara came with us. However, children were not allowed on campus; so we took a hotel suite in nearby Watsonville, south of San Francisco, found daycare for Sara, and commuted to the mountain each day for our sessions.

There were some lectures on theory and method, but most of our work was experiential. We came from all parts of the world: India, Australia, England, Canada, and many states. Day after day we met in groups and did therapy with one another under expert direction, not simulations or roleplay, but intimate, personal excavation with the raw material of our lives, at times working as therapist, at times as patient. The intensity of this program overwhelmed us with a concentrate of professional information and experience which could be integrated gracefully into our work only gradually over time. On a personal level it catapulted Jackie's and my relationship forward with little mercy, bringing us face to face with the differences, insecurities, and sexual tensions which would also take us years to work through.

Jackie kept a journal of the experience, two hundred pages of description and insight. It spoke with enthusiasm and anguish about her self-discovery, her growing differentiation from me, and emerging dreams ("maybe go back to college...maybe a new job...maybe stay home with Sara...do photography..."). It was entirely devoid of religious language, guilt-free, self-occupied.

Although I did not keep a journal, I was just as self-occupied, scrambling to adjust to a new profession, and emptied of religious faith–now that the assumptions had proven false, in Jung's language, that the truths and ideals of life's morning would serve as before.

At the same time, we remained family, devoted to baby Sara, urgent about reinforcing our marriage, admonished by our therapists to learn to play together and not work so seriously! We loved California and had some wonderful times driving down the gorgeous coast between the cliffs and the ocean, eating at Fisherman's Warf in Monterey, poking around Carmel with little Sara strapped to my chest. We also had cold-shoulder days and a number of memorable quarrels.

Back in Duluth, Jackie and I, together with Shirley Levine and Brenda Schaeffer, who had also signed three-year TA training contacts, organized the Duluth TA Seminar to educate other mental health workers. Our contracts required us each to run two therapy groups using TA as the primary modality; and, since Shirley, Jackie, and I all did this through the Human Development Center, there were for a while up to six group therapy options running concurrently there, and something of a shortage of customers, since most clients at this clinic preferred individual therapy. Jackie's main job duties at HDC were with school and children programs; and mine, at the Harmony Club, were in organizing social and recreational activities for adults with serious mental illness, such as schizophrenia and manic-depressive disorder. However, as we began to gain expertise in formal clinical work, both of us began to overlap with the work of the Adult Team and offer group therapy and eventually individual therapy. Soon I was taking one day a week of "on-call," meaning a full day of availability to respond immediately to any "walk-in," anyone who showed up at the front desk with an urgent request to see a therapist.

At one point, Jackie and I decided that, since we were both in training together, it would be natural for us to work as co-therapists in marriage counseling sessions. We tried this for a while at HDC, but our insecurity and competitiveness, as well as some of the strains on our marriage, made for poor chemistry. We quarreled after most sessions, as soon as the clients were out the door, about who interrupted whom, and so on. The experiment ended quickly, and we would not try to work together again until twenty years later–when we had more skill and our marriage had mellowed.

Chester Creek House required less of us than it did in the formative years of the community. It had been nearly four years since its founding, and it continued to be a vital place, always changing. Bob and Patsy and Kiya had built a cabin on the Lester River, twelve miles out, and were living there as country cousins. They made their eighty acres available as common property, and Jackie and I built a little one-room cabin with a half-loft a quarter of a mile upstream from their place. We called it our dacha. It took a lot of work to finish and maintain, and we had to haul food and water a half-mile through woods when we spent a weekend. Our Chester Creek friends had helped us drag all the lumber, cement, shingles, and four-by-eight siding sheets on a toboggan during the winter to get everything in place alongside the river for construction in the spring. It turned out to be a sweet little place with a window seat, a Hoosier kitchen, and a Franklin stove. We would spend quiet winter weekends reading, summer days fishing the river and exploring the woods.

New members moved into Chester Creek House. Vern moved into Blue's old room. Bill moved in and soon married Lynn. Dave and Trudy came with their gigantic St. Bernard for a few months while they were preparing to open a second community house several blocks away. Kris and Cassandra moved out to a beautiful log cabin they had built in the woods.

Eric and Vernal Bogren had been our closest friends outside of the household since Jackie had first met them at her Welch Center seminar before we were married. They were attracted to Chester Creek and community but lived seventy miles away. Eric was a mining engineer at the Hanna Research Lab, Vernal a nurse and textile artist. They had adopted babies, Kert and Ann, the year Jackie had first met them. Now they were on an old Finnish homestead farm with eighty acres, preparing to share their land and form community. They visited Chester Creek often; and Jackie and I, in turn, would spend weekends at their farm every two or three months. These were long hours of slow conversation, simple, good meals, deep sharing, warm hospitality. We talked a great deal of what people in mid-life are concerned about: job, leisure, money, children. Also about art, carpentry, writing, world travel. Of course, we had no idea then that one day we would live there. They would give us their house. They would move to the remodeled barn. We would talk of growing old together.

Sara was now beginning to crawl. There was no strait jacket binding this girl. Jackie and I began to muse about taking some time off away from Chester Creek House. Jackie called it "nesting." Bill and Lynn offered to sublet an apartment they had been renting. We decided we would do it-take the summer off, be a family of three in a pleasant, spacious duplex, and come back in the fall.

It turned out to be a very a hard summer. Externally, everything in our lives was going well, but our inner lives were roiling. Was this something like a second adolescence, this moodiness, this abiding dissatisfaction and irritability? We could have fun together, delight in our daughter, get excited about plans and possibilities–and yet there would be this sub-octave drone of disquiet. At least, that is how I remember that summer; and it was something like this for Jackie, too. We were distracted, absent, not really happy. And resentful, that too. It was not totally mysterious; there were real conflict issues between us, which I will keep tucked into the privacy of our remembered pain.

Yet we were nesting, becoming family. Sounds cozy, but maybe that was part of our discontent. We now were out of the family–the family of the church, the family of social activists, the family of Chester Creek...is this push to move out of family what so annoys surly adolescents? We were alone here with each other. "Is this all there is?" Perhaps a numb panic.

Hard to believe it was so, for midsummer we decided to look for a house. This meant we decided not to return to Chester Creek, did we realize that? It started with an idle chat with our friend, Mary Graf, who introduced us to the notion of "fixer-uppers," houses that go for a song because they are in bad shape. It was the only way we could think of buying a house, for we had almost no savings. We started shopping, got a feel for prices, learned about financing, worked with a realtor. My mother was probably only too happy we were moving in this direction and offered "an advance on your inheritance" plus a loan at regular interest. Jackie and I took on house hunting with gusto and dragged the poor realtor through all the options in the east half of Duluth for weeks until he said he had run out of listings and suggested we take a month off and let some more come on the market.

We did this and went on vacation with my brother, Quinn, and his family and friends on a lake on the Canadian boarder. We had a miserable time, ill at ease with each other, Jackie and I, poor company for the others, no doubt. After the month cool-off , we tried to get hold of the realtor but could not reach him; so we struck out on our own; and three house tours later we put earnest money down on the perfect place: 30 West Arrowhead Road, sold by owner, $27,500, contract for deed. Goodbyes to Chester Creek Community. We moved into our home September 1st. Another seismic shift.

....

We had such a good time together looking for a home, cooperating so well. Do we exaggerate the unhappiness of that period? Just glance at the pictures in our photo album, even those taken after we took possession of the house. I look drawn, pastey, sad–not quite there, as though I had just awakened from a nap. Jackie appears self-possessed and smoothly beautiful. We are positioned side by side, holding our child, pretending for the camera. We look like we have not been feeling well. That period? What was that period–when was the onset? How long did it last? Impossible to say when this life began to appear very different from what each of us had expected, but there were early moments: our religious doubts, the deaths of our fathers, the eclipse of faith, a new appetite for middle-class lifestyle, becoming parents, entering therapy.

It is much easier to say how long it lasted, this period of unhappiness. I told Sara about it in an entry into her big book exactly one year later. Here is what I told her in July, 1975:

I have been spending a lot of time with you these days because I am on vacation. I love to be with you, Sara. And I love to be with your Mom. Before writing I re-read some of the preceding passages, because it has been over a year since Jackie or I have written in this book. In the last entry, Jackie alludes to the difficult time she and I were having in our relationship–in our *marriage, to be explicit. It was a very painful and testing summer and fall for us. I wonder how much of that you experienced and how much of it you have incorporated permanently into your nerve system, Sara. I wouldn't mind telling you the details of our struggle when you are old enough to appreciate them, but I don't want to write them down on paper. I imagine you as a teen ager asking me or Jackie what that summer of '74 was all about. Anyway, the reason I bring it up at all is to tell you what our home is like now–and the contrast is profound. Jackie and I are at a new level of deep love for one another. Our life together has been beautiful and happy the past weeks and months especially–since last November. You are really surrounded by love in our home these days. We both love you **so much!** And I really love Jackie! She is so beautiful, such a fine wife. We three are very happy these days. I hope we remain so and become even happier as time passes.*

"Since last November"...that would have been two months after we moved into our home. Neither Jackie nor I can recall, thirty years later, what the turning might have been; but there is the documentation.

....

   The next two years of our lives were more uneventful than any up to this point, just as we had wanted it. Jackie planted a vegetable garden in the front yard. I built a little red rowboat in the back yard, with Sara handing me the screws faster than I could keep up. We had great parties in our basement and invited all our HDC colleagues. On payday we would stop at the liquor store after work, and I would shop the shelves for a new kind of aperitif or liqueur and learn how to make Rusty Nails and Tequila Sunrises. We had a well-stocked liquor cabinet; and when guests came, I would hear myself asking, just as my dad had, "What can I fix you?" as soon as they were in the door. We spent weekends with Eric and Vernal on the farm, and they came for visits to our home. We went out to relax at the dacha; and Sara would sit in the sunshine on the window seat cushions, carefully selecting red raspberries from a bowl while she turned the pages of her little books.

   In September the dacha burned to the ground. When Jackie got the call at work from the horrified young friend who had been using it, she said to him, "Oh well, David, that's okay." I stopped by her office later, just down the hall from mine, and she told me. I said, "Well, that's okay. It was getting to be too much work anyway." Abject David wanted to know what he could do to atone for the disaster. We said, "Paint our house this summer. We will buy the paint." He did and found peace.

We visited our mothers in Chisholm and Soudan, went camping in the Boundary Waters Canoe Area, went on road trips. Winter evenings Jackie and I sat by our crackling fireplace studying the large amount of required materials for our contract with the International Transactional Analysis Association. In February of 1976 we went to Chicago to take the national written exam in Transactional Analysis. Both of us passed. Then we prepped hard for the last hurdle, the oral exams to be held in Chapel Hill, North Carolina. Our state supervisors and trainers came to Duluth to drill us and run through mock exams. The four of us in training quizzed and drilled one another. All four of us were pronounced competent and ready by our supervisors.

The TA orals were held during a national conference, the last step to recognized clinical proficiency after three years of anxious, hard work. We were about to come into our own as psychotherapeutic professionals.

My exam was scheduled before Jackie's. I entered the hotel room where my examining board of five sat in a semicircle. I was nervous but confident. They were gracious, reassuring, and asked me to open by telling about my work. I told them about my work at the mental health center and my work with schizophrenics, not using the words "Harmony Club," because I wanted to present myself as a therapist, not just a group worker in a socialization program. That deceit and inflation of my resume ruined me. The examiners began to ask me technical questions about schizophrenia, bipolar disorder, and major depression. I did not know anything about these disorders, nothing beyond running recreation groups. I did not know their etiology, course, prognosis, treatment. A day would come when I would know all this, be able to train others, diagnose conditions for insurance reimbursement. But this day, I sat there blocking, fumbling, running dry. They were gentle, tried to give me hints for my answers to their probing questions, even tried to coach me; but it was evident that I did not know what I was talking about. This had nothing to do with TA, and I had set them on this track. Finally, they stopped, and I could not believe what I was hearing. Five times I heard the word "deferred" as the vote was taken.

I left the room in a daze. Jackie was coming toward me, looking tense: "How did it go?"

"I failed."

"Oh, Phil!"

She went into the room next. She told the board of examiners at once what had just happened, how she had met me on the way in, how shaken she was. They asked her what she needed at that moment. She said she needed a space of quiet before she started. And she needed them to gather round her for a moment to support her. They were impressed with her, glad to do it. They were, after all, therapists. When she began to answer questions, she did very well. She passed with flying colors.

I went out and bought a pack of cigarettes and began to smoke again. That evening I got drunk. The next morning I left the conference a day early, changed my plane ticket, and flew home alone.

When I got home, my mother and Jackie's mother were there babysitting Sara. I was consoled in my shame and emptiness. I was glad Jackie was not there.

At work my colleagues and my boss, Al Brown, comforted me and welcomed me back. They let me know my failure did not in the least affect my standing with them. When Jackie came home, she was sympathetic about my disappointment but also resentful at not feeling free to celebrate her success.

I knew that I was handling this setback without dignity and did not care. The orals examining board members had tried to be encouraging, assuring me they had fully expected me to pass as I entered the exam, still considered me a good therapist candidate, but did not think I was ready and urged me to try again in October. I should have accepted my humbling and taken the exams again. Instead I decided to quit the ITAA and go my way. I did not need their credentialing for my job, after all, and resolved to shift my interests away from direct counseling toward program development and administration. This turned out to be a successful career decision, albeit prompted by wounded pride.

In the fall Jackie began working on a Master's Degree in Human Development through an external program with St. Mary's College in Winona. For the next year and a half she would continue her fireside studies, apply her therapy work as credit, and meet with a college supervisor. Instead of a final thesis paper, she produced a film with music and narration called "All Us Kids Are Okay." It was a study of her work at Center School. She says this was, in a way, a recovery of her own childhood, an understanding of child needs and struggles from the inside. She showed how children responded to group activities which redirected their energies, using art, photography, and experiment and giving them words for their emotions. The film complemented her collaboration on a teachers' manual of resources for dealing with the emotional life of children. Another product she developed was a large poster called "Taking Care of Yourself As You Care for Your Child." On a densely packed grid format it correlated child developmental stages according to Piaget, Erickson, Berne, and other experts with relevant emotional self-care advice for parents. The poster went through several reprints and was stocked for sale at the national ITAA headquarters.

Meanwhile, HDC had reassigned my co-worker in the Harmony Club, Mary Sippel, and me to a year of program development for adults with chronic and persistent mental illness. It resulted in the design of a very successful psychosocial rehabilitation center we named Independence Station. Mary was my senior and would have been a natural to lead this project, but she had decided to take a different job. I became the Program Director, a position which eventually led to my becoming the director of all adult services for the mentally ill in three counties and one of the three Team Leaders at the Human Development Center.

....

One day after work, Jackie spoke to me about a teenage girl she had seen in therapy needing foster home placement. As so often happens with us, what started as casual conversation ballooned into a great undertaking. We made inquiries; and, within weeks, we had become foster parents with PATH–Professional Association of Treatment Homes. This was a private, for-profit organization specializing in placement of older children and teens with behavioral or mental health problems. The foster parents needed to be part of a treatment team, beyond providing board and lodging. We were qualified. Donna (not her actual name) joined our family, to Sara's delight, an older sister. Donna was easy to live with; her problems were not behavioral. She was pleasant, warm-hearted and helpful. Later in the year, a second girl came to live with us. Barb, too, was friendly and fun, but she was a runner and had fled from thirteen placements before ours. Our task was to break this streak, and for several months we thought we might just do it. But one day, Barb was gone.

The social dimension of PATH was good for us. Roger and Melanie Allen, among our very best friends, were part of the network. Parents were required to meet monthly for support and training. Jackie and I, as mental health professionals, provided some of the education. PATH families would recreate together and go camping. Jackie was on the board at the state level. When Donna's steady date, Randy, became her fiancé, we invited him into our family circle and the following spring blessed them onward at their wedding.

But now, after all her work, Jackie was getting tired–burned out, she says, from study, counseling, teaching, parent training, working with difficult kids. She resigned from her job at the Human Development Center in order to get some rest, spend more time with Sara, do some photography. It was not long before she started getting calls: "Are you still doing any counseling...?" She agreed to take on one or two clients at first, and see them in the finished basement of our house with its private, separate entry. Some were nuns or former nuns or clergy, aware of her background. In time word-of-mouth recommendations brought steady referrals and she found herself in private practice.

Probably Jackie was not the only one getting tired. This time of our life is something of a blur. I was never one to keep a diary or journal with any regularity; I have done it in fits and starts and often would pour out my mind or my soul in circumstantial journals at hand–the Chester Creek after-dinner entries, the letters-to-Sara book, a travel log. Jackie and I started a travel log the summer of 1978 when we decided to take a vacation trip out west. It surprises me when I read it now to see that I was pondering explicitly the textbook issues of mid-life. But before telling that, here is a bit of background for this trip.

One of us came up with the idea of getting a motor home, getting away from it all, and heading out east to Quebec or west to the Pacific. We still had little money saved, nothing that would allow that. But Mary and Fred Sippel were selling their truck-chassis motor home for $4500, and it would be perfect. We decided to risk it, went to the bank, talked them into lending us that amount on a ninety-day note, and made the deal with Mary and Fred. We would take the trip, sell the motor home as soon as we got home, and pay back the loan–all within three months.

So, our shared journal starts this way:

6/4/78 She was thirty the last time. I was thirty-one. We set off carrying our home on our backs in bright orange packs, set off standing alone and vulnerable alongside Highway #2 in Wisconsin. Now we are preparing to go again–this time on Highway #2 in the opposite direction: across Minnesota and into North Dakota. This time we go with the vulnerability of a tank, carrying our home around us in a rolling hulk as we move. Seven or eight years have passed since we took to the road, the open road, and wrote of what we called "Our Adventures." Why so long? Well, we have not been without adventures in the meantime . . . (It would appear) we have moved into conventionality and conformity. When we hitchhiked to Europe and North Africa in 1971, we earned less than 1/3 of what we do now. We lived in a commune. I had a marginal job in the peace movement. We were childless.

Today we own our home, have a four-year-old daughter, two foster daughters; Jackie is in private practice as a psychotherapist and I am director of a mental health program–and we have just bought a motor home. Getting here has been an adventure, and it seems we did not need to travel for it. Yet we have traveled: some months in Watsonville, California, Chicago, Raleigh, Atlanta, New York, Philadelphia–but these have been work-related, part of our gradual process into stability, conventionality, middle class and middle age . . .

*I am thirty-eight now and she is thirty-seven. I know that much is finished and will never again be revisited. I know that the choices are fewer and some of the risks could be terminal. But I also have a sense of the future at thirty-eight much keener than I did at thirty-one. When I was younger–especially in my early to mid twenties–the future spread out before me like a panorama, like a vast uncharted wild, and I could go anywhere and **everywhere.** Now the future is more determinate. I do not know what it will be, by any means, but I know–and sense–that I cannot go **anywhere** and certainly not everywhere. I will go to certain spaces and have certain experiences, and they will be every bit as fascinating as those left behind, I have no doubt. And the future is coming soon, I know. And it is all that separates me from being dead. And done. **That** is what is so different now.*

Strange it is that here, mid-course, I am with my wife and child, huddling in, wrapping myself round with a house and a garden and a profession and– and–. I have the sense that I am gathering in, consolidating–no, crouching to spring. This may be the remnant of a boyish romantic fancy, but I sense that my life is soon about to open out again and surge forward.

....

Jackie had already crossed over into the future. She had returned to church. Silently (that is to say, unknown to me) and separately (as was becoming more frequent) she had re-embraced her faith. I was not happy about it. What ultimately brought her to this turning was a client. She had been working in therapy for months with a woman caught in years of crippling depression and suicidal ideation. All Jackie's loving efforts to guide her through the windfalls and tragedies of her lifescript into redecision and commitment to live were not enough. This woman was clinging to her therapist for life–and yet she herself said, "It is just...not enough." Then one day her client came for a session, and Jackie could see at once she was changed. She was at peace.

"What happened?" Jackie asked

"Come and see," she said.

Jackie was hesitant yet curious about the suggestion that she accompany this client-friend to a prayer meeting. How simplistic. Reluctantly, she complied; and, as she tells it, "As I came through the door into the prayer meeting–whoosh!–it was like a wave hitting me, and I nearly fell over!" She stayed and began to pray, and returned, and returned. She began to go to Mass at Holy Rosary, and there in the front pew she saw a bald, middle-aged lawyer, singing with joy, swaying slightly, hands raised in prayer, a face glowing like that of an archangel, Mike Cohen. "There is a man who believes," Jackie said to herself.

I did not like it a bit. However, I decided to go to Mass with her at Holy Rosary each Sunday "out of friendliness–out of wanting to be a decent fellow." I did not want to aggravate this split in our family: Jackie taking Sara to Mass week after week while I stayed home and read the paper. So I went and sat in the pew; but I did not believe any of it.

Jackie let me be, but I felt I was losing a friend. Here is a passage from her first entry in our motor home travel journal. Passing through

Montana into the Rockies, she is envisioning doing a photo study and writing a book:

> *...The theme of my book has not been decided. I believe that this trip will spell out what I am looking for, that is, recapturing our basic child energy that is within and responding from our insides out as children–which is what gives us our feeling of aliveness, centeredness, awareness that we lose touch with as we "grow up." Being "as a child" connotes faith, a sense of wonder, awe and fantasy or mystery. Yes, this theme is awakening in me, I am sure. My faith also includes a dimension of life that these mountains, the ocean, and the vastness of our earth and sky are enlivening in me. Without some spiritual dimension in our lives, life becomes only three-dimensional; whereas it is multi-dimensional.*

The three of us had a great trip. Sara and I agreed to collaborate on a guidebook when we got home to be called *Best Slides and Swingsets of the Western United States.* We visited friends in Seattle, meandered down the Pacific Coast, went to Mass with my sister, Marilynn, and her family in South San Francisco, crossed into Mexico at Tiajuana, got ticketed and had to bribe a cop to let us go, scurried back across the border and made our way to the Great Sand Dunes and the Grand Canyon and returned in time to sell the motor home for $4500 and pay off the bank note.

We were back, we thought, to normal life–although what would be normal about taking on another foster daughter (also named Sara) who was sixteen, defiant, deceitful, and surly/sweet? She came with a boyfriend who hung around, and soon it was apparent she also came with a baby. As her due date approached in early winter, we learned it would be two babies. Angela and Robert were born premature and frail at the end of November. Robert died a day or two later. We brought Sara Henderson (not her actual name) and her daughter home with us and parented them both for the next year.

For the most part, life at home was apparently stable; but Jackie and I were diverging at the core of our marriage. We generally got along well and provided a happy home for our two Saras and the baby. But there were the exceptions, teeth-clenching quarrels and fury. Once, in a rage at something she said, I wildly struck out at the kitchen wall and smashed a lamp fixture to pieces and left the empty brass base dangling from wires below a gape in the wallboard. Almost in that very moment I was pierced by the enormity of what I was doing as I saw her clutch our own daughter, Sara, to her chest. My hand hung bleeding.

Often we would ask forgiveness of each other, sometimes delayed hours or a day, and always we would forgive. What could I have meant by that very odd writing of the summer before in the travel journal?

> *...the choices are fewer and some of the risks could be terminal...I will go to certain spaces and have certain experiences, and they will be every bit as fascinating as those left behind, I have no doubt. And the future is coming soon, I know. And it is all that separates me from being dead. And done.*

What wildness, what desperation in those words! What was I thinking? I had been drinking quite a bit. After work my staff and I would often stop downtown, and regularly I would call Jackie from the pay phone in the bar to let her know I would be home "pretty soon." One night I drove home alone late from a party at someone's house out in the country–and I could remember leaving, and remember pulling onto the gravel of our driveway, but nothing in between.

It came to a head on May 17, 1979, after a cookout and party I had hosted in our back yard to honor all the student interns and community volunteers who had worked with my staff during the past year. Jackie had joined us for the party but had withdrawn to the house after a while. When the guests were gone, she came at me fiercely. I defended and blustered, acted indignant; but it was no good. She let me know she would not go down this road with me. She would not!

At three o'clock in the morning Jackie was out walking up and down the street crying. Then she called her friend, Connie Burdick–the same Connie who had helped her in the classroom when she was a nun, who had gotten her the job at HDC, who had babysat her daughter for a year–woke her in the middle of the night and poured out her broken heart, knowing she had to make a decision about this marriage.

In the morning I left for work without seeing her, knowing that the flooring under my feet had given way and I was ruined. I saw that I had become a moral wreck and resolved that, no matter what Jackie did, I would change my life. At work I went through the motions in a daze. The clock slowed down. I could not wait to get home. I did not know if I would find her there.

She was there. I said I needed to talk to her. I told her simply that I saw I had become a bad man. My life had become what she might call "sin." I said I was very sorry and, no matter what she might decide, I would begin to become a good man. I knew it was a lot to ask, but I begged her to go with me to the Marriage Encounter.

She had not been expecting any of this and knew it was not an act. But she was hurt and wary; and following through on the Marriage Encounter, scheduled to start that very evening in a motel conference room downtown, was out of the question–that went without saying!

Ironically, we were already signed up. A friend had talked us into going, insisting it was "to make good marriages even better, not for couples having trouble." Both of us initially had said no. We had years of that kind of communication and relationship training through our jobs and did not need more. Besides, this was a religious approach; and I, especially, had not been interested. Jackie came round first and had asked me to reconsider. I had been grumpy and reluctant but in the end gave in, and Jackie had sent in our names and a deposit. We were expected at the registration desk at seven o'clock that evening. Now *I* was pleading, and she was ready to be a no-show.

The Marriage Encounter did not heal our marriage. It simply caught us as we were falling into a heap, held us in warm arms Friday night, all day Saturday, until we came out Sunday afternoon, tear-stained and upright. The format was simple: a panel of trained couples talking intimately about their own marriages on a range of topics from the everyday to the profound. No group work for us but husband-wife sharing in privacy on a simple assigned question. This was called "ten-and-ten": ten minutes for each of us apart to write thoughts/feelings on the topic, ten minutes to swap notebooks, read the other's writing and discuss. (Sometimes a thirty-and-thirty, later even a ninety-and-ninety.) By the end of Friday evening, Jackie's steely resistance to me had melted. I spent a good part of the weekend weeping. By Saturday morning I had begun to believe, to recover my abandoned faith. By afternoon I was praying–for the first time in six years.

One might think that the usual order would be: I believe, then I convert, then I kneel. However, *metanoia* often has this biblical pattern: I have a change of heart and mind. Then I begin to believe. Then I pray. The grace to turn comes before the grace to see (ask Paul, ask Augustine.)

On Sunday I said to Jackie. "You and I are at peace. Now, the first thing I have to do when we leave here is go to the bishop and be reconciled with the church."

Instead of going home, we drove directly to St. Francis House, the residence of Bishop Anderson, and rang the bell. He was just sitting down in the living room with a few friends to watch *Sixty Minutes* on TV.

I asked him, "Bishop, sorry to interrupt. Could I talk to you for a minute?"

"Sure, Phil. Come on in here. Nobody will be coming through here." He led me into a long, narrow side room and sat at one end. I took a chair by the door.

"Bishop," I began directly, "I have only run into you a few times around town over the past five or six years, but you always invited me to drop over sometime. Well, I am not coming here today for a social visit. Bishop, I have been away from you and from the church for a long time. I am here because I want to be reconciled with you–and with the church."

(*...then his son said, "Father I have sinned against heaven and against you..."*)

Bishop interrupted in his casual way–it took me by surprise–as though we were having a perfectly ordinary chat. "Sure, Phil. That's good. I suppose I've been a prodigal father maybe and, well, we can get this fixed up...."

(*...but the father said to his servants, "Quick, bring out the best robe..."*)

Then he did the most extraordinary thing. He stood up, crossed the room, and sat down next to me. He reached up, placed his hand on my head–and I nearly swooned as I heard him saying, "May our Lord Jesus Christ absolve you, and by his authority I absolve you from every bond of excommunication, suspension, and interdict, to the extent of my power and your need. Finally I absolve you from your sins, in the name of the Father and of the Son and of the Holy Spirit."

I had not asked for the sacrament, had not known I was confessing. The next moment he was on his feet, reaching out to shake my hand:

"Good, Phil, great! Give Bernie Popesh a call sometime this week. Come on down to the Chancery Office and talk to Bernie. He'll get you fixed up."

(*"...It was only right...your brother here was dead and has come to life; he was lost and is found."*)

EIGHT

A Sign on the Lawn

The compass swing of my conversion took place in a few hours. The arduous movement of turning marriage and family life–like a loaded ore boat on the Great Lake–took the next two years. Jackie and I strained to recover our original dedication to service and build a new marriage spirituality. For guidance we instinctively looked backward–to the piety of Catholic traditions and to our mythic wedding-day gesture of stepping down from the head table to wait on the guests. It came more readily to her, already returned to Christianity a year and buoyed in the joyful, hopeful enthusiasms of the charismatic prayer renewal which was prominent in Catholic life at this time. I found the insistence and language of this style awkward and aggravating, much in conflict with the residual skepticism I felt from the preceding "religionless years," when extensive reading and reflection on comparative religion and natural science had confirmed my doubts about faith. Yet I was eager to comply now, straining to make whatever adaptations might be needed to restore my integrity in our marriage, hopeful that, by prayer and practice, I would eventually come to a genuine faith.

The ups and downs of this struggle are documented in extraordinary detail in the love letters we wrote to each other daily. For three years after the May, 1979, Marriage Encounter weekend, we continued the practice we had learned there of "doing a ten-and-ten." Every morning we would take up our notebooks, agree on a single-sentence question (such as "How do I see God working in our marriage?" or "How do I feel when you criticize me?"), write our reflections on it in the form of a love letter for ten minutes, exchange notebooks and read, then discuss for ten minutes. By the date of our final entry in 1982, there was a stack of fourteen spiral notebooks filled with the outpourings of our mid-life hearts.

Jackie: *June 17, 1979--Sitting with you last night and experiencing how divergent our interests are, I am reminded how much I would be missing in life without you in my life. Your curiosity about the world, your resistance to pat answers and your probing mind give me a broader base of understanding of the world than I would have alone. My mind and way of being are more accepting, poetic, appreciating and less critical–tending to unite rather than take apart. You are more constant; I am more fluid. I am more open to new ways of seeing things; you cling to powerful structures of thought from which to see the world. I tend more toward experiencing and working out a process; you seem to be able to glean a great deal by vicarious experiencing, mostly through books.*

Phil: *June 3, 1979--What just happened in our talking about the passage from Acts is an example of how I feel when I think you criticize me. I thought we were reverting back to our camps, our chosen positions–you espousing religious enthusiasm, me espousing common sense materialism.*

Phil: *June 29, 1979--I still feel my heels dig in, my defenses go up these days when you say, "Do you want to pray...?" or when you begin to tell me how you see things in the eyes of God or when you make exclamations that are religious. Very often you bring God into a topic we are talking about and often stop for us to pray, right in the middle of it...I usually feel jarred by that and prefer not to pray but to keep talking.*

Phil: *June 2, 1979--(to the question about God's presence...) Sometimes I can appreciate it, sometimes do without it at this middle-age period of my life. What I mean is that, in my childhood and youth, feeling God's presence was something I was trained in and depended on for identity and confirmation. I think in my old age feeling God's presence will seem important for a sense of sustenance and security. But in middle age I had come into a sense of my own powers. I had developed several careers; I had found and kept a wife; I had a child; I was earning money to support us; I had a house, a car, etc. In other words, I knew how to be a man; and it seemed to me that I was able to stand and move through this world. The experience of my conversion shook me to my roots. This is something of the meaning in what I said to you at the time of my conversion: "I can begin to grow old now."*

I have felt okay without God's presence. Strong, contented, happy. But now I do not want to be without it. I have come to see that, without it, our relationship nearly came to tragedy. It was when I was strongest that the flooring collapsed from under me, and I saw my structure fatally flawed.

In this last entry it seems I was under an illusion that mid-life as a crisis was now over and I was entering the sustaining and secure third stage of life. Not so. We continued mid-life, a reactive version of it, as the story ahead will show. This entry also reveals that I valued my return to religion mainly for its stabilizing effect. At that time I could not know that, with aging, I would become less religious, not more so.

Almost at once, I busied myself with the formalities of reconciling with the Church. In response to a question about "What place does the Church now have in our lives?" I wrote to Jackie a letter which further exhibits the contrasts of my conversion motivations: the return of idealism, a desperate need for companionship, and fear of the abyss:

July 28, 1979--Church is very important to me; it embodies the search I have been on so long. Church means many things to me: It means meeting with God; it means rising above the banal and the immediate, rising beyond what the Hindus call "maya" (illusion, which all the world is) to what is essential. It means liturgy, prayer, the Word of God. It means losing myself in that which is greater than I. And all of this I share with you. I think of you as my sister with whom I walk hand in hand, two kids needing to stick together because the way is long and the woods seem deep and dark and maybe filled with wolves.

Applying for laicization (formal authorization from the Vatican for my "reduction to the lay state," which was required before my excommunication could be rescinded and validation of our marriage in the Church allowed) was a degrading process. I did not mind, however, for I was already humbled and eager to take some punishment. The first step was easy enough, a formal letter to Bishop Anderson summarizing my

life story, my decision to be a priest and later to marry, my repentance
and request for reconciliation. It allowed me to speak to this good man
from my heart:

> *...Directly from the Marriage Encounter we drove to your house, even be-*
> *fore going home. You received me like a father and you forgave me. Please,*
> *Bishop Anderson, do whatever you can to help Jacqueline and me to be*
> *restored to full communion with the Catholic Church. Thank you for ev-*
> *erything.*

The next step was a lengthy interview with two priests trained in
canon law at the chancery. I had been in the seminary with one of them.
They were personally respectful and sensitive; but the interrogation
guidelines from the Vatican which they had to follow were invasive and
probing, sniffing about for inadequacy, moral weakness, and lack of faith.
They scheduled me for examination by their consulting psychologist.
They took down contact information in order to solicit testimony from
my mother, my sister, my brother. They wanted a letter from my "former
therapist." So I contacted my old friend, Marsh Ward, who wrote:

> *I saw (Mr. Solem) for six hours in all. He presented himself as a young*
> *man of strong conviction and idealism who was radically changing his life*
> *style and was needing a therapist more as an objective point around which*
> *to pivot, than a healer of a sick person. I saw no signs of mental illness or*
> *character disorder. Emotionally he was distraught, feeling some anguish*
> *about his decisions, an anguish made all the more painful by his continuing*
> *strong faith and positive regard for the church.*
>
> *As we moved into therapy we discussed many unresolved issues of*
> *autonomy and authority that remained with his own father, who was then*
> *dying. These issues, of course, were parallel to his struggles in the church.*
>
> *He was able to separate from his father and as a free adult return and*
> *effect a reconciliation with him before he died.*
>
> *Since then, I have seen Mr. Solem mature a great deal, both in his*
> *work and in his personal life. That he seeks now to reconcile himself with*
> *his spiritual self and with his church, I believe, is further evidence of this*
> *growth.*
>
> *In conclusion, I view Mr. Solem's struggle for the past few years as*
> *one of identity. His idealism and energy has perhaps made the journey more*

complicated than it needed to be, but who is to say? He seems to be more
content with himself now, and ready to move on to further service.

By the end of October, the application for laicization was complete,
and now we had only to wait for a response from Rome. We waited
impatiently, for the irregular status of our marriage in the eyes of the
Church was presenting obstacles to several efforts we made to render
service. Rome, however, would not speak for eight years.

The first obstacle came that summer when we asked to serve as a team
couple in the Marriage Encounter movement. At first the state board was
favorable because of our intensity and professional experience; but, on reconsideration, they...unfortunately...had to reject our request...because...
we were "not in good standing with the church (sorry!)" They would be
glad to have us serve as the recruitment couple in the northeastern part
of the state. Crestfallen, but grateful for the consolation prize, Jackie and I
prepared to work hard for the next two years, recruiting other couples to
attend Marriage Encounter weekends by giving pulpit talks in churches,
passing out literature, launching advertising campaigns, setting up in-
home info meetings.

Next was something more ambitious. Eric and Vernal were visiting one weekend. As we sat in the summer sunshine after breakfast
that morning, they fell to talking of their days of service in Ghana with
the West Africa Teacher Corps, working with Father Hotze, whom they
called Christ-like, one of the heroes of their lives. As so often happens
when we talk travel with Vernal and Eric, plans began to hatch. We began
to dream of overseas service work, perhaps in Ghana with Father Hotze,
perhaps in neighboring Ivory Coast or Nigeria.... I could get leads on opportunities from Dauda, a young student intern from Nigeria, working
with my staff at Independence Station just then. It had been ten years
since Eric and Vernal had been with Hotze, but they would write him to
explore the possibility.

By lunchtime Jackie and I had a decision: the next stage of our lives
would take us with Sara to Africa or some Third World country to do
volunteer work. Our foster daughters were still with us, but Sara Henderson would be a legal adult in September and planned to move to her
own apartment with her daughter.

A month passed, then came a reply from Father Hotze. His situation in Ghana would no longer make it possible to place a volunteer family. So at once we turned to Maryknoll. We were quite familiar with them, an American Catholic missionary organization of nuns, priests, brothers, and lay people working worldwide with the poor, sick, elderly, and war-zone refugees. They had an enlightened and respectful approach to culture, economic issues, and social justice, combined with a humble presentation of Christian witness. Jackie and I wrote to headquarters in New York expressing our interest in the lay missioner program and, when the reply came, immediately applied. Jackie, Sara, and I were then invited to a screening interview at the nearby Maryknoll house in St. Paul, Minnesota. It amounted to a relaxed chat and dinner with several of the priests and the strong suggestion that our services would be welcomed in their overseas programs–very likely in Tanzania. As we returned home, excited and trembling, I began thinking of studying Swahili. Once accepted, we would be going out to Maryknoll, New York, after the first of the year for a period of training in preparation for a three-year assignment.

It was suddenly moving fast, and there was much to resolve in the next few months: our foster daughters' departure, Jackie's clients, my job at Independence Station, the Marriage Encounter recruitment we had just undertaken, attention to our mothers, our family, our friends. And Starloc.

I had just started a business. Two years earlier I had come up with an idea for an invention, a star-finder. I refined and simplified it, built a crude prototype, and took it to a patent attorney. After a year of patent search, drawings, applications, revisions, and a couple thousand dollars, I was awarded a U.S. patent for "A Device for Identifying and Locating a Star in the Heavens." Then, over the following year, I devoted most of my free time to learning how to become a manufacturer and businessman: taking a short-course in small business startup, ordering pamphlets from the Small Business Administration, buying a hundred pounds of cold-rolled steel strap, ordering a hundred twelve-inch celestial globes from the Replogle Company in Chicago, special ordering ten-thousand (minimum allowed) inch-square red plastic tips from a firm in Missouri, combing the Thomas Register at the library for camera tripod suppliers, printing up business stationery, brochures, and a fifteen-page owner's manual, setting up a marketing plan.

In June, 1979 (two weeks after the late-night showdown between

Jackie and me triggering my abrupt conversion), the first photo ads for Starloc appeared in *Astronomy, Star and Telescope,* and *Star and Sky* magazines. Orders began coming in, one, two a day. *Popular Science* magazine featured it in its "Roundup of New Products and Developments" section, and *Newsweek* included a description in their *New Products and Processes* international trade newsletter: "The Starloc consists of a locator device that pivots around a 12-inch celestial globe mounted on a tripod. The system sets up in about a minute and is extremely easy to use. The locator is first set on the North Star and the Big Dipper. Since the celestial globe represents a mirror image of the stars in the sky, positioning the locator-band ring on each desired star on the globe aims the sighting tube directly at the same star in the sky. Price: $59.95."

Soon I was getting inquiries and orders from all over the world: Germany, South Africa, Kuwait, Venezuela, France, New Zealand, Uganda, Hong Kong, England. I received inquiries from firms in Sweden and Japan about importing the product. When I shipped Starlocs to Malaysia and Australia, I had to add special instructions for using it at the Equator or in the Southern Hemisphere. I spent evenings and weekends in the basement hand-fashioning the globe cradle and sighting-tube spider, bending, riveting, spray-painting, packaging. I had never contemplated an overseas market and had to make shipping charge adjustments, consider credit card availability, wonder how to move to a more sophisticated production capacity to supply stores and importers.

All this was building just as Jackie, Sara, and I were deciding to leave the country for three years in Africa. It was not a difficult choice because, at this point, my heart was not in becoming a businessman but in becoming a Christian. For us this implied a life of service, which now meant going with Maryknoll to Tanzania, or wherever they wanted to send us. It was clear: I would let Starloc go. By September, only four months into the venture, I pulled the ads in all three magazines. I would respond to inquiries and orders for the next four months until we went to New York for training. I would use up the remaining inventory. We would go to Africa.

That same month, however, I took a call at work from the Maryknoll father we had dined with in St. Paul a few weeks earlier. There were problems, he said, at the headquarters level–uncertainty about whether I could be in the program as long as my status with the Church was unresolved. Yes, he agreed, it might help that my application for laicization was being sent to Rome now, yes, that might help. It was not Maryknoll itself that would have a problem with this, he assured me, but I had to understand that many of the bishops in these overseas countries were very conservative and would not look kindly on hosting a married priest.... He urged me not to worry, he did not see it as an insoluble problem....

At the end of October a letter came from Maryknoll, New York, letting us know it was an insoluble problem. We would not be able to join their lay missioner program. The next morning Jackie suggested for our ten-and-ten letters to each other this question: *"What am I feeling about the letter we got from Maryknoll?"*

> Phil: *October 30, 1979–Dearest Jackie, I am feeling very bad. The busyness of the day with all the pressing moment to moment demands have not yet taken over to numb me to what I am feeling deep inside.*
>
> *Images of a door being shut, just as we are about to go through. I want to serve the Church and feel I have no right to do so. I picture us reluctantly getting back to work in PATH and starting to take foster kids again, and I feel crushed. I know a big part of our wanting to go away was to go away. Life seems to be going along: you seem cheerful, Sara seems cheerful. I feel cut adrift, floating, aimless, going through rituals, contained and properly sober on the outside, screaming on the inside. I don't know the face of the Church anymore; it has shifted to a dream image and looks alien. Then I reflect on what is really happening, and I know it is I who have changed, not the Church. I feel caught in a vise of punishment and think, "This can't be!" At the same time I think I am just pitying myself; many others have it much worse.*

I did not want to give up and argued that we should try other avenues. I could talk to Dauda about Nigeria; we could look into the Methodist World Service or other service groups, like the Peace Corps. But Jackie wanted to go as a missionary with a Catholic program, she was clear about that. And Maryknoll was probably the most liberal group available. If they could not accept us, none would. So we simply lost heart and let it go. In the backwash of this disappointment, I had lost heart about Starloc, too, and continued to let it shut down.

....

Surely for me, going to Africa had represented a way out of fatigue and endless, hopeless responsibility, a mid-life start-over. I frequently wrote to Jackie about overwork and tiredness:

Sept 25, 1979 Fatigue–and anxiety about fatigue–are with me constantly. The weekend was a break, but I really worry about not seeing any longer-term reprieve. Perhaps it is not only fatigue but scheduling every minute of the day and week and constant responsibility. I am losing my ability to play. I look forward to some decisive major change in this pattern. This is no way to live. Hope always seems about a week away, but that is carrot and stick....

October 11, 1979: I feel sad, cut off, and awoke this way–aware of the burden of my past, my choices. Aware that I am 40 and my life is, perhaps, half-over and I am here only for a short while. Already my life is nicked and battered. Eager to complete my life, to finish it out, short and patched-together as it is. I see my life like one of Sara's art creations, a picture drawn, a package wrapped, well intentioned, crumpled, sloppy, cute.

I had thought we would leave all this, just pack a few suitcases and walk away, just the three of us, turning off the lights, shutting the door behind, and stepping onto the open road.

I can understand the man who leaves the house for a few minutes to buy a pack of cigarettes and is never heard from again.

Instead, we moved inward, the three of us. We converted the spare bedroom in our house on Arrowhead Road into a poustinia. "Poustinia," as we learned from reading the book of that name by Catherine deHueck Doherty, is the Russian word for "desert place," the image in Russian Orthodox spirituality of a small retreat house, the forest cabin of a recluse, the prayer hut of the *staretz*, or of the ordinary devout believer. Jackie and I made a desert of this room, emptying it of all but two side-by-side chairs, an open bible on a pillow, a crucifix on the wall above it, a plant and a candle. Two or three times a day we would come together there to pray the Divine Office of the Church, to meditate, to write our ten-and-ten letters to each other. Off the small room was a clothes closet, now emptied. Six-year-old Sara claimed it as her poustinia and brought in a small stool, a pad of paper and a pencil. She would often join us in silence, solemn as a monk, at times taking up the pad to scratch something like this fragment: "Dear God, take awy hour sits and don't lead any robers to us this is the word of the Lord."

I wrote to Jackie,

The door to Maryknoll is not open...we have nowhere to go, no plans we can lay hold of...eager to make a poustinia and get the office books...the idea of God I had in the past five years–those religionless years...was much more cosmic and apprehended in stars and quantum mechanics and fields of energy, layer upon layer that makes this world (my stars, my fermions, and bosons and quarks!). It is still so for me: that is where I look for the mystery. But then comes along this clear, unique scripture (I John 1:1-7) that says, yes, and that God appeared among us and his name was Jesus.

I feel some great relief, as though an answer were given to a question I had decided had no answer. I realize, Jackie, I don't tell you much about the deepest parts of my faith. I am glad I am doing it now. I love you! Phil.

Somewhere in this period, when doors had closed and we sat in silence in the poustinia, I began to find a genuine spirituality. Gone in my daily letters to Jackie was the ambivalence over her effusive intensity and my awkwardness with prayer and Jesus-talk. A sense of peace and spiritual energy settled in.

The staff I supervised at Independence Station could see I was a changed man. They were not altogether comfortable with it. I was discreet but did not keep my light under a bushel, and I could see signs that my new religiosity annoyed them. At one point I hired a fervent, born-again Christian, the first person of that sort on staff, and it did not go down well. I had sternly instructed him on boundaries and prohibition against evangelization and praying with clients, but I soon began to get complaints from staff and clients. His missteps were not egregious; but, in the end, he did not survive the probationary period; and, under pressure, I fired him. Although I continued to be promoted to positions of greater authority and responsibility at the Human Development Center in the coming years, the relationship with my staff, once chummy and collegial, grew more formal from this point on.

....

One day I sat down alone in the poustinia and wrote a long entry in

Sara's book, the large black book of letters Jackie and I had been writing to her off and on since she was *in utero*. Perhaps I wrote it as much as a parable to myself as to her, to resolve the tension between belief and knowledge, between myth and fact, which so troubled my inner life on both sides of the conversion-event at that time–and which troubles me to this day at age sixty-seven. Here is the parable, a true story, on which I still meditate as I write:

December 16, 1979

It is Advent. We have been preparing for Christmas in the most beautiful family way that I can remember. You and I had a conversation the other day which I would like to record here, because it seems to me it might have been a landmark in your development.

Background. You have been coming home from school lately with stories you accept unquestioningly and devoutly–about the obedience and docility of St. Theresa–and most recently about St. Nicholas. I am not sure who tells you these, the nuns or the lay teachers, it doesn't matter. I am a little uncomfortable with some of the things you are apparently told, so heavily moralistic and unrealistic. But I do not get too worried, because I know you well and know that you have a good grounding in reality and common sense and know how to think well and to observe and to take care of your feelings healthily.

Well, all this is off the point. You came home recently talking a great deal about St. Nicholas shortly before Dec. 6 (his feast day). St. Nicholas and Black Pete, who puts "a coal or a stick or a wire in the shoes of kids who have not been good!" I have not heard of Black Pete since I was a student in Belgium and used to watch humorous skits of St. Nicholas, the bishop, and his obnoxious, villainous sidekick, "Zwart Pieter," who would badmouth the children and get booed, while the genial bishop would give presents. I had not realized how important this story from school was to you; but Jackie did. On the morning of Dec. 6, as we awoke, she said, "Oh, we forgot to put something in Sara's shoes!" I had put you to bed the night before and knew that you had not taken care to put out your shoes by the door for St. Nicholas. So I thought this Nicholas story was just a story to you. But Jackie thought otherwise. So we scurried around for something for the shoes before you woke up. Jackie found a vigil candle and a tiny key and I dug up a sucker I had been carrying in my coat pocket and 25 cents; and these we put in your shoes. Then we went to your bed singing "Jolly Old St. Nicholas." You awoke and immediately looked distressed and muttered, "Didn't St. Nicholas put anything in my shoes–?" Then you looked over to the doorway, and your face changed; your eyes opened wide and a look of happiness came. You ran to the shoes and were delighted. I was surely glad we had followed Jackie's instincts.

Now, even at this point, I still thought that you did not really believe it was St. Nicholas but were just carrying out the fantasy as you do with so many play things. Then a day or so later, as I drove you and Sara Wasserman somewhere in the car, the two of you were arguing about who brings presents. Sara W. authoritatively declared that St. Nicholas did not put presents in shoes but <u>parents</u> did. You were shocked and offended and were sure it was St. Nicholas himself. It went like this:

"St. Nicholas couldn't do it! He's dead."

"That doesn't matter, Sara! He still does it."

"How can he put presents in your shoes if he's dead? He lived seventy–no, four hundred–three hundred years ago. He's dead now!"

"He<u>does</u>, Sara! It isn't our parents, it's St. Nicholas."

"It is, too, our parents. Isn't it, Phil?"

I was silent, pretending to ignore you both. I did not want to side with either of you on this one.

Then came the conversation I mean to write you about. About a week later, I was putting you to bed; and, as ususal, you asked for a story. As usual, I felt out of stories but required to dream one up. Then I remembered St. Nicholas and recalled a legend I had heard about the historical bishop, Nicholas. I told it something like this:

In the old days, people used to choose their own bishops. They would pick a man who was wise and good and declare him bishop. This is how it was in a town called Myra, far across the ocean, about sixteen hundred years ago. There was a man named Nicholas who was a good and holy Christian and followed the way of God. The people called out, "We want Nicholas!" And so he was named bishop and ordained. Not long after, there was a poor man named Theocrastus who lived in Myra and who had three daughters who wanted to get married but could not because their father was so poor he could not afford three weddings. Theocrastus and his problem was known to the good bishop, Nicholas, who decided to help his neighbor. The people of Myra had given Nicholas gold and presents when he had been made bishop. Now he took three bags of gold and disguised himself and went out late at night to the home of Theocrastus and threw the three bags of gold into the window, one for each daughter. Then he went away quickly, thinking he had done his good deed without being known. But a young boy had been watching and had recognized the man at the window as the bishop, Nicholas. The next morning you can imagine the joy of Theocrastus, his daughters, and all the household when they found the three bags of gold. They said, "God has dropped this gold upon us!" Then the boy came to them and said, "No, I saw that it was the good bishop who came here secretly last night to do good." So Theocrastus and all his family went to Bishop Nicholas and said, "We thought at first that it was God himself who dropped this money upon us, but now we know it was you who did us this kindness, and we thank you from the bottom of our hearts!" But Bishop Nicholas said, "No! No! Do not thank me. Give thanks to God, for it was God who gave you the gold. I am only his servant and the messenger he sent. All good things are from God. Give thanks to him!" And then the people did, and gave thanks to God, too, for giving them a holy bishop. The end.

Well, Sara, you and I then talked for a while longer, and suddenly you wanted to know where Black Pete fit into this. I said he did not fit in at all, because, whereas St. Nicholas was a real man who lived in a real city named Myra a long time ago, Black Pete was not real but was just "pretend."

To my surprise, you looked stunned, then hurt; and you said, "But Sister Jude said so! She told us about Black Pete!" All of a sudden I had the sense that you and I had stepped into an important moment. "No, Sara," I said, "Black Pete is not real. He is just a story." Somewhere between a whine and a cry you said, "Then Sister Jude tricked us. That's mean. It's not nice to trick little kids!" I was really very amazed that you believed all of this so thoroughly. I thought Black Pete and St. Nicholas filling shoes were, for you, in the category of Winkie and Humpty—consciously imaginary. Not so.

I said, "Now, wait a minute, Sara; Sister Jude didn't <u>trick</u> you. She told you kids a story with part of it true and part of it 'pretend.' That's not trick- ing. That's telling a story. We all do that all the time and it's okay to do it." I could have stopped there, but I had the nervous sense that this was a privi- leged moment. It was risky, but I went on: "St. Nicholas was real. He lived and died about sixteen hundred years ago in Myra. The story I just told you about him might have really happened, I am not sure. I heard it told about him. But Nicholas died sixteen hundred years ago, so he's dead. He is with God now and so he is very much alive, even though he died. But, you know, don't you, Sara, that St. Nicholas himself did not put that candy and key and candle and quarter in your shoes the other night, but that Mom and I did..." here your eyes widened again, but you seemed to be listening hard to me, so I continued. "We put those things in your shoes; but really they came not from us but from God who gives all good things. You remember in the story how the people wanted to give Bishop Nicholas credit but he stopped them and said 'No! Give credit to God, for this is from him.' It is the same thing here, Sara. These gifts in your shoes are from God who gives you all you have, and we—Jackie and I—are only his servants and messengers; and we put them there in memory of the holy bishop, St. Nicholas; so, in a way, it was St. Nicholas who put these things in your shoes. This part is true. The Black Pete part is only made up, like witches and goblins and hobbits and fairies. You know they are not real, don't you? Only imaginary?" You slowly agreed, and I could see that you were understanding—pretty much— and accepting. Then I went on to Santa Claus and told how that name was just another way of saying "Saint Nicholas," and I said that most of what was said about Santa Claus was not true but only a story and that it was okay to tell stories like that (Jesus himself did when he taught the people) with part of them true and part of them "pretend." St. Nicholas was a real man, I repeated, and what is important to remember is that all good things are from God.

From your face, from your eyes, I saw that your world was back in order and you could go to sleep in peace. I sang you, "For you are my God, you alone are my joy, defend me, O Lord..." You went to sleep.

....

Jackie and I were sure of our direction, we just did not know the way.

Years later I would write a novel and dedicate it to her with a frontpiece inscription by the Spanish poet, Antonio Machado:

Caminante, no hay camino.
Se hace camino al andar.
("Traveler, there is no road. You make the road as you go.")

This was our experience. A few months earlier, we had been ready to abandon house and property to serve in Africa. Now we reversed course and began to cast about with a series of efforts, any one of which would depend on long-term commitment to this house.

First we invited our mothers to come and live with us. They were great friends, Frances and Mildred, widows living alone in opposite ends of the Iron Range. Whenever they got together at our house to care for Sara, they had a wonderful time. Like this:

They are riding in the back seat of the car, Sara between the grandmas. My mom starts a story.

"So the pig said to himself, I think I will go to town to buy a newspaper. And he took up his walking stick and put on his blue hat, and out the door he went."

"No, wait Mildred. It think it was his red hat."

"No, Frances, I'm sure it was his blue hat."

"No–I don't think so. The hat he put on was red."

"No, Frances...."

And Sara between them, wide eyes looking up, head swiveling back and forth with the argument, mouth slightly open.

....

We had a fine house and wanted more family. We asked each other in our morning ten-and-ten letters how we really felt about inviting our mothers to live with us. We made plans to remodel. We agreed we wanted to bring our mothers into our home and care for them as they aged. But this was not something *they* wanted.

Just as well, perhaps, for it looked as though our responsibilities to Sara Henderson and Angela were not yet over. They had been living in a small apartment in the East Hillside for several months since they had left our home. Not doing well. Sara was not stable, and there were a lot of parties, people hanging out, heavy cigarette smoke; and baby Angela looked depressed, runny-nosed and sick. Jackie had been stopping in to check on them regularly, and one day she asked if we could take Angela back to our house for a week or so for some regular food and rest and attention. Sara H. agreed, admitting that she was not yet up to being a mother.

We now had a baby in the house again. Sara H. would visit from time to time, and so would Mike, the father, although they had long ago stopped talking about being family. Neither were forming a bond with her. Angela, it seemed, was ours. Our relationship with Sara H. grew tense, and the security of Angela in our home depended on the moods of her mother. Jackie and I decided to try to adopt Angela, if possible, and proposed this to Sara and Mike. They were not a couple anymore, in fact, never saw each other outside of our home. During a long, moody meeting one evening in February they both agreed to give us permanent custody of Angela.

Jackie and I retained the legal services of our friend, Mike Cohen, who began to explore Minnesota statutes on "open adoption," a cooperative legalization between natural and adoptive parents without the intervention of a placement agency. Angela, formerly our foster granddaughter, would hopefully become our daughter. Little Sara would have a sister. We began to allow ourselves to love her and think of ourselves as a family of four. We had virtually raised this child in our home from birth. Now she was fifteen months old, and we would be her father and mother. As PATH foster parents, we accepted official placement of Angela once again, while adoption action was pending. This was the situation for the next six weeks.

Sara H. visited at times. We tried to include her in our family life and wanted Angela to know her birth mother. However, our relationship with adolescent Sara continued to be testy, and now she used the child as a pawn in quarrels with us. She would casually let us know she was changing her mind about the adoption, then, a day later, get over her pique and say she was back on board with the plan. Meanwhile, Mike Cohen was still uncertain about the legal feasibility of open adoption; and the ups and downs of our understanding with Sara H. kept us on edge. Jackie, especially, was becoming emotionally exhausted. One day, our friends Roger and Melanie, also PATH parents, dropped by to visit and found me upstairs comforting Jackie, who was draped across our bed crying.

"You are tired, Jackie!" pleaded Melanie. "You are just worn out. You can't keep doing this. We have been watching you guys for weeks now and are worried about you."

"This isn't going to work," said Roger, rubbing my shoulder. "It just isn't going to work."

I guess we should have seen it all along, but we were too close. Roger and Melanie came at just the right moment and did what friends do. We knew they were right. Jackie phoned the PATH social worker, who in turn contacted the St. Louis County Welfare Department, who in turn contacted Sara Henderson and had her sign papers. A day or so later, Jackie and I held each other, sobbing, as we watched a county social worker carry our daughter, Angela, down our front walk and out of sight. We had no idea where she would go, what would become of her. For the next twenty-five years.

Our ten-and-ten notebooks indicate that, not long after this, we were trying to decide about taking into our home "unaccompanied minors," the technical term used for teenage Vietnamese "boat people" who were among the waves of war refugees literally washing up on Asian shores in expectation of relocation in America. The tone of what Jackie and I wrote to each other indicates that we were weary and hopeful that this cup might pass but willing to take it if offered.

Fortunately, it passed; and, instead, we worked with our church to sponsor an arriving Laotian refugee family. This began a long and happy friendship with the Phommachack family of seven, who came to Duluth in May at the invitation of Holy Rosary Parish. They arrived from a camp in Thailand with a few suitcases. Our committee rented a house for them, furnished it, gave them cash, clothes, food, found the father, Som, a job as a dishwasher in a Perkins Restaurant, enrolled the kids in school, and tutored them all in English. Others did much of the organizing legwork. Jackie, Sara, and I became the family most personally involved with them as friends on a near daily basis. We often ate with them, laughed and garble-chatted, had them over to our house. I took Som to his job, only two blocks from mine.

Eventually, when they indicated they wanted to become Catholic (that is to say, become part of the community which had welcomed them–sort of Catholic Buddhists), we gave them "instructions" in the Catholic religion. This was not easy to do; for, even after a year, their English skills varied greatly (from very good in the children and teens to almost-none in mom and dad). Sara, Jackie, and I relied a lot on charades to communicate the subtleties of Catholic dogma. We remember one moment of eminent success in explaining the life of Jesus. We were telling the story of the raising of Lazarus, getting nowhere by talking and talking, and once again falling back on pantomime. We were at their house. I stood and vigorously pointed to my chest and said: "Jesus! I am Jesus." Then pointed to Jackie: and said: "Lazarus! Friend. Friend of Jesus. Lazarus sick (Jackie coughs violently). Lazarus dead. Dead (Jackie closes eyes, hangs her head sideways, her tongue lolling out). Lazarus in the grave. Dead! Buried." Sara pushes Jackie, eyes closed, tongue out, into the clothes closet and slams the door. I again: "Lazarus dead, buried. Four days. One day. Two days. Three days. Four days, dead! Then Jesus in a loud voice (I shout in a loud voice) LAZARUS! COME OUT!" The closet door flies open. Jackie, smirking, eyes open, shuffles out of the closet like a mummy!

Well! Their Laotian eyes opened wide and their seven jaws dropped. "Ooooh." They got it! They got the Christianity idea.

At the Easter Vigil, Bishop Anderson baptized them all.

So, those were our friends, Som and Khamphone and Keomanikham and Khamphouvanh and Saykam and Vanechay and Khamleck. We loved them. They loved us.

....

It was spring now and just a year after my conversion. We were at peace in our family and happy. Sara was in the second grade at Holy Rosary School. Jackie had a regular clientele of people coming to our house for therapy. Most of our social life now involved church people, from the parish, Benedictine nuns, the bishop. We sometimes gathered in the mornings for Mass at the bishop's house and afterward lingered in his kitchen for bagels or muffins and coffee before going off to work. My regular routine was to walk down to work from our house through the UMD campus, down along the Chester Creek gully, to Independence Station just across the alley from the Human Development Center. After work I would take the bus home up the steep hillside. Sometimes I would bicycle both ways, getting a strenuous workout climbing homeward.

One hot summer day, for some reason, I had Jackie's bike. After work, I pedaled the straight, level stretch along Second Street, then turned uphill pumping hard toward Fourth Street. Breathing hard and sweating, I leaned the bike against the stone wall and entered the cool of the echoing cathedral, empty, full of summer light on the yellow-pink marble surfaces. I walked far forward, to the side, and sat. I had the place to myself. So quiet now, only the shushing of blood in my body, slowly settling. I talked in my head a bit, I suppose, that is to say, prayed. Listened to the quiet. Thoughts. One thought came–you know how thoughts just come by–this one: Maybe we should sell the house and give the money away.

I got back on the bike and pumped uphill, pulled into our yard and lay the bike down on the grass. I went into the house, greeted my love, and flopped on the living room rug, breathing hard, feeling the sweat run along my temples. She was sitting in the rocking chair I had made her. She asked about my day.

I said: "I stopped at Holy Rosary on the way home. The thought came to me while I was praying there, we are sitting on about thirty thousand dollars of equity in this house. Maybe we should sell the house and give the money to the poor."

Jackie said simply, "If that is what God wants us to do, I am open to it."

....

We had been pondering ways of forming community again, and surely that was what had been behind our invitation to our mothers to come live with us or to bring others into our home. The charismatic prayer movement in which we took part was giving rise in those days to a movement of lay religious communities all over the country. In May we had driven to Notre Dame, Indiana, with Bishop, Sister Mary Charles, and Sister Joanne Crowley for a national Catholic charismatic conference, three days with thousands in an arena, singing, swaying, handraising, speaking in tongues, hearing prophecy, witnessing healing and slaying in the spirit. In June we had been weekend guests at the Bread of Life Community in Deerwood, a small Minnesota town. Most of these covenant communities were quite conservative in style and theology, a mix of Catholic traditionalism and evangelical Protestant pentecostalism. They fostered a network of families and mixed communal households under strict, centralized authority, advocated male headship, separation of gender roles, loyalty to church hierarchy, biblical authority, and direct Holy Spirit inspiration. Some were large, with several thousand members, such as Word of God in Ann Arbor or Servants of the Lord in Minneapolis to which we would briefly somewhat apprentice ourselves. However, the rigidity and conservatism of these groups left us with misgivings; and we would in time seek out community mentors more open and mature.

At the end of that summer we began an explicit process of discernment. Expressions such as "...what to do with our lives..." and "...the prospect of giving our house away and forming community..." appeared in our ten-and-ten notebooks. Regarding the question of selling our house and giving the money away, we agreed on these steps:

We would make no final decision till spring, nine months away.

We would pray and fast.

We would consult others, especially people more likely to question or oppose this idea.

We would trust our feelings (Does the idea continue to attract us or begin to fade?)

We would watch for a sign.

....

I was at work one day–perhaps it was September or October–and Jackie called, laughing. Laughing, so much that I had a hard time catching what she was trying to tell me:

"Phil, you're not going to believe what just happened!"

"What?"

"I went over to the Phommachacks this morning between clients–I had a two hour break. I couldn't have been gone more than forty-five minutes, an hour at most. Phil! When I got back there was a FOR SALE sign in our yard!"

"What!"

"A FOR SALE sign planted right in our lawn, a big one hanging from a wooden post dug into the lawn with a shovel."

"Wha–? Who–?"

"I looked up at the sky and yelled, 'You're really funny!'"

"Where...?"

"East-West Realty. For Sale. Phone number. So I called them and said, 'You know that house for sale on 30 West Arrowhead Road?' The woman said, 'Yes, are you interested in it?' I said, 'Yes, I am. It's my house, and it is not for sale.' Silence at the other end for like a minute! Then she said, 'Oh, I'm so sorry! It's a mistake! We'll have somebody come right out and take the sign down!' Isn't that *wild*?"

....

No one came to take it down for three days. We let it stay there, and surprised friends and neighbors came asking us where we were moving and when.

All right, so now we had #5 on our list. That did not trump the first four; we would still give it time, pray, get advice. Signs can be coincidence, you know; and, even if they're not, interpretation is still necessary. We would take our time. But we were excited!

Jackie: *October 22, 1980–...selling the house...excitement and anticipation...given how many houses are on the market these days...*

Jackie: *November 5, 1980–(addressing the open topic "Someday why don't we...") Sell all we have, give to the poor and follow Jesus. Writing this is difficult....perhaps the step we are moving to make in the spring is the beginning of the response we need to make.*

Jackie: *November 8, 1980--(addressing the topic " The next thing I want to shop for is...") You probably know already that I don't have any desires for any furniture as an expenditure, but what I do want to plan for is a number of tapes and books for a library for clients. I am so aware of the poverty of people I work with in the area of God, theology, prayer, spirituality....One thing I want to look at in the near or far future is getting a good radio. Other than that I feel content to rest with what we have.*

A radio. All she wanted for herself was a decent radio. We were on our way. We sought out Sister Alicia, an elderly nun of Jackie's order who was now living down in the Central Hillside, poorest area of town, spending all her days knocking on strangers' apartment doors, offering friendship and kindness, visiting the lonely and sick, getting cash, furniture, clothing to people in need. We asked her how we could get started. She did not have any suggestions. "You just do it," she said. We were not ready yet. We still lived up on the hill, in Hunters Park, on Arrowhead Road. We had some things to take care of first.

One of them was the formation of community. We organized a series of meetings, repeating the process that formed Chester Creek Community. Most of the participants were from the affluent Holy Rosary area on the east end of town. Our first idea was to cluster in rented apartments in the Central Hillside and borrow or rent space for community gatherings. However, we soon had our eyes on the empty Sacred Heart Convent. This was a huge, red brick, three-story building that rose from the hillside. It had been built at the beginning of the twentieth century for the Christian Brothers who taught in the diocesan school which took the rest of the block. Mid-century the brothers were replaced by Benedictine Sisters who made the residence a convent and ran what became the parish elementary school. Now the school and convent stood abandoned and empty in this deteriorating part of the city.

Jackie and I approached Father Gerry LaPatka, the pastor, with our idea of forming a lay religious community in the old convent. He was well known in the charismatic renewal as a devout priest with healing gifts and was receptive to what we had to say but pointed out that he was being transferred soon and any decision would be up to the parish council and his successor, Father Jim Crossman. This was promising. Jim and I had worked together as pastor and co-pastor at St. Anthony's before my marriage. We were good friends.

Eric and Vernal came in from the farm to join us on the first tour of the convent. It was a damp, overcast Sunday in February. As we unlocked the door with a borrowed key, we were met by a smothering sense of vacancy and gloom. Only one room, still used weekly by a small prayer group, had any feeling of presence and furnishing. The rest of the building, with high ceilings, gothic windows, wide hallways, and oversize common areas felt cavernous. All had been built for a community of men at the turn of the century. On the second floor, a dozen empty, narrow bedrooms formed facing rows along a hallway, wide as a street. Halfway down was a room of toilets, shower cubicles, and two rows of sinks bolted on either sides of a partition wall. On the third floor, a large, empty chapel, two large, empty rooms, a plugged fireplace, and one smaller, more attractive room, with wainscoting, tall, gothic windows and a glorious view over the city to Lake Superior.

"If we come here, I hope we could get this room." said Jackie.

I glanced at her sharply in surprise. She had seemed deflated during the tour, murmuring her sense of desolation to Vernal as we walked room to room, overcome by the ghostly mood of the place. We were glad Eric and Vernal were with us, accompanying us with the warmth of their friendship as we explored. We did not feel so much alone.

The next morning, as we awoke at home, the ten-and-ten question we put to ourselves was "How do I feel after seeing Sacred Heart Convent last night with Vernal and Eric?"

Phil: *February 13, 1981: Dear Jackie, I had some of the feelings you described as we were touring the building, a sense of dismay at how large and institutional it seemed. I tried to picture nuns like Diane living there. I tried to imagine a number of people living there with us and had a hard time picturing us filling it up. And the contrast with our cozy home, or any cozy home that we would make if it were smaller and more home-like. I wondered if it were possible. And I thought of how strange and different that this would make us, much as Chester Creek did. And I thought of the nice things Joan Mork said about clients coming into your home would be lost in that place, to some extent.*

On the other hand, I thought of poverty, and this is it. I saw the neighborhood as I looked out through those dirty windows. I wondered if this is what the Lord is calling us to.

And I saw how disturbed you were, Jackie. I was concerned–not worried, for I know that you are seeking God's will in this as in all things; but you seemed hurt and sad; and I thought, "What kind of a home will this be for her?" But I know that Jesus is calling you, Jackie, in some strong ways.

I do not feel impatient and zealous and willful as I have at other times in my life–when I married you and, before that, when I gave all my money away, and when I resigned from St. Anthony's and moved into the Lutheran Student Center. I am amazed at how smoothly our initiatives on community and Sacred Heart are falling into place. I pray for the continued grace of detachment so that my bias and willfulness does not take over like a grip.

I intend to stay attuned to you, Jackie, and to watch and listen and pray with you. I am concerned that you might be afraid of me, that I might get you into something you will regret. I love you.

Jackie: *Feb 13, 1981–I've described pretty much of my feeling of loneliness, fear, oppression with letting go of what I have come to love–our home, our possessions, our place in the world. I began to envision despair, bleakness, flatness, hardship and trial of being in a place that is so depressing to me and people who I do not choose to be with.*

Since then I experience a call within me to grow, stretch, strip away willingly whatever encumbers my relationship with God. I desire to do this even though my feelings bombard me, even in sleep. I dreamt that I was in a kind of hand-to-hand combat with Satan, who was stalking me, pushing pins into every inflated, vulnerable spot that I have. I felt strong, decisive, willing in my dream, certain of God's strength, wanting to die to myself and bring new life to the world.

Seeing the convent needing so much care and feeling an urgency within me to make it a place where people would want to come–pleasant, simple, attractive, and spirited–I have already begun to place furniture here and there, to paint, scrub, and place flowers and plants, clean windows, let the light in. So I know there are some ways the Lord has already triumphed in me.

Phil: *March 30, 1981–Last year at this time we were between Angela's leaving and taking in Vietnamese children. I guess our mothers had just said 'no' to living here. As I recall, we were not very eager to take in Vietnamese children but were doing it out of response to a need. Similar to what we are doing now in our moves toward community. We keep going into hard things, Jackie, walking toward intense relationships and personal involvements (with our mothers, Angela, boat children, and now the Monday night prayer group.) This morning this all feels rough and sticky and dirty–like hands in clay. Can it be right or healthy for us to keep pushing ourselves into these demanding and unfulfilling situations? And now we are trying to sell our house. We are doing this, Jackie, to seek the Kingdom of God first, to seek Jesus. I need you in this; I feel that very much this morn-*

ing. This is something we do together. I have a deeper and deeper sense of our vocation to marriage. I love you.

Phil again: *April 25, 1981 ....we get along good and move together in the same direction like a couple of draft horses pulling a wagon, each responding promptly to the tug of the other...*

....

We put our own FOR SALE sign out on the lawn. Not as nice as the one East-West Realty had, but this time we meant it. We wanted to sell the house ourselves and set up a couple of Sunday open houses. Realtors called looking for business saying, "Don't you realize how many houses are on the market at this time? At least a thousand. You are going to have an awful time doing this by yourselves in this market."

Late on a Sunday afternoon, the last stroll-through couple said they wanted to make an offer. We quickly came to accord: $43,000, contract for deed, sign-over of the six percent mortgage we were carrying, final balloon payment in eight years. Sue and Pat, young couple. Sue said, "I was getting disheartened. We looked at an awful lot of houses, and so many of them were selling because the owners were divorcing. When we came up onto your porch and saw the Marriage Encounter decal pasted to the window glass on the front door, I just had a good feeling."

Now we had to confirm that we had a home in the Central Hillside. Jim Crossman came as the new pastor; he said, "Sure. Of course." We met with the parish council and formalized our proposal: We would move into the convent with others, pay no rent but pay all heating, utility, and maintenance costs, save the parish money and reverse the property deterioration. They seemed a bit puzzled but found no objection. They wanted to think it over and check into a few things, but, well...it seemed like we could go ahead with our plans as long as we negotiated an understanding with the Monday evening prayer group that used the building.

Jackie and I began attending the Monday evening prayer group regularly, about a dozen people who gathered in the front room of the convent. We said we wanted to come regularly to pray with them; and, at the same time, we laid out our hopes for community in this place. How could they not let us join them for prayer? But they were wary of our intentions, distrustful that we had come to take leadership. It was a group organized in the style of many charismatic prayer gatherings at the time: male headship, strong authority leadership style. We were a couple with an agenda, older and more experienced in religious life, and seen as a threat. We had to go carefully. One of the women, letting me know she thought we were a bit pushy about building community, offered a mild scriptural rebuke:

"Remember. 'Unless the Lord builds the house, those who build labor in vain.'"

"Yes," I said, "that is right."

And where was Sara in all this? A line in one of our morning letters says simply: *"Sara is open and ready to move."*

The ten-and-ten question for June 26, 1981, was "How do I feel about saying a last goodby to this house today?"

Jackie: *These last three weeks have been filled with a great deal of change and work as we are moving to the Sacred Heart Convent. There has been so much uncertainty about whether we could go there, when we could, if we were accepted; and here we are, our last day, day after the Parish Council meeting where we were not only accepted into the convent and parish but affirmed in our desires to serve the people of that area.*

I am feeling weary of cleaning and packing boxes, of details of closing this chapter of this wonderful home, but my heart is eager to move on, despite my feelings of nostalgia as I think of all the blessings that came to us in this home. But now, after a year of prayer and preparation, I am ready—well, almost, after more boxes and details. But spiritually, emotionally, psychologically, physically, I am ready...I will not fear but hold tight to His hand and yours, my love. This is a wonderful adventure on our journey back to the Father. I love you. Jackie.

Phil: *I am ready to say the last goodby, to look around, to take one last bike ride in the neighborhood and to leave. When we do, I don't expect to look back with misgivings or longing. I want us clearly to remember that what we are doing is the work of God, following where He calls and not just looking for the most comfortable nest for ourselves.*

No sooner will we leave than we will have to begin finding our bearings in a new place. I wonder: how will we bathe? how will Sara begin to find new friends? how will you see clients? But all that will come in its own time without trouble.

It was good for us to sob and grieve over the ending of this stage of our life last week—and over the end of our life in this home. We <u>are</u> leaving home. We are moving on where we must. I am ready. I don't feel deeply sentimental about this. I think we have our traveling clothes on; and we would <u>really</u> be uncomfortable now if we sat around and did not leave. I love you! Phil

NINE

Community Again

*W*hy this recurring interest in community? Most people we knew thought home and family the normal way to live. We kept going back to intentional community, the gathering of strangers to shelter under a shared ideal. Probably it was the imprint of monasticism on our childhood imaginations. Monks and nuns were the spiritual athletes, heroes in the history of sainthood, those truly serious and willing to give all for the kingdom of heaven. The very austerity of the life redoubled the appeal rendered accessible even to the timid by the prospect of not going alone but by joining a band of fellow pilgrims moving in one direction, bonded under a rule and a leader, thinking alike and feeling a similar stirring of heart. To join a peaceable army, that was it. Perhaps that was what drew the young people we had found clustering by the thousands around the remote monastery of Taizé during our travels in France. Or the efforts I had made as a young priest to cultivate a local nonviolence movement by gathering supporters around a dedicated communal household like a medieval town around an abbey.

Jackie had gone to the convent in the middle of her college days and, for nine years, submitted herself to its sixteen hundred years of monastic tradition. I had spent the twelve years of my adolescence and early manhood in the Catholic seminaries modeled on monasteries with obligatory celibacy and obedience, regular hours of prayer and chanting of the

Divine Office in somber Gregorian modes, study of theology and church law.

Now in mid-life, we were about to move into community again, bringing an expired convent building to life with men, women, and children living together, single people and families. This would not be the last time. Five years into the future we would move to Eric and Vernal's farm and live in community with them and our neighbors. Another five, and we would affiliate as Benedictine Oblates with the Monastery of St. Scholastica, Jackie's former home.

We came to this next stage in our lives with experience from Chester Creek House. Thomas Merton had encouraged my notion of monasteries with families and celibates living together. The covenant communities rising from the charismatic prayer renewal provided some models. Now, as we prepared to form a new lay religious community at the old Sacred Heart Convent, Jackie and Sara and I began to travel about the country to learn what others were doing. We had already spent time at Bread of Life in Deerwood and Servants in Minneapolis. In the spring, with our house on the market, we flew to Cincinnati to study New Jerusalem and consult with Father Richard Rohr, its founder. At the end of May, after our house sold, we went to Sojourners in Washington, D.C., an ecumenical community formed by evangelical Protestants, dedicated to social activism. That summer, just after we moved into Sacred Heart, we took a vacation trip to Madonna House (founded by Catherine deHueck Doherty) west of Quebec, a L'Arche household (founded by Jean Vanier and focused on sharing the common life with people with developmental disabilities) in Ontario, and Menominee River Fellowship, an ecumenical lay community in Michigan.

Back home (was this home? this towering brick building on the hillside which had appeared so vast and vacant when we first strolled through?) problems and promise were waiting. Two men had moved into the convent with us at the end of June, both from the Monday night prayer group. One stayed only a month or two. The other, going through a divorce, rigid and judgmental, staked his claim on his second-floor room, refused to join the daily life of the community as new people began to join, contributed no work or money toward the venture, and would not leave, even after a year, despite repeated requests from the group that he do so. He was a dapper middle-aged figure who went to and came from his job, ate by himself, and lived as a cold, resentful shadow, seldom seen. His ally, the leader of the prayer group which met there, continued to oppose us with pious, sententious rebukes; but eventually he went away. We were mystified at this opposition, not sure how we had offended. Perhaps it was that we had taken leadership.

These were only a few stones breaking the river current. For the most part, church friends from around the city pitched in to help remake the building. Crews gathered on the weekend to paint, scrub, wash, haul, and decorate. Mary moved in, then Annette. We began to host community potlucks; and the large dining room was often filled with guests, the kitchen clattering with food prep and cleanup, the wide stairway and two stories above noisy with the stomping and yelling of kids. Ginny Storlie had been sent across the street from the chancery office to see if we would consider a part-time community member, since she lived with her husband in Grand Rapids but was in Duluth half of each week for her job as director of diocesan education. We couldn't imagine what a part time member would mean; but after getting to know Ginny, a mature woman with grown sons and life experience like our own, there was no question of her being a house guest. She became one of us and remains today one of our best friends. Next came Father Pat C., a priest of the diocese in alcoholic recovery and without assignment. In time, Mark M., Jim K., Mary S., Mike B. joined us. Except for Ginny and Fr. Pat, the community was growing mostly as young Catholic men and women, spiritually seeking, idealistic and devout. Then Sister Jeanne M., an older nun on loan from an order in another state, joined us. Quite different from Chester Creek Community, this one was, from the outset, taking the form of a mixed lay religious household, married people, a child, single adults, a nun and a priest. We established a daily prayer regimen based on communal prayer of the Divine Office, morning and evening. We ate the evening meal together, had weekly house meetings, sponsored a weekly potluck supper to draw in people from the neighborhood, and celebrated religious festivals with fanfare. Father Jim Crossman from the church across the street activated the third floor chapel with the Blessed Sacrament in the tabernacle; and each Wednesday he celebrated a noon Mass there followed by a simple soup lunch which Jackie prepared for anyone in the neighborhood who showed up. The area churches and social service agencies soon began sending us people in need of food or temporary lodging. And refugees.

Carmen and Leonidas appeared at the door, scarcely speaking English. They had fled Cuba, posing as degenerates eligible to join the notorious Mariel Boatlift, on which the Castro government exported boatloads of the country's criminals, prisoners, mental and moral misfits to Miami where they were accepted as asylum seekers. After months of marginal survival in Miami, Carmen and Leonidas dreamed of getting out, going anywhere. They had managed to get together enough funds for an old car and literally took a map of the United States and blindly poked a finger into its middle. The finger landed on Duluth, Minnesota. A week later they pulled up to a cheap motel in the center of our city and put down the last of their cash. In the morning, they went out to get their bearings and saw, just two blocks up the hill, the pointy towers of Sacred Heart Church, to which they went to find the priest and ask for help. Father Crossman sent them to us.

They lived with us for two months in the suite of two rooms just off the kitchen. They were stable, wholesome people, helpful and friendly. Although they remained guests, they joined in all meals and work and became one of us for a while. When Carmen's pregnancy began to show, they asked Father Crossman to marry them. They were able to set up a little shop in the neighborhood, import cheap clothing from sources in Miami, and move into an apartment on their own.

Hassinol was a refugee from the Cambodian killing fields. He had survived the massacres of Pol Pot by playing dead and waiting for nightfall, then traveling many nights to safety. He was a quiet, serious, sweet-faced young man with passable English. He had a ready, warm smile that would lead you to think that his life had been serene. How he came to us, just before Sister Jeanne moved in, we don't remember; but he came as a refugee guest and stayed on quietly and peacefully to be a full member of the community for years. He was easy to love.

There was the guy from Chile who showed up at the door. A wanderer, alcoholic, shattered, another informal refugee, no doubt. It was the period of Ugarte Augusto Pinochet's cruelty. Carlos–was that his name?–did not talk about it. He just stayed a day or two and disappeared without a sound.

Oscar, a refugee from El Salvador, had fled the threat of death squads which operated in the shadow of the right-wing government's military. It was difficult to learn his story during the months he lived with us because his English was poor, and he was nervous and edgy. He had no plans; he was on the run. He reminded me a lot of the young men I had counseled who were struggling to get to Canada during the days of the Vietnam War.

Edmund and Elizabeth were not refugees, far from it. Jackie had taken a call from Father Noel Stretton, the pastor of the Cathedral Parish, asking if we could host a couple from–she understood him to say "from China." Their name was Kwaw.

"Yes, Noel," she said, "send them over."

A half hour later, she looked down from our third floor window at a taxi stopping before the house expecting an Asian couple. Out stepped a short, very black man impeccably dressed in suit and tie. After him stepped a woman, equally black, swathed in gloriously yellow-red-orange-green-blue kente cloth, a swirl of the same color turbaned on her head. The country was Ghana–in West Africa.

This was Dr. Edmund Kwaw, physician, well connected internationally in the Knights of Columbus. This was Elizabeth Kwaw, Director of Secondary Education in Ghana. Why were they coming to us for lodging? They had come to Duluth to enroll their son, Isidore, in the university pre-medical program and were running out of funds, not because they were poor–in fact they were quite affluent–but because of a currency exchange problem they had encountered with limits on the amount of Ghanaian sidi they could transfer.

Jackie welcomed them in and assured them they could stay as long as they needed. She gave them the two rooms off the kitchen, recently vacated. They were a charming addition to our community life, cultured, intelligent, gracious. Jackie explained that we invite all guests to join us not only in meals, prayers, and socializing, but also in household chores. This sent Elizabeth into peals of laughter, slapping her knee and pointing at her husband wearing an apron and working a kitchen broom: "I *never* thought I would live to see this day! To see Doctor Kwaw sweeping the kitchen floor!"

They introduced their son, Ike (Isidore), who had already settled into a dorm room. He was open, very comfortable with himself, easygoing and friendly. In the two weeks they stayed with us, Edmund and Elizabeth became our good friends. Ike came to refer to himself as our "African son." He spent much time at the convent, joining us for meals and celebrations, practicing his music (an outstanding pianist!), going camping with the community. We have maintained contact with Ike for over thirty years now. He became a brilliant medical researcher with a specialty in nephrology, working on a second doctorate, and owner of two clinics in Los Angeles. Twenty years later, Edmund and Elizabeth would return the hospitality to our daughter, Sara, when she would decide to take a summer break from college and travel alone to Ghana.

There were always transient house guests. Usually they were broke, hungry, and homeless, often mentally ill. Vincent Eric for example (he said that was his name, although to others he said it was Eric Vincent–and we came to suspect it was neither–it didn't matter) showed up needing a place for a few days. He was tall, good looking, a bit disheveled and carried a small suitcase. He stayed about three days and was generally a pleasant companion, an engaging raconteur whose tales would eventually ramble and unravel in a most cheerful way. He did not carry clothes in his suitcase, only old food, which he did not tend to. Once he opened the suitcase by the front door hallway, and a minute later someone on the third floor yelled down, "Hey, what's that awful smell?" One morning I came down to breakfast to find Eric Vincent standing in his socks on the kitchen table removing all the fluorescent tubes from the ceiling fixture. I shouted that he get down from there! He affably assured me that it was all right, and he continued his project, giving some word-salad reason for taking out the lighting. I commanded him, cowed him into submission, and he meekly climbed down and returned to sanity with no hard feelings.

Marilyn and John, middle-age vagrants, were regulars. They traveled about the state, although John said they had a home in some small rural community. He did all the sensible talking. She had schizophrenia and was floridly delusional most of the time. Marilyn confided to our Sara with the utmost seriousness that she had twenty-nine children. They would turn up unannounced about once every six months. We grew increasingly uncomfortable with them, as it became clear that John was as mad as she, was abusing our hospitality, could not be trusted. We eventually refused them entry, and one night had to go to bed with John

out in the middle of the street at midnight, locked out, shouting obsceni-
ties up at an unresponding building.

In the meantime some new community members prompted the community to reconsider its identity. Lance was the first member who was
not Catholic. Was this a Catholic community? Was denomination part of
who we were? We had assumed so as we built much of the prayer life
of the group around the Mass, the Blessed Sacrament in the chapel, and
the liturgical Divine Office of the Roman Church. Yet our presence to
the neighborhood and the world was open and inclusive. So, we agreed,
Lance was one of us, and not expected to be Catholic. Same for Hassinol,
for that matter.

However, the question returned when Franny came. She slid into the
community in a gradual, unobtrusive way by being a guest who stays
on until she is functionally a part of the core group. Fran had been living near Duluth with a fairly dysfunctional family who had been part of
a small Pentecostal free-church group. The parents of the family were
unemployed, their four children undisciplined. One of the children had
taken matches and burned their house to the ground. It was the last
straw for their born-again church people who no longer welcomed them
(perhaps, to be fair, much as we had to do with Marilyn and John). The
burned-out family and Fran were sent to us. The family was truly chaotic, and we found ourselves organizing the parents as well as the unruly
children. Fran had probably been a stabilizing influence while she lived
with them; but now she tended to separate from them and identify with
us. We were able (just barely) to tolerate the family of six for about two
weeks, feed, house, clothe, and direct them, until, with the help of other
community agencies and some church volunteers, they were relocated
to a rented house in another part of the city. Fran did not go with them.
She was happy to be in this new spiritual community of believers who
"sought the face of the Lord." Fran had the saved-true-believer's irritating habit of not speaking straightforward English but a kind of hallelujah
dialect. When she meant "I think that...," it would come out "The Lord
has put it on my heart that...." Instead of "I have decided...," we would
hear "I am under the Lord's conviction that..." The adjectives "good" and
"bad" were routinely expanded to "of God" and "not of God."

Catholics did not talk this way. So were we a Catholic group–and
was Fran a member of this group? Well, after she formally asked to be-

come a member of the Sacred Heart Community, we had a discernment meeting and agreed that she would join us, clarifying at the same time that we were an ecumenical religious community.

This was not an academic question. As we began to get more involved in social service to the neighborhood we found it useful to present a flexible identity rather than a denominational one. This became clear as we started to think of the large, shuttered, school building next door as a resource. Jackie began working with a committee of people to organize a soup kitchen there. It was an ideal location, in the poorest area of town, accessible to street people, the homeless, and apartment renters living on food stamps. The building still had a commercial grade kitchen which had been certified for hot lunches when the school had been open. The Duluth Air Force Base up on the hill was just closing, so all its kitchen supplies were donated to the soup kitchen–pots, pans, heating trays, dishes, silverware, brooms, mops, everything. Local restaurants donated food, supplementing the government surplus food program, and the Twig Bakery donated day-old bakery on a regular basis.

The soup kitchen was not started by our community–although Jackie worked on it from the outset. The organizing committee wanted her to be the project coordinator, but she declined because she had her full-time therapy work and the daily demands of tending to guests and visitors at the convent house while I was away at work at the Human Development Center.

One day I was reading an editorial Bishop Anderson had written in the diocesan monthly magazine, calling for a service of support to pregnant unwed girls and women facing difficult decisions. I told Jackie about it and suggested that the school next door could be used for more than a soup kitchen in the basement, could in fact be opened up as a center for all kinds of services. She and I began thinking of a number of possibilities: a free clothing exchange, drop-in center, employment service, rooms for support groups,.... Suddenly she said to me:

"Call the bishop. Tell him these ideas."

"Now?"

"Yes, now. Call him."

"But, Jackie, it's late."

"It's not late. Call him."

So I did. Bishop Anderson said, "Sure, Phil, great, great, write it down. We'll talk about it. Write what you're thinking down. Good, Phil, good." Click.

We did. And we called a few others–Sister Joann Crowley, Sister Mary Charles, Roger Allen–and we called the bishop back and pinned him down to a time for a meeting. A small board was formed: the bishop (nominally–he never attended meetings), Roger, Sister Joann, Joel Cooper, myself, a few others. Jackie preferred to stay with her work on the early stages of the soup kitchen project. Sister Joann came up with a startup funding idea: the Catholic Extension Society headquartered in Chicago.

We had a board; we had a concept–a ministry center in a poor neighborhood. We needed a name, and here is where the flexible identity issue came into play. We would be using diocesan and parish property and resources and applying to a Catholic foundation for the initial grant. Yet this would not be a denominational program or service. We would in time need non-denominational funding. The church would support but not own this project. Sister Joann suggested "Damiano Center." St. Francis of Assisi, the little poor man, had received his call from the living crucifix in the crumbling church of San Damiano. Who would think of this as a Catholic name? Only those to whom it meant something.

The Extension Society gave a $30,000 startup grant, which allowed us to hire Jim Dwyer as the Damiano Center director and Fran as the custodian. Jim was the best choice we could have made. Over the years he kept his eye on the core mission of providing a wide range of services to the low income residents of the neighborhood, secured a broad range of ongoing public and private funding, and oversaw the filling of that old building with services for people in need.

Only a few of the people from our community house were actively involved with Damiano, which was something of a disappointment to Jackie and me; for we had hoped that direct service to the poor might emerge as our community's primary mission. She herself worked at the soup kitchen as often as she could, assisting the rotating shifts of volunteers from the area churches. I helped out occasionally. I stayed on the board until we moved away. Nine-year-old Sara, Jackie, and I took our turn spending the night at the Damiano emergency shelter the year that experiment was tried, staying awake to supervise, chat with the sleepless, and lock out the noisy drunks and fighters.

Today, twenty-five years later, the Damiano Center is still a vigorous resource in the city, with soup kitchen, clothing exchange, Kids' Café, community garden program, housing service, and emergency resources for homelessness, addiction, domestic abuse, mental health problems, public assistance, transportation, and more.

The three of us felt relief when a second family decided to join the community. Pat and Andrea came with their two-year-old son, Devon; and during the first week in the house, Andrea gave birth to Molly. Pat was Sister Mary Charles's nephew, and this family was dear to her and to Bishop Anderson.

Jackie and I thought back to that overcast day when we had first inspected the convent with Vernal and Eric and recalled how it had seemed hollow as an empty airplane hangar. We could not imagine filling it with life. Now there was life on every floor, in nearly every room, and light and color and warmth. Again and again we heard from Jackie's clients and from visiting friends and guests that they felt an immediate sense of peace as they came through the door. It was home, and we were family– almost the full range, an infant, children, young adults, parents. Only the elderly were missing; but that changed when Bob, a widower, joined us. He was a very kind and gentle man, a grandfather to the children, a devout believer, our dog's best friend.

A few of the early members had moved on by this time (Father Pat, Sister Jean, Jim), but the household stabilized at about sixteen. That we truly enjoyed and respected one another is clear to me in the memories I hold of our long lingering after dinner around three long tables shoved together, easily chatting, teasing, getting rowdy and outrageous. No one seemed in a hurry to leave the table; and, when we did, it was to crowd into the large kitchen where two dishwashing stations had to be set up to keep the cleanup moving.

....

Interwoven with all this we had a family life. Sara caught the city bus at the stop a half-block down the hill and rode it across town to Holy Rosary School every morning. Clients found their way to the old convent and poured out their stories to Jackie hour after hour, initially in the room I built on the third floor, later in the suite off the kitchen when guests were not there. I walked the mile-and-a-half to and from work at the mental health center every day and had increasing responsibilities as Team Leader for all programs for people with major mental illness, and supervision of staff at sites in three counties. We visited our mothers in Chisholm and Soudan regularly and allowed them to feed and take good care of us when we arrived tired out at week's end. We took summer vacation trips, paddled, portaged and tented in the Boundary Waters Canoe Area, maintained a social life with old friends from the Hunter's Park and Holy Rosary areas.

Every few months we would drive seventy miles west for a visit with Eric and Vernal on their farm. Of all our friends, we probably shared most interests and values with them. The four of us could spend long hours on quiet weekends talking about leisure and work, simplicity of life, jobs, art, service and children. These visits were interrupted, however, during our first year in community, when they left to live and work in Papua New Guinea for three years. At the end of the second year of their stay, they returned home for a break and spent the Christmas holidays with us and the community before going back to Lae for their final year. When the three years were over in January, 1985, they came back to the farm; and, of course, we went to see them while they were acclimating from the tropics to Minnesota winter. Vernal casually said:

"Why don't you consider moving here? We could be community here and grow old together. You could have this house, and we would move down to the barn which we have been remodeling into living space for years now."

"We have talked about it," Eric added. "It is a serious invitation. You would be welcome."

"Oh, that's a lovely invitation," one of us said, "but we have a home and a commitment to our community in Duluth. And we are city people, really. All our service work is in the city."

"Well, take this snapshot of the house here, and put it up somewhere in your bedroom. And just look at it from time to time and think about it."

This was typical of our unique relationship with them, the way major undertakings could begin with a casual comment–such as Eric's suggestion we go to North Africa instead of Norway, or our plan to go to Africa with Maryknoll, or our decision (five years in the future) to move to Japan for a year after a chat over morning coffee. We entirely understood their own decision to go to Papua New Guinea for three years. Their dominant motivation was to raise their children outside American culture during their prime years of adolescence. Both had been adopted as infants; Ann was black, Kert white. To begin with, Vernal and Eric did not know where they would go–finding jobs overseas would specify that–but they were clear that it would be to a part of the world where the population was non-white. So, of course, we talked a lot with them about child raising and adoption.

....

But that is not where we got the idea–not that we know. It happened more serendipitously while Jackie, Sara, and I were at a Holy Rosary School fund-raiser bazaar in May of 1982 (by this time Eric and Vernal, Ann and Kert had already been in Papua New Guinea for four months). I was working in the school kitchen, flipping hamburgers or washing dishes or something. A guy I know, Jim Tonko, leans over to me and says:

"Wanna see a picture of my new daughter?"

"I didn't know Joanne was having a baby."

"No, she's not–not yet. Here, I'll show you her picture." Out of his wallet he slides a snapshot of a pretty, dark-complexioned little one. "Pretty?"

"You're daughter? Are you adopting her?"

"From Columbia. She's coming in a few weeks."

After the bazaar, as I started the car for the drive home, I told the story to Jackie. Sara listened from the back seat. Then Jackie said, " Phil, I think we should look at the possibility of adopting." That simply. And I said something like, "Okay."

Ten-and-ten letters to each other, June 2, 1982, on the question *"How do I feel about adopting a child?"*

Dear Jackie, I do not feel a lot of excitement about it, mainly, I think, be-cause it seems so unlikely that it will happen....life seems full of activity and responsibility now and my feelings tell me to let well enough alone. Yet my fatherhood responds strongly...yet I feel resistant to the practical work to get this going–trips to St. Paul, paperwork, etc.

Dear Phil, There is certainly no need within me to pursue this issue, except that it seems to pop up here and there and, when it does, I pray about it and ask for doors to open or close. I notice that neither of us have done anything about checking out with each other about time we'd go to the Cities for a meeting....Are you willing to go?

Letters to Sara in her big, black Sara Book. From Dad: *August 26, 1982: It has been a very full, happy summer for all of us...your week at the Y camp, a week with us at Art Dale's cabin, Kee Tov, on Lake Vermilion, a week with your cousins when you stayed with Jeanne and Darrell and then Melissa's staying here with you for a week, two weeks in the Barn Program with Sister Mary Charles, and nine days with us and Shelty in Winnipeg camping, swimming, going to Folklorama....There was the weekend we spent with Mark in the Boundary Waters on the North Kawishiwi out of Ely and the weekend with Phommachacks at Timberline Campground. It has been a time of big changes for you with friendships. You have been in the process of saying goodbye to Sara Wasserman who is moving away; and last night you were angry because President Reagan did not answer your protest letter you wrote him about his budget cuts which forced Sara's dad to move to the Cities. You are often saddened by people you love leaving your life; you often miss Sara Henderson, and last night you recited a list of other people who are leaving: Bishop Anderson (resigning this month), Mark (going to the seminary), Annette (talks of leaving the community), Mary L. (leaving the community and getting married). The hope for an adopted sister has become very important to you–someone who will stay, be part of our family. Your infatuation with the movie "Annie" is the dream of the orphan girl, Little Orphan Annie, and especially the little Molly in the movie whom she protects. You have seen the film three times and read the book; and you talk about the story and characters a lot.*

Remember when we three made the firm decision to go ahead with the adoption? We were at the spring in Soudan, filling water bottles for our water supply at Kee Tov. The spring trickles slowly, and we were wrapped in leisure and unhurried. You, Jackie, and I stood around the car by the spring, waiting for the bottles to fill, and talking about our feelings about adopting a young girl. You were all for it without reservation. Jackie, too, was ready to go ahead. I needed time to talk out my uncertainty. I could see you did not like this because it sounded like "no" to you, and you seemed to be trying hard not to argue about what I was saying–my concern about the responsibility, my question about whether I could love a new child enough, and so on. But then I said the positives and ended with, "Okay. I am ready. I want to adopt a daughter." You were overjoyed! We all are. After that, Jackie and I registered with Children's Home Society, and this past Monday we filed the application. You seem to have a new sister on your mind most of the time now. You have adapted a song from the movie, "Annie," and Jackie or I will come upstairs and find you in Jackie's office sewing clothes at the sewing machine and singing "Maybe she reads/ maybe she sews/ maybe I'll make her a closet of clothes;/ maybe she's smart, smarter than me/ I don't really care as long as she's with me./ Now, there's good times and bad,/ the way it ought to be. / Come now and be my baby–baaaaby." (You have these words written down with some misspellings on a sheet of paper with "For my sister" written at the top.)

Letters to Sara in her big, black Sara Book. From Mom: *October 31, 1982--Actually this is Halloween eve, and we are sitting in the community room, each working on something: Papa is writing in your new sister-to-be's book like this one. You are writing a letter to a friend that you made last night at Mary and Corey's wedding, and I am writing in your book....We are together eagerly awaiting a long-desired sister. We have gone through our fantasies of what that would be, and we know that we are open to good times and bad. But, until she is actually here and we know that she belongs with us and we with her, we still have many anticipations and even worries, at times.*

I've been very involved in your struggles to grow, to learn difficult new work in school, to get along with friends. You have many normal uncertainties, and I remind you that your uncertainties are okay, that you are loved by us, by God, and by others, though some people may have difficulty knowing how to show it....We shall dance again tonight, and we will be taking you tricks-or-treating to friends' houses soon.

I feel so much love for you and want to encourage you to grow, to trust, to love. You are a good daughter. During the week that Papa was at the monastery on retreat, you and I had many special talks, and we slept together every night. I felt very special love for you as we did things together, you and I. Now I will go and help you make a witch's costume. You are practicing your witch's cackle already I hear from the sounds floating up the stairs. I love you dearest Sara!

Letters to Sara in her big, black Sara Book. From Dad: *January 8, 1983: ...We have a referral for adoption! We know who your sister will be. Her name is Kim Eun Joo. She is seven, going on eight. Yesterday we got the biodata and pictures of her. As we drove here to Camp Wanakiwin last night, you and Jackie and I agreed that her new name will be Maria. What do you think of that? You are Sara Maria and she is Maria Kim. Today Jackie and you and I all wrote in her book–a big blue one, just like this black one–which we started for her.*

....

Letters to Maria in her big, blue Maria Book.

October 31, 1982–I wish I knew what to call you; I wish I knew your name....I have been thinking about you a lot...I don't even know if you understand English....I don't even know if I dare call myself "father" to you yet...

From Mom: *November 20, 1982–Dear Daughter, This time of waiting for you is a time of longing, just as it was when were waiting for Sara to be born...*

From Dad: *January 8, 1983–Dearest Maria, Yesterday we received the important envelope and excitedly tore it open to see you for the first time. You are beautiful! How happy we are to see your face and to know your name, Kim Eun Joo. We welcome you, all three of us, with full hearts...We are overjoyed!*

Two days before this, I got a message to return a phone call to Steve Blons, our social worker at Children's Home Society in St. Paul. He had just been at our community house three weeks earlier, December 14, to do the home study. When I returned his call I was worried that there might be a problem, and I was very surprised when Steve said, "I've got a referral for you."....One of the reasons it was a surprise, Honey, is that we had been told we should be prepared to wait a bit longer for an older child. We had asked to adopt a girl between the ages 5 and 8, normal and healthy. We knew our daughter would come from Korea....

Our whole community has come together this weekend to stay at Camp Wanakiwin, near Barnum. We are huddled around the fireplace in this drafty lodge as I write. Jackie and Lance and Mary Schmitz are snoozing in chairs beside me with open books on their laps. Mark and Charlie are out skiing. This morning we skied around the edge of the whole lake, about a two-hour trip. We eat well and read each other stories. And now, when all is quiet, I write you this letter. These letters to you, Love, will not cross great distances to unite us, as letters are meant to do. They will not travel to you. You will come to them. They will cross the years of time, and someday you will read them when you know English, when you have grown up a bit and can understand some of this. And you will learn how our love for you began to grow in our hearts. I love you, Eun Joo–Maria. Your father, Phil

We did send her letters with pictures of us tucked in, real letters forwarded by our adoption agency to the Korean agency in Seoul, where a social worker brought them to her in the foster home and read them out in translation. Jackie sewed her a gray stuffed dog and sent a little suitcase of warm traveling clothes with Steve Blons who would be going to Seoul.

From Jackie in her big, blue Maria Book: *March 14, 1983–My dear daughter, Maria, I am writing to you from Minneapolis where I am spending time alone with God at a monastery in preparation for your coming to be family with us. I know that my special task for the first few months will be to welcome you, make you comfortable within our household, our neighborhood and especially our family. I expect that I will be with you many hours a day, sometimes teaching you our language, sometimes playing with you, sometimes just being quiet with you. I want to be very present to you, to assure you of our welcome, to love you very gently but intensely so that all the wounds of your abandonment will be healed. I want to be there for you.*

I have been growing very much since your sister, our first daughter, Sara, was born. I had many problems to work out with her because of my many struggles inside myself. Sara and I are now very close, love each other intensely, and choose to be open to each other's hurts and joys. With you, too, Maria, there will be struggles. We will work hard together to find our way into each other's hearts. It is our work, but it is also a work of God. The

Holy Spirit will be instructing us in the way of love and we shall listen and grow together.

I am writing now because I just came back from a wonderful walk around a small lake near here. I was praying my rosary very specially for the people God put in my heart at the moment. Suddenly, a huge jet crossed the sky high above, there was a loud boom! as it broke the sound barrier, and I felt you drop and plant in me. I cried out: "Maria!" and tears flowed down my cheeks. I prayed to our blessed Mother Mary, Jesus's mom, after whom you are named, to give me the love for you that I needed in order to heal all the hurts and fears of your heart. I thought of you there, waiting, having just had a visit from Steve Blons (or maybe even at that moment visiting him there in Korea) and getting our letter that I wrote telling you how eager we were to have you come, and our little suitcase with some new clothes to wear over here in case the weather isn't quite warm yet. Sara had also included a lovely toy that we were sure that you would like. That moment was very precious to me because I believe our hearts met in prayer then....I will write more as I pray to our dear Lord about you, my love. Mom.

The grandmas made the two-hundred mile trip to the Minneapolis-St. Paul Airport with us. It was March 26. The last winter storm was moving in. The reception lounge at the airport was packed with families awaiting babies from Korea. The wait seemed endless, the weather turning very foul. Finally, someone called out, "There it is!" and we all surged forward to watch an ever-so-ordinary Northwest Airlines plane taking its sweet time creeping along the tarmac in the gray dusk and driving snow. After another eternity, they started marching through the doorway into the terminal lounge, along the roped-off walkway, women cradling babies, babies, a dozen, maybe fifteen or twenty of them, babies. Last of all came a gentle woman leading by the hand a small girl, walking *"...and I don't remember much else, but I know that we surrounded you and approached you shyly and carefully. Jackie, Sara, our mothers–I remember them all around you, tear-streaked faces. And your face, darling, so sober, impassive, so unresponsive. You allowed yourself to be led. You took our hands when we took your little ones and you did not pull back. I reached out to touch you, and I had the sudden memory of how I timidly reached out to touch Sara for the first time in the delivery room when she was born. Jackie put her arms around you and took you up onto her lap. There were cameras going and people bustling around and getting in the way, and we sat on those plastic chairs and looked and looked and stroked you. A woman came over and told us she had been your escort on the flight. She said you had been sick in the first part of the flight, probably excitement, grief, the first plane ride. But she said you had gotten over it (an eighteen-hour flight). Then we found Steve Blons and hugged him and cried some more. He told us a bit more about his visit with you and your foster mother in Seoul, but we could not communicate much except emotion. He said he would come to see us in April. I signed a paper someone gave me saying we had received you. Slowly and confusedly we began to get ready to leave. I think we did not want to. I know I wanted to stay on there and not go anywhere. But there was nothing else to do. You were holding your stomach now, feeling sick. We had given you some Korean soft drink we had bought and some other presents. You were wearing the clothes Jackie had bought for you and sent with Steve a couple of weeks earlier."*

I ran to get the car filled with joy. I ran. The snow had now become a storm, and traveling was slow and treacherous. You sat on Jackie's lap. I forgot to say that, in the airport, Mrs. Hyun Sook Han, the Korean social worker with Children's Home, spoke with you and interpreted for us. She introduced us each to you, and you told her you recognized us from the pictures we had sent. The escort also told us that when she met you on the plane in Korea you pulled out our pictures and showed them to her.

So home we drove in the storm at 35 mph on the freeway. Cars were in the ditch to the right and to the left; a couple dozen accidents we saw on the way. You had spoken scarcely a word. After an hour or so, Jackie said you seemed to be relaxing in her arms. You dozed. You awoke and she played with you with the little stuffed dog, pretending that it was licking your face. Then you smiled. And soon we heard your little laughter. It was only a few minutes more and you were playing wildly with Sara who was leaning over from the back seat–a hand-slapping game–then throwing the stuffed dog back and forth. When we stopped for gas, you went into the gas station hand-in-hand with your sister, and she helped you spend your first nickel on a mint candy, which you lost in the snow before getting back in the car. You were giggling all the way. It was a long, slow trip in the storm. We got home at 11:00 P.M. and the members of our community came downstairs to meet you. After something to eat we took you to bed. Jackie, Sara, you and I knelt in the chapel before the altar and the crucifix. You bowed your

head and closed your eyes. We wondered who you are and where you have
been....

The next morning, we just idled about the house, settling in, letting
Maria get used to this big place, these many people. Maria was with us
in the community room kneeling at the large doll house I had built for
Sara several years earlier, a pretty, three-foot high light yellow structure
with real shingles on the roof that resembled a bit our old house on Arrowhead Road. Sara was out of sight in her (their) bedroom for the moment. Maria's first word came, called loudly: "Aniya!" I knew at once
what it was. Children's Home had given us a little booklet with everyday
Korean words we might need. Maria had just called: "Elder Sister!" Soon
she was speaking also to us: "Amma. Appa."

Maria's first two-and-a half years in our family were in the Sacred
Heart Community House. She began school right away at Holy Rosary
starting in kindergarten, and the following fall began first and second
grades in an accelerated program to bring her grade level up to her age
in the next few years.

....

The community itself was going through a period of maturing, then
renewal, before coming to an unforseen end. A year after Maria came,
Yadira Arevalo arrived, a young catechist, who had fled the civil war in
El Salvador after receiving a death threat from the right-wing government's military. She had made her way north through Guatemala and
Mexico to California and settled in Los Angeles for a time before taking shelter from the American government in church sanctuary. Jackie
and I had joined the Duluth Sanctuary Committee six months earlier and
worked to establish a coalition of local churches which would stand in
solidarity against the efforts of the U.S. Immigration and Naturalization
Service (INS) to arrest and deport these refugees from El Salvador. The
Reagan Administration at that time supported the existing government
in El Salvador and did not grant asylum status to refugees from the death
squads entering the United States illegally.

A nationwide network of churches and synagogues was formed to
counter this policy with civil disobedience in offering sanctuary to these
refugees, actually housing them in churches, and invoking the inviola-

bility of sacred space against arrest by the INS. Church personnel and committee volunteers knew they themselves were also risking arrest and prosecution by this action. At one point we had a momentary scare when the federal government launched a series of simultaneous arrests of pastors and congregants participating in the Sanctuary Movement on the West Coast, in Oklahoma, and elsewhere. I felt a sharp pang of fear when I heard the news on the radio, now that I had a wife and two daughters, a fear that I had never experienced doing civil disobedience as a celibate priest. However, the government apparently thought better of proceeding against a national network of church people and dropped charges.

Three congregations agreed to take the risk as the Duluth Interfaith Sanctuary Committee: the Friends Meeting (Quaker), the First Unitarian Church, and Sacred Heart Church. Father Jim Crossman agreed that she could live in the church itself if a threat from federal authorities appeared imminent.

Yadira Arevalo was a great gift to us throughout 1984-5. She was a bright, intelligent and very articulate woman in her early twenties, petite and attractive, who told a compelling story. She was not afraid to tell it publicly, increasing her personal exposure to arrest, and cooperated eagerly in our campaign to get the word out about the U.S. support of an oppressive regime implicated in shadowy death squad activity and disappearances. She lived from house to house with members of our interfaith committee, always ready to bolt for Sacred Heart church in crisis. For a short time, she stayed with us at the Sacred Heart Community House. The INS never made their move, and in time the civil war in El Salvador ended.

Yadira came to visit us one last time when we had moved from Duluth to Eric's and Vernal's farm near Bovey. She came with the two attorneys who had worked pro bono with the sanctuary committee, Jean Boler and Louis Smith. After that, she returned to Central America and began to build a life.

Ironically, at this period when our community was cohesive enough to share in the risk of this venture, we were also experiencing disorienting questions about continuity. These arose from both internal and external developments. The internal problems were normal uncertainties to be expected in a maturing process: leadership challenges, ambivalent commitment to group rituals, what we call ourselves ("Sacred Heart" had always been thought provisional), what our focus and purpose was.

The external uncertainty came when Bishop Anderson retired. The Vatican appointed Bishop Robert Brom to replace him. When he arrived, Jackie and I requested a meeting at the chancery in order to welcome him, inform him about our community and the Damiano Center, and invite him to dinner so he could get to know the people living across the street from his office in church-owned buildings. He was polite and urbane but signaled from the first that, with his appointment from Rome, came the directive "to do nothing *contra legem*," and that, in fact, he had come not to continue his predecessor's casual style but to clean up.

In short order it became apparent, not only to us but to the people of the diocese, that we had been sent not a shepherd but an apparatchik who began to create divisions, shuffle pastors, alienate dedicated parishioners with insinuations and mild denunciations, and generally dismantle much good work that had been done. At Holy Rosary, the bishop's cathedral parish, which we still attended regularly, many of the hardest working parishioners left, some to find more hospitable Catholic parishes, some to join Protestant churches.

Naturally, we in the former convent expected our days were numbered. But nothing came, no eviction notice, certainly no acceptance of our dinner invitation, nothing but Father Crossman glumly showing up one day, apologizing that he was under orders to remove the Blessed Sacrament from our chapel.

Our community decided to enter a process to clarify our purpose and develop contingency plans in the expectation that Bishop Brom's hatchet would fall on us. After all, we asked one another, should the identity of our community depend on the availability of this old convent? Over the years we had affiliated with other groups like ours around the country in an association called Community of Communities. Jackie and I had attended annual meetings of this coalition in the inner city of Detroit and on a lush campus of Hope College in Holland, Michigan. We now requested consultation from colleagues at the Menominee River Fellowship in northern Michigan. They sent Joan and Steve, a husband-wife team, to spend a weekend with us, listening, assessing, coaching, sharing their experiences–helping us through an identity crisis.

Jackie wrote in her personal diary,

Our situation in this house at this point is very precarious. We received our second letter from Bishop Brom telling us the conditions under which we can stay here month by month. Fr. Jim's response was 'We need to pray and fast.' So Phil wrote a wonderful announcement to be sent to a number of people, Bishop Brom and Fr. O'Shea (the chancellor) included, inviting people to fast and pray with us. The response was unbelievable: calls, visits, promises of prayer came in steadily and most especially concern of others about what is happening to these buildings and the ministry that goes on here. This mailing announced a Day of Listening, not for discussion and planning but for common prayer, silent reflection, and discernment.

The morning of that Saturday arrived sunny, chill, and bright. It was January 7, 1984, early in our fourth year in the old convent. An overnight heavy blanket of thick, wet snow had fallen during the night. We were making preparations for the retreat program scheduled to begin at noon. At 11:30 A.M. Jackie was just returning from an errand at the Damiano Center through our connecting back yard. As she passed from the yard beneath the back porch, a massive three-storey wooden structure attached to the rear of the convent with landings and stairs to serve as a fire-escape to each storey, she heard a sudden cracking and splintering, then a roar and a shuddering above and around her. Frozen mid-stride, she had only time to think: "This is it. This is how I die." And she watched the lumber and snow rain into the yard, beams, planks, shingles, sections of stairway. The snow-laden roof had buckled and torn the third-floor landing away, sent it crashing into the second-floor landing, pierced it in places, destroyed its railing, but then heaved outward with a glancing blow, and the whole confusion sprayed out across the yard. We all heard it from within the house, came running to the kitchen and met Jackie, shaky and white-faced, coming though the back door.

We, who had reason to give credence to "signs," were certain we had our sign. The bishop and the chancellor of the diocese would certainly notify us that they could not allow us to stay, now that part of the building had collapsed, now that there was no fire escape. Liability, insurance,....

To our amazement, we heard nothing from them. If this was a clear

sign, its interpretation remained inscrutable. We waited and watched–
and stayed on for another year. It was as though nothing had happened.

When the porch fell, I decided to go on retreat with a total fast to
fashion a written proposal addressing our questions of identity, purpose,
and direction. After three days secluded in a motel room, I returned to
the community with a four-page draft for discussion leading to a char-
ter. Several months later a single-page "Statement of Commitment to our
Community" was agreed upon by the members; and on Easter Sunday
we all assembled in the chapel and signed our pledges. This document
was framed as a flexible and personalized statement of intention concerning membership duration, relationship, prayer and spiritual growth,
simplicity of life and service. Husbands and wives co-signed one another's statements indicating mutual agreement.

None of this held us together. Within a month or two Pat and Andrea said they needed their own place with Devon and Molly and would
be moving on. It was disheartening to us all after they had so recently
pledged to stay for the coming year. Yet Jackie and I could understand it,
having left Chester Creek ourselves at about the same stage of our family. The disappointment did not weaken our resolve. People were still
coming to join us, and we expected a long future either here in the old
convent or elsewhere. However, the end, not yet in the headlights, was
coming. Neither the collapse of the fire escape nor an eviction notice from
the bishop brought it on, nor our failure to clarify our vision nor even
our incompetence in properly naming ourselves. Surprisingly, it was the
beauty of Mexico, the radiant peace of its poor.

....

When Jackie attended the 1984 annual conference of the Association
of Christian Therapists, her professional organization, held that year near
Mexico City, she met a priest and several community organizers who
lived with the poor of the capital and the *campesinos* of the surrounding
countryside. She asked them to show her the barrios where they worked.
They took her into Los Reyes, introduced her to the projects of building
small economic cooperatives in Christian base communities, and invited
her to return with her family to volunteer. When she brought the invitation home, Sara, Maria, and I were all for it. We planned a six-week
summer trip to Mexico and began preparing that spring by holding a se-

ries of informational meetings in and around Duluth to acquaint people with the "south-north dialogue." This was to be an effort to tie affluent Americans of the north into the grass-roots economic development of Mexico and, at the same time, to open a conduit for a kind of reverse missionary movement whereby the gospel simplicity of the poor of Mexico would be an evangelizing influence on the rich of the north. During these public talks, Jackie managed to raise over six hundred dollars in orders we would take with us for fabric and embroidery goods produced in Mexican village cooperatives.

U.S. Interstate 35 starts in Duluth, Minnesota and ends in Laredo, Texas (or vice versa). It was an easy three-day drive in our new-used Pontiac. Beyond the border were rougher roads, stunning landscape, no unleaded gas, kids in Monterey or Saltillo swarming our car to sell papers, vegetables, or Chicklet gum, men on ox carts or donkeys, a good night's sleep in a spare motel in Matehuala. Approaching Mexico City on our fifth day, we deflected toward the west and climbed the beautiful mountains toward the small town, Villa del Carbon, which would be home. We kept a family travel journal, and all four of us made entries and drew pictures in a rainbow of colored inks. Maria (now ten) wrote:

I like Mexico. We do work for peopel. and we help peopel. I like this Sara (eleven) wrote: This trip has gotten me very excited. On the way we saw some very beautiful and interesting sights...most of the time Maria and I would rest or read...as we got closer and in the State of Mexico it topped off all the sights we've seen on our trip here. The mountains I think were the most beautiful, shades of purple, blue, red, pink, and gray and many, many more....

Our hosts and bosses were Mario and Estelle Carota, Canadians from Prince Edward Island, in their sixties who, after raising nineteen children (some even their own) and spending a life working in social justice causes were now living here to develop the cooperatives. A wealthy Mexican friend had offered us a two-room house (in Minnesota we would call it a cabin) at the back of a larger property. Villa del Carbon, a clean town with a pretty, shaded plaza would be our home. Our work would be out in the rural *pueblocitos,* not quite villages but scatterings of shelters (scarcely houses), where poor women and children, mostly, lived while their men were fifty kilometers away in Mexico City trying to scratch a living. Jackie's work would be to help the *pueblocito* women develop embroidered fabrics and mine would be to assist one of the few men in the area to finish off the community workshop and build rough-lumber furniture for it. Sara and Maria would spend some of their time with the more prosperous families in the town, playing with their children, spending overnights in their homes and some of their time with us out in San Salvador getting to know the children of the *pueblocitos*.

....

At this point it is better to let verbal snapshots from our family travel journal tell the story of this richly textured experience which would change the direction of our lives back home.

Phil: *Thursday evening we went to San Salvador, a pueblocitos just twenty kilometers from Villa del Carbon. It is a strip of bumpy, rocky, washed-out road on a mountain ridge lined with huts, shacks, sheds where people live. There are always people moving along the road, tending sheep or driving oxen or leading burros laden with sticks or bags of pulche (alcohol drink made from cactus). Many children everywhere, turkeys, chickens, goats, horses, dogs wandering alongside or on the road. We met Andreas and Sofia Gonzales and visited their spare home. He is president of the eight or ten person cooperative, one of the first formed by Mario in the area. The meeting by candlelight was a picture of base Christian community, starting with a prayer by the leader, then each person in turn praying spontaneously around the circle, missing no one. Then a reading from scripture and again around the circle for each to comment and refer the text to their daily life. The issues are: no work, scarcity of land, high cost of living, sickness, family hope for future in the cooperative.*

Saturday: Jackie, kids, and I drove in to Mexico City—actually to Satellite City on the outskirts to buy fabric for the cooperative. Driving is horrendous through the most teeming, squalid, smog-choked, littered, noisy areas I have ever seen. The 48-kilometer trip took two hours each way. We bought about $80 of fabric and returned.

Monday and Tuesday: I worked all day both days helping Andreas plaster the wall of the San Salvador workshop. Hard, heavy, dirty work. Each day I eat at about one o'clock with Andreas in his house. Sofia cooks and never eats with us, keeping a ready supply of tortillas. Marcella serves.

Jorge, Augustin, Miriam and infant Mario eat with us. Sofia cooks with wood over an open fire. The smoke rises to the ceiling and escapes where it can, through the many holes and openings about the roof. Sometimes it fills the front room where we eat and the door and windows have to be opened. Tortillas and beans always. Sometimes also soup or rice. Always the heavy black mortar basin of fresh salsa. We drink tea or strawberry pop. The meal is quiet, casual. We talk of work or of the food or watch the children. Miriam keeps us entertained, asking me questions in baby-Spanish, patting her brother Saul on the top of the head and talking about her "hermanito gordito" (chubby little brother). The food is good. The tortillas never stop coming. I feel full quickly, and this meal keeps me for the rest of the day, no need for supper. Even though the work is very hard and heavy. I sleep well and wake refreshed, only slightly hungry, ready for another day of heavy work–shoveling cement, hauling water from a ditch a hundred yards away, lifting eighty-pound bags of cement to my shoulder to carry to the building again and again and again. I get so dirty that yesterday on the way home I stopped to wash the lime and cement from my hair in a rain-swollen, rushing, yellow-brown, muddy stream in the ditch. There is no bathtub, no shower in our cabin. I learn to bathe slowly and carefully with cold water, soap, and washcloth.

Jackie: *Embroidery is a lost art, at least in my life. The last time I did such a thing was when I was eleven or twelve, about Sara's age. Now I am trying to show some new stitches to a group of women who know only the cross-stitch; and this happens between their running home for something or changing diapers on one of the niños who sit on the dusty cement floor as we work...all my books of embroidery are coming in handy to spark some desire in them to try something new. Time will tell how much we accomplish. Tuesday, got to San Salvador and did a photo study in Sofia's, Carmela's, and Francesca's houses. It was hard because they are so conscious of their poverty; but they were so humble, allowing me to see them as they are in their dire circumstances. They have so little, but their patience, love for each other, and humility make me feel less before them. I have come to love them very quickly, though our conversations are very limited. When we greet, we kiss each other on the cheek, and this is warm and sweet....Somehow my spirit has grown stronger here. I feel so content and at peace, creative and relaxed. I feel God's presence and power each day. I am thankful for all we are experiencing and the people and country we feel so at home with.*

Phil: *We spend lovely, peaceful days at San Salvador in the workshop. Andreas is putting the finishing cement on the walls. Jackie sits at the big table I built and writes or embroiders, waiting for the women to appear to embroider. Maria and Sara sit and read or stitch. I hammer and saw and plane another table and the benches–thick, long, rough lumber. The women come with their children: Sofia, Francesca, Erlinda, Carmella, Alvina. Sometimes only Sofia comes. They embroider quietly. I carpenter noisily. We talk now and then. Today, before they came, Jackie, Sara, Maria, and I had a beautiful walk into the ravine behind the workshop, a long, steep road paved in stone diving deep into the valley. Lush, gnarled trees, flowers of bright orange and purple and white, yellow and fuchsia. At the bottom, a small aqueduct, and above it a cascade tumbling down from a great height. Along the road, small, scraggly patches of corn banked and terraced against the hill. No people.*

Sara and Marcella teach each other English/Spanish. They make long lists of words and point and tell each other the meanings. Marcella has to finish chores first, that is, working in the maize. Sometimes they embroider together. Maria sticks to herself pretty much, or to Jackie or Sara. Last night Maria and Sara performed a delightful puppet show for us dramatizing the arrival at Villa del Carbon and the problems of language.

This is definitely the rainy season, that is to say, the muddy season. Red clay clings to my boots and doubles their weight. Mice in the cabin. One became so tame that today I poked him to make him move, but he wouldn't. Then he climbed into our garbage, so I clapped a bowl over it and carried him and the garbage out to a ditch where trash is thrown. But tonight there are two more mice wrestling on the kitchen floor.

Shops in Villa del Carbon: the carniceria with huge quarters of beef hanging from meat hooks near the ceiling, rods of sausage wound round and round a rack, all meat out in the open for–how long? What ever happened to food poisoning? On the other hand, when we want to buy a chicken for supper, we are told "only in the morning." No chickens in town except in the mornings. Mañana. Unless we want to buy a live one. The items we buy are always tallied on a scrap of paper or the edge of a newspaper. Don't give too big a bill; not much change available. Our regular stops: the food stores, the hardware store, the panaderia where we daily buy biscuits, muffins, and, best of all fresh bolios–warm, crunchy, tasty rolls baked twice a day.

Riding on the Villa-San Salvador bus makes me feel like I am in a movie. No muffler. None of them have mufflers. Dirty, battered, cluttered bus. Wide aisles so people can put boxes, animals, packages down. The bus heaves and lurches. When full, men pack on beyond capacity and dangle from the doorways. They jump off while the bus is in motion. The driver is cheerful. The windshield is cluttered with decals and fringes. Always a crucifix and usually a few pictures–the Sacred Heart or Guadalupe.

Animals: On the road to San Salvador sheep graze. Burros, horses, oxen, pigs, turkeys, geese, chickens. Along the highways men drive burros carrying bundles of sticks covering their backs like a roof, the kind of sticks the second little pig made a house of. I learned it is leña, firewood. Food is cooked on open fires in the campesino homes and a supply of firewood is a daily concern. Burros also carry canisters of sloshing pulche for market. Pulche: "You can get drunk cheap here," they tell me. Twenty pesos a liter: about eight cents. Animals roam free. As we sit in Andreas and Sofia's front room at table, a turkey struts and gobbles through.

In the squares and on the streets in towns and country villages, women tend their food stands where they sell tortillas, quesadillas, enchiladas, roast corn. They set up metal fire pots, feed the small fires with wood or charcoal, put a round metal sheet directly over the fire and fry or cook their food. Always there is a case of soft drink nearby. Refresco they call it, and it is everywhere, mostly manzanita (apple-flavored pop) or sangria, also Coke, Sprite, Pepsi, and Orange Crush. They drink it throughout the day and at meals. I have never seen a Mexican drink water. Pop is the drink of the poor.

....

We went to a lot of other places during these six weeks, big places–the pyramids at Teotihuican, the volcano Popocatepetl, the elegant government resort at Oaxtepec, Cuernavaca, Chapultepec Park in the D.F. Little places, other pueblocitos–El Calvario, San Ysidro higher up at the end of a dirt track. But all that is less important to tell than the following two experiences:

One morning Jackie sat outside the workshop waiting for the women to come. Alone, all quiet. She gazed out at the thrumming indigo-blue mountains across the valley from this ridge and away. She was awash in beauty, at peace. She had not realized how much life at home in the city, in the community house, had been draining her. I have always been saved by beauty, she thought, and here again.... It would really be all right, actually, if the women did not come this day...but, of course, they would come....

Another morning–Jackie was back in town–and I, Phil, was sitting in that same place outside the workshop at my appointed hour, waiting for Andreas to show, waiting to begin the day mixing cement, hauling water. Old Mariana also was there, Sofia's mother. I sat on the ground beside her companionably as she waited for the rattletrap bus to Villa. She lifted the towel from the metal bowl cradled in her lap and showed me the blue maize grown in her garden.

"What will you do with that in town?"

"I will take it to the man who grinds it to flour."

"And then?"

"Then I go to the plaza and begin to make tortillas."

"Where is your fire pan? Your wood?"

"In Villa. In a box near the plaza. We all keep our things there. I cannot carry it back here, of course. I go every morning."

"All day?"

"Yes, all day."

"Look, I think your bus is coming."

Down the dusty road it wobbled with noisy flatulence, crammed with people, men hanging to the open door to avoid spilling out. Mariana gripped her pan of maize and stiffly rose and took a few steps forward. The bus did not even slow; it rattled right past us. She stood looking after it a moment, then turned, came back and sat down on the ground beside me. I looked at her brown, creased, Aztec face for a long moment. It had not changed from what it was a moment earlier when she and I were speaking.

"Mariana. You missed your bus."

"Yes."

"When will another come?"

"In about an hour."

So we sat side by side and continued to wait.

....

The last entry in our family travel journal:

July 17, Wednesday. I am writing this at poolside in a Holiday Inn in Kansas City. The trip homeward has gone fast. Jackie and I are doing a lot of inner-space travel–thinking about job, community, friends, the image of living on Vernal's and Eric's farm....The miles outside the car fly by. We talk, we pray, we tell Maria and Sara long, very long, stories. So far we have told: The Hobbit, the life of Gandhi, The Sorcerer's Apprentice, the Killing Fields of Cambodia, The Witness, and pieces of The Mutiny on the Bounty and Moby Dick.....

....

The six weeks in Mexico had allowed us to step back from the intensity of our lives in household community and get a sense of what we really needed. "Quiet" was the word that arose. Quiet and time. The five-day drive home with our girls in the back seat gave us the space to frame the question: What would it be like for us to move to the country, work only half-time, and live a more contemplative life?

A month after we returned, we phoned Eric and Vernal and asked if their invitation to us still stood. It did. And they really would give us their house? They would.

We let our community know what we were thinking and drove to the farm the next weekend to work things out with our friends and their neighbors. I gave three months notice at the Human Development Center. Jackie began to give her clients notice. Eric and Vernal needed three months to finish off their living space in the barn and make room for us. We needed it to finish with our community, our service work at Damiano, our friends.

The community members, most of them, decided to continue on as a community at Sacred Heart. We notified Bishop Brom that we were leaving but stressed that the community was intact. It brought a terse letter: "...we do not find it honest for the diocese to sponsor something so undefined and without connection to the Catholic Church into a tax-exempt status. May I ask you, please, to meet with Father O'Shea to arrange for closure of the convent when you move."

TEN

Putting Up Firewood

Now began our time of settling. The stream had been rushing so. The time had come to put a little dam here and make a little pond, a place of quiet waters which would nourish slow growth and maybe feed the crops.

When we first came to the farm, Jackie would sit for hours looking out the window, nursing her exhaustion. She felt bruised, depleted, a failure. I did not see this at the time, did not understand it. You're tired, yes, I thought, but why failure? How did we fail in leaving community to seek a more contemplative life in the country? For her it was more the sense that the needs she had slammed against in the Duluth Central Hillside were so much more than what she had to give–the soup kitchen, the transients and refugees who came through our doors almost daily, the burned-out family we could scarcely tolerate, the mad and hostile people against whom we had to barricade our doors, her community's precarious uncertainty, the suffering of her clients and of her own Korean daughter, whose only luggage at arrival was grief. Jackie was in menopause and going through her own mid-life crisis. It took her years, she would later say, fully to leave Duluth and be at home here.

Her struggle was internal, for the farm's environment was certainly welcoming. The house Eric and Vernal gave us had been built around 1910 by Finnish homesteaders named Wirta. Thirty yards away was the log barn turned into their home by raising one side of the roof to make a bank of windows along the hayloft wall with a south view across the marsh onto Blackberry Lake. Downstairs, where there had once been cows, Ann and Kert now had bedrooms; and later Vernal would convert that area into an artist's studio. The understanding we had was that the house and yard around it was ours, a verbal life estate. Legally the entire sixty-five acre property remained in their names. Our children would have no claim to the house after us, nor theirs to the house as long as we were in it.

Across the open fields, at the edge of woods a half-mile away, lived Gayle and Gary with their three children in one direction and an aged brother and sister in another. Waino and Marie Karjala were original pioneers in the area still actively farming in slow motion the land their father had settled in 1904. These four families, Bogrens, Edwards, Karjalas, Solems, were now "the community," more than neighbors. We clustered at the end of a mile-long, dead-end road among lakes, open land, bog and woods.

The evening after we arrived, there was a lively party at Gayle and Gary's house celebrating a birthday of someone in their Edwards-LaPlant clan; and their log house was packed with neighbors and relatives, thirty or more. There was food overflowing, singing, guitar-banjo-mandolin-fiddle-playing, and dancing. These musical parties happened frequently, for any birthday or graduation, or sometimes just for fun. On other occasions we met other neighbors for miles around at the old Trout Lake Town Hall, where the ancient cast-iron barrel stove, American Flag tacked to the wall, and 4-H club meetings for kids Sara's and Maria's ages looked like a Norman Rockwell back-copy cover of *The Saturday Evening Post*.

At five-thirty every morning the big-belly milk truck would roar down the road to pick up the milk from Waino and Marie's herd of a dozen cows. At seven-twenty a panicked cry of "Bus!" would ring through our house and I would shout up the stairs in vain one last time that the girls were to come down "Now!" to get at least a bite of breakfast before bolting out the door. When the orange bus rumbled past our house, the girls still had about two minutes while it slowed at the end of the road to pick up Aaron and Naesa and Ben Edwards, then gingerly backed away from the dead-end and turned, trying to stay out of the ditches, before charging back to a stop at our house for Ann and Kert, Maria and Sara.

Maria was now in both second and third grades at Connor-Jasper School in Coleraine. Sara was in seventh at the middle school in Bovey.

What we called "the farm" was no longer a working farm, although Vernal kept a few animals– a clutch of unnamed chickens, a vicious rooster, goats named Apple, Mwelu, Kai, and a lovely rust-colored male dog named Rosealice. As Jackie and I strolled in the mornings on the gravel road, admiring one neighbor's horses, another's herd of cattle, looking this way toward the pine woods to spot the eagles perched in a tall scrag, that way through luminous fog over fields toward the barn, the bog, and the lake, we could not believe our good fortune–that we lived here. No longer weekend visitors on this serene and beautiful land, we were home.

It more than offset the physical austerity. Before moving to the farm I had made a number of weekend trips from Duluth to put up a winter's supply of firewood and insulate the roof of the house. There had been little between us and the stars than roof boards and tar paper. We heated the house with a single wood stove, backed up by a fuel-oil Jungers stove when we were away from the house for more than a day. Our two families shared an outhouse between the barn and the house. When the hole filled up every few years, Eric and I would dig a new one twenty feet away and wrestle the old wooden two-hole structure to its new location. Vernal and Eric had electricity in their barn-home but chose to carry their water in buckets from a deep-well hand pump nearby. Our house had electricity and running water and even a shower from a sandpoint well in the basement, but the water it gave had high iron content, which stained the porcelain sinks and turned Sara's blond hair bright orange when she washed in it. It was important enough to her to restore her natural color that, even on the coldest winter mornings, she would bundle up and trudge across the yard to pump and lug back two buckets from Bogren's clear-water deep-well for her hair washing. We did have a functioning indoor toilet, but there was no functioning septic system to receive what it produced, only a primitive cylindrical holding tank buried alongside the house, which had to be pumped out every couple of weeks when the toilet was used regularly, an unbearable chore when the December-January temperatures plunged to thirty degrees below zero for days on end.

After the raucous milk-truck-school-bus start was over, our days were serene. Often we would go to the barn for coffee with Eric and Vernal or they would come up to us. As before, we spent long hours talking, simply enjoying one another's company. At times we would go down to Waino's and Marie's for coffee, an experience, Eric observed, like visiting another country in an earlier age. Often we got together with Gary and Gayle. Our families would go out to the woods together to cut our Christmas trees and have a winter picnic in the snow, work together to make maple syrup in the spring, gather in late summer to help Waino and Marie put up hay and later in the fall to set snow fences to keep the road from drifting over in winter.

Always we gathered and celebrated the holidays. Thanksgiving dinner each with our own extended families, dessert at Gary and Gayle's. Our kids put on plays for us at Christmas, and then we exchanged presents. On Christmas Eve in 1993, my present to each of them was a little booklet which I had edited and desktop printed called *Meetings in the Outhouse*. The introduction explained:

> *This little booklet is a transcription of notes and messages written in a spiral notebook kept in the old outhouse between the Bogren-Swift and Solem houses on the farm. In it over the past seven years have been written a variety of messages by those living at this farm (Eric, Vernal, Kert, Kerstin, Charlotte, Maria, Sara, Jackie, Phil) as well as friends, neighbors, and guests. It is interesting that little mention is made of the big events in our lives (Eric's treks in the Himalayas, New Zealand and Alaska, Vernal's extended stay in the Queen Charlottes, Solems' bike trip in Europe, Kert's wedding, Charlotte's house-building). Much is made of the everyday, of the passing of seasons, of pondering and philosophizing, of conversation. This is a picture of life at the farm.*

A sampling:

> *The sunrise is breathlessly blowing clouds into our still-grey sky. Orange rarely feels cold, but it is meeting the steel-grey sky with a clash that looks so much like applause.*

> *I am writing this by the light of the half-moon, which is in Gemini now. Tomorrow I think she will be in Cancer, right in front of the mouth of the Lion.*

I hear the woodcocks. This morning I heard the geese, an owl, and many other birds at dawn.

It is statistically safe to assume that outhouses (choose one): 1) rarely 2) occasionally 3) frequently blow over.

I think Halloween is a greater threat to outhouses than wind.

It smells funny in here. Oh well.

This book is like the graffiti in the girls bathroom, except the girls bathroom is better.

What does the graffiti in the girls' bathroom say? –well, never mind.

Phil, graffiti in a public women's bathroom often is about 1) feminism, 2) lesbianism, 3)ecology. What is in men's bathrooms?

1) violence, 2) homosexuality, 3) insults, 4) phone numbers, 5) religion.

SCHOOL'S OUT! I'M SO HAPPY!

This is a good little house. Interesting that the true community house is not a dining hall or gathering room, but a small place where none of us ever meet.

June 14 This is the day that the song "Morning Has Broken" was written about. It is spring and summer together and everything's dewy fresh. And the mosquitos have arrived to assure us that it is not yet heaven.

Dear Jackie, Last week there were no mosquitos but similar weather to this. Was that heaven?

Possibly. At least a foreplay–I mean foretaste.

I think of winter often these days. I think of it as a relief from this damp, juicy, crawling, tickling, hot, ever-growing season. Yes, I think it is important for us to be among all this, for the chemical reactions to be tumbling over each other and multiplying. This is nutrition for the cold season, like the nutrition in the dank, sweet hay which will feed the cattle some morning when it is 30 below. So it is in us. We are partly growing, partly marinating, partly fermenting here in the tropics.

7/30/87 This weather feels similar to Papua New Guinea's climate today. For supper I'm making hot fish curry to keep me in the mood.

Summer is here, almost gone.

How is it going? Summer, I mean. For me, it's been my favorite summer. Because it's HOT. You?

*No, this is not my favorite summer. Too hot and muggy and rainy and tornadoey. Too much life. Too real. My body often feels very funny in this summer. Too many mosquitoes. Too much real life. I retreat to the radio programs where people with mellow, competent voices tell me of things going on far away that are interesting and dangerous and mischievous. And I read books about life and danger. Better yet, I write a book full of danger and life and death. But this summer? This summer is coming **too close**. It touches my skin with warm, sticky fingers. It doesn't let go. It stands too close and looks into my eyes and breathes into my face. It doesn't respect my personal space. I have to step back a pace or two, polite and irritated.*

Welcome home, Jackie!

It is raining steadily. The sunflowers I see from this outhouse door look like patient horses in the rain, waiting for the sun to return. Long wait. Yes! Welcome home, Jackie! We missed you so!

Last week I measured my woodpile with a tape measure and computed what that was in cords (5.6). Then I put the stove pipe in my new stove. Saturday I cleaned out the chimney from last winter's creosote. I climbed up on the roof and looked out at Blackberry Lake–beautifully blue, rimmed by auburn, ochre, palegreen trees–as I cleaned the chimney. Today I pull up part of the garden and read over the new stove instructions. This week I froze beans and canned plums. I worked hard. But I wasn't frowning. I was smiling, I think, and whistling at times.

Schools out pretty soon! I am getting sooo enc en excited!!

Me too! Maria

Me too! Naesa

Me, too! Phil

School is fun, exciting. Boring and ok.

It seems to me, having been away 10 days, that we go away partly to more enjoy coming home. Sometimes we can't see straight becuz "home" is so close. Backing up and seeing from farther away makes me see what treasures I have. I think we've found the field where the pearl of great price is buried. It's good to be home, Friends! You animals, this includes you.

Thank you Jackie for the good words. One of the "animals" has chewed a significant piece of your apple tree. I will give you money for a 2 yr. replacement from Guerney ($15) and my apology. Today I'll get a collar & chain for Apple (the culprit) and make sure all 3 are always tethered. One's behavior is always affecting another, I see over & over. My care less ness cost you. Sorry. Fortunately Eric told me about the tree. I hadn't noticed, of course.

I just made $150,000 on the stock market. Interesting.

Thanks, Vernal. I just take it to mean I let go of whatever isn't there for me, but I accept what you offer with thanks.

3/21/88 Changed a flat tire this morning. I'm thinking about changing the location of the bird feeder. I hesitate to, now that lots of birds are coming to it. But I want it closer to the house so we can see them better. Two eggs from the chickens this A.M. Let the goats out for fresh air. Have to put them back in their pens soon. I'm sure they're eager for warm weather. So am I.

Pencils are more dependable than ballpoint pens. Even though ballpoint pens have beauty of design with only one moving part, often that is one too many and it breaks down. Pencils came first, are more basic, and have no moving parts. Like goats, they take regular tending, though (sharpening), and that is their drawback. It is the choice between basic methods and progress through technology. The horse or the automobile.

3/22/88 Phil & I just returned from a walk in the springlike countryside. We heard crows and woodpeckers & had to take our jackets off. Emmmm-mmmmmm!

Good morning Rosealice. Christ is risen!
Good morning Mwelu, Apple, Kai. Christ is risen!
Good morning Red, Black, White, and Rooster, you who crowed for Peter. Christ is risen!
Good morning Shelty, Tiger, Carmel. Christ is risen!
Good morning Darrell, Jeanne, Mandy, Melissa, Frances, Mom, Sara, Maria, Jackie. Christ is risen!
Birds of the air, good morning. Bugs and creepers, good morning. Wild animals that howl and sniff and prowl around us, good morning. Christ is risen!
All you angels and saints praise the Lord, for Christ has risen!

He has risen to save us all and to bring us to life again, for we will all die, but we, too, will rise again and live forever at the heart of God. Christ is risen! Alleluia!

And for Him we give thanks for creation great and small! We give thanks for farm, family, friends, and fine feathered fowl. We give thanks for He is truly risen!

There is a sharpness, a hardness to the light in early mornings now. A sign of fall. The air is chill and businesslike, moving about. Where are those unwelcome days of fat, unmoving heat that nearly killed us with their boredom? Gone.

The dog, Shelty, likes to chase sticks. I myself have no interest in chasing sticks. But, at the end, they say, we all have to be ferried 'cross the River Styx. Some dogs are prophets showing us in their foolishness what lies ahead.

6 more days till school starts

Are you looking forward to going back to school?

Kinda

What clothes are you getting?

Sunflowers are bowing their heads, bent-shouldered, waiting for the end.

Phil's 1ˢᵗ radio novel program was wonderful. I am proud.

Thank you. I am pleased.

My heart warms hearing

Bless your soul, Eric, and thank you for the new latch on the outhouse door.

You know, I've been thinking–I don't think we're going to get out of this alive!

What good are stories? What good are pictures? They can't tell you what God is. All they can tell you is what God is not.

I think stories & pictures can tell more than what God is not. And I myself do not too much care what God is. The IS is enough. Same for stories and pictures. The event is enough for me.

Once upon a time, God appeared to a man. He said, "Got a smoke?" "Sure," the guy said, and he gave Him a smoke. "Thanks," God said. "It's okay," the guy said.

Quite an event.

4/3/91 Transitions are very demanding of energy as we become new or changed to accommodate life. The wind, cold & snow yielding to sun and greenery causes me to change gears, change clothes, change modes. Changes! Eric & Vernal are gon e now for 2 years. Charlotte is moved in and relishing the land. Sara is about to graduate, while Phil, Maria, and I are preparing to leave the country for Japan for God knows how long. No small things. Besides that, Waino and Marie are talking about the future of their land as they see their lives narrowing, slowing. Who we shall all be when we reconvene is anyone's guess.

....

When we decided to move to the farm, we did not know how we would make a living but were confident each of us would find something. We were determined to keep our living costs low, owning only one car, having no mortgage or house payments, maintaining a frugal budget, so that we could keep our resolve to work only half-time. I was fortunate in finding a job as administrator of a new group home for people with mental illness scheduled to open in Grand Rapids in a few months. The newspaper ad said they were looking for a program director. When I applied, I said I was highly qualified and very interested but would only accept a half-time position. Immediately I got a phone call from Del Sand, the owner of Hecla, Inc., a for-profit company developing group homes around the state. Del had attended a major workshop on schizophrenia I had organized and chaired in Duluth the year before and had seen me in action. He scheduled an interview and said, "I am sure we can work something out." When I met him at a motel in Grand Rapids for the interview, I was puzzled to find he had his new program director with him–the position for which I thought I was interviewing. It was not much of an interview, a negotiation over coffee actually, and I met the woman who would be my colleague and friend, Marian Barcus, the administrator of Esther House, still under construction. Del's offer was that, although I was a dozen years her senior with many more years of experience in the field, I would be her assistant. I was delighted, and pointed out that, whereas Marian was upwardly mobile on her career path, my aspiration was to be downwardly mobile. In other words, I valued time over money and prestige. I would be happy with the number-two job.

Del was an imaginative entrepreneur and was always on the lookout for creative talent. A few months later, after he had met Jackie at one of our administrative staff retreats to which spouses were invited, he offered her a job on the spot.

"What would you want me to do?" she asked him in surprise.

"I don't know yet. We will work something out. I will make a job for you."

But Jackie turned him down. Some of her clients from Duluth had followed her, and her reputation as an excellent therapist had preceded her. She had work almost as soon as we arrived, and she was not looking for more when Del offered. Instead, she hired our new friend, Gary Edwards, to turn a little dry storage shed just outside the door of our house into a work studio where she could see clients and do art.

Eric and Vernal, too, had tailor-made their jobs. She had founded the Itasca County Hospice Project several years before and continued to work as a hospice nurse. On a volunteer basis the two of them had also created Nightingale, the county's first crisis-line/information and referral service, which later was renamed First Call for Help. Eric gave up his engineering job at the Hanna Mine Research Lab to be a house husband and later teach metallurgy at the University of Lae in Papua New Guinea. When they returned from overseas, he picked up occasional Hanna consulting projects, worked for a while in Labrador, and eventually found he could make a year's income in a couple of summer months at a commercial fishery in Alaska. Vernal worked as the fish camp nurse several summers, but art is her true work. She is a gifted artist with a Masters in Fine Arts from Cranbrook Academy. Her primary medium has been batik which she studied at its source in Indonesia. Today she sells work all over the county and is shown in museums and fine galleries.

So these were our interesting friends who lived in the barn across the yard–with whom we often had morning coffee–who had given us their house. We all agreed that time was worth more than money. We believed in living fully now, not waiting for retirement. With a quieter life out in the country, Jackie and I found ourselves in a way more productive. She continued to work on her photography and had access to the darkroom at the local community college. She decided to take a part-time job as a hospice social worker for a number of years (joining Vernal, hospice nurse, and Gayle Edwards hospice volunteer coordinator). Half-time work allowed me to take up the pleasure of physical work, repair and maintenance about the farm, work I might have hired someone else to do if I were occupied with a career. I grew strong cutting, hauling, splitting firewood. I put a metal roof on the house, replaced all eighteen windows, put down oak flooring, renovated, re-wired, re-plumbed, rebuilt.

"They have machines that do this, you know," Gary said to me as he watched me digging with a long-handle shovel seventy-five feet of trench six-feet deep for a water line from the house to a new sand-point well I had pounded.

"I know, Gary," I answered. "But the soil is sandy here and the digging goes easy. I have time, and I don't mind the work. I just dig each day until I get tired and then let it go till the next day. I started as soon as the frost was out of the ground–probably will finish by July."

I did finish, not only the water line trench but the hole for the thousand-gallon septic tank and the hundred feet of drain field running out from it. All with one shovel. I was proud of that. Our family then no longer used the outhouse.

....

We had a burst of cash for all these projects from the retirement fund I withdrew upon leaving my job in Duluth. We had decided to live without the security of savings. Perhaps it had been the decision to sell our house and give the money away or living with the very poor of Mexico for a few weeks or moving to borrowed housing in the convent which had separated us from the conventional wisdom of financial security. Even now our friends had surprised us with a house, a yard, a beautiful countryside. A financial advisor would headshake at this and lecture on our responsibility to plan for the golden years. First we should have projected retirement income needs and expectations for a comfortable lifestyle maintenance. Then we should have adhered to a regular savings investment schedule to assure that comfort. Jackie and I did not take this advice, but it is not that we did not plan for the future. We did not expect to put our kids through college. Rather, we thought they would work their way through, and we would help out from our current earnings at the time as best we could. Besides, our low income and lack of assets would be to their advantage in applying for student loans. As for our golden years, we thought these were the golden years. When we became old, a lifetime of simple living and low income would be our best preparation for a Social Security budget. We expected to be content with what we would have. We expected old age to bring fewer needs, less activity, less travel, fewer responsibilities. There would still be music, libraries, conversation, friends, family–one another, we thought.

A second bundle of money arrived during our second year on the farm, the final balloon payment from the sale of our Arrowhead Road house. However, we did not see that as our money and sent it on to its owners–in Mexico and Bolivia.

On the other hand, around this same time, Jackie and I did make a short stab at becoming capitalists but failed. Eric had mentioned to us that there was a new Iron Range project for encouraging local business startup in Keewatin, a small mining town thirty-five miles away. He thought it might be an opportunity to manufacture and market my Starloc invention. We made the contacts and soon formed an enthusiastic partnership with four other entrepreneurs (without business experience), which we named Range Options.

During the next year, we six developed a business plan, hired consultants from a Duluth marketing firm, borrowed $10,000 from the bank, bought production equipment and set up a factory floor. Jackie and I put in our last $5,000 from my old retirement fund. We made long-range development plans for other astronomy products: school educational packets, audiotape sky tours, and more. The Range Options partners were long on enthusiasm and ideas, short on skill and luck. The marketing consultants gave sloppy advice and did not red-flag flaws in our business plan. We went into production and began mail order selling–a few Starlocs. As the months went by, the cash flowed out, the orders did not come in, and I began to see the writing on the wall. One day I said to Jackie, "You know, we lose money on every Starloc we sell. Maybe we should reduce our losses by trying to sell fewer." We went to our partners and tried to convince them we were headed toward ruin. They would not see it and urged a "stay the course" approach. Jackie and I resigned. A few months later, the whole enterprise folded.

It had been fun, and it only cost us five grand and a little disappointment. Jackie took it in stride, and I was not much troubled either. She had liked the creative and social part of this venture. I enjoyed being the inventor but knew I had little talent or interest in marketing. So I stayed with what suited me more and began to write the novel I now had time for. I have been writing stories, telling tales, ever since I was a boy. Now I was ready to spin a long yarn.

Years earlier my friend at Chester Creek House, Mary Schmitz , had given me for Christmas a blank journal book with a quaint cover picture of two oval rocks painted like owls resting amidst tree trunks, leaves, and grasses. The thought had flashed through my mind: I will write a story about these. Now, seven years later, I sat down at the computer on a day I was not scheduled to be at Esther House and began to write *Owlstones*.

Each morning on days off I payed out the tale, making it up as I went, like the hundreds of little Sara's bedtime stories. The first page

said, "*Owlstones*, by Philip Solem–dedicated to Jacqueline with love."
The second page quoted the Spanish poet Antonio Machado: "*Caminante
no hay camino, se hace camino al andar–Traveler, there is no road; you make a
road as you go.*" At the end of two and a half years I had thirty chapters.

At the beginning, I did not know what owlstones were. By chapter
eight, where they first appeared, I still did not know. Toward the middle
of the book I began to understand them. I wrote not knowing for more
than a chapter ahead what would happen, who would appear, where
this travel-tale was going. Jackie, Sara, and Maria would sit by the wood
stove and listen to me read aloud as the chapters clattered out of our
dot-matrix printer one by one. I would take the latest down to Eric and
Vernal, knock on their heavy barn door and call out, "Morning! Itasca
County Outreach Reader here. Can I come up?" And they would call me
up and put on the coffee and settle in for another episode.

When I finished the last page of the novel, I went out into the yard to
tell Eric. He said,

"Come on. I am going to take you into town and buy you a Lala-
paloosa Sundae at Bridgeman's to celebrate." I thought to publish the
novel, but rather than search for an agent and publisher, I read it as a se-
rial on KAXE, our local community radio station. My half-hour readings
ran four nights a week at the supper hour, from October to December.

Reflecting on that work, I have come to realize that *Owlstones* was in
many unintended ways a long dream. Today it seems to me a subliminal
telling of our story–Jackie's and mine–in a form that I scarcely recognized
as such at the time. Only now, twenty years later, as I write *this* narrative
of our lives, *Such a Road*, do I begin to decode some of the meaning and
symbol embedded in that tale.

It is the story of a young man, Nome Ogrodni, who is sent out by
a father, for whom he feels both resentment and respect, on an undefined journey to save their ancestral estate named Brighthome. His quest
takes him on a search for "the dangerous man" who seizes and binds
him to his cause by fear and hostage. Nome fails his commander's orders and becomes an aimless fugitive. (The owlstones appear. What are
they? guides? guardians? tricksters?) His path crosses that of Ravenna
Rosealice, herself a fugitive from a despot, fleeing her home to save life
and honor. Nome observes her peril and follows to protect her but sub-
sequently is protected by her. They meet beyond The Plains of Wildness,

haunt of sighing, keening, malevolent spirits, and join forces with other companions in Ravenna's ancestral homeland which has recently become a war zone. There Nome meets "the dangerous man" once more, but he is dying of war wounds (owlstones appear). He reconciles with Nome and asks him to complete his legacy by writing his story. Ravenna and Nome agree to leave this country and travel on together. They wander a long, peaceful way; threat and conflict seem to have lifted and faded (owlstones appear). They come to the fishing village of Quiet Waters by the sea and marry. They go on to Brighthome and are received with joy by Nome's mother and father. However, Brighthome does not survive; it is undermined by a subterranean river, diverted by their enemies; and the beautiful old house collapses. Here is the 257th page of this book, the last:

They were refugees now. The four of them and the dog, Chindit, were driven in a cart to within an hour of the border and dropped off. The last stretch they would walk, for they were approaching the Tosar border station. When they had discussed crossing the border, Ravenna, remembering their entrance only days before, had said, "We don't dare go through that way!"

"No, we don't," said Nome. "This is the time when we are going to have to take the long way around through the spruce bog. It will be rough going, and it looks like we may be doing it in the dark. Wet and scratchy and mucky walking in there, Mo. Are you up to it?"

"Yes," his mother answered quietly.

"Then, Fa, I suggest we go to Farmer Hite's and ask if he can put us on the best way around the border station. There might even be paths."

"Just what I was thinking," said his father.

As they walked along, they watched the sun setting and realized that the border station would be closed to them at this hour, even if they had chosen to go that way. The farmlands and holdings appeared poorly tended and scattered, and the tamarack and spruce bog took on a wild and over-grown look. Finally the weathered buildings of Hite's Farm came into view on their left, looking ancient and abandoned in the twilight.

They turned in at the farm road. Baron took the lead, thumping along with his walking stick; and Rena, wearily struggling under her pack, hurried to keep up with him, with Chindit, ears back, trotting alongside. Nome and Ravenna followed, side-by-side.

Two dogs rushed out from Hite's Farm bellering and lunging forward with murderous yowling. The travelers stopped. Wilman Hite, squinting and scowling, ran into the open holding an ax. His tangled beard, down to his belt, wagged and twitched as he ducked his head down and thrust it forward trying to see who was attacking his farm.

Baron Ogrodni took a step forward. "Call off your dogs, Hite!" he shouted. "We need your help!" Not waiting for an answer, he turned and beckoned his family to follow.

Rena looked fearfully at the dogs, then followed her husband. Ravenna and Nome also stepped forward, first looking ahead to where Hite was standing, then glancing sideways apprehensively toward the dogs. But they could see no dogs. They only saw two small, feathered, stony shapes that stood staring at them, unblinking. These turned suddenly and began hobbling and tripping forward beside them toward Hite's Farm.

....

Jackie and I had come here with our daughters to this farm, as we often said, to slow down, work half-time, and live a more contemplative and prayerful life. Jackie continued her regular practice of prayerful journaling. Each morning, for the first few years, she and I would rise early, read scripture, meditate, and walk together the mile of our road praying aloud as though in conversation. During this time I received notice from the bishop that the pope had finally approved my application for laicization filed eight years earlier. We had stopped thinking about this, and it scarcely affected our lives or our activity at our church in Grand Rapids, where for some time we had been lectors and Eucharistic ministers at Sunday Mass. Our attention was not on church life but on deepening the inner life. The active life of service and involvement in projects of charity and justice had moved to the background with our move here; the contemplative life had come foreground.

One very important experience for both of us was a conference on Eastern and Western spirituality held at the College of St. Scholastica in Duluth in 1987. We attended workshops on Buddhism, Native American spirituality, Jewish and Sufi mysticism, and Zen. But what most impressed us was the person and message of Father Thomas Keating, a Cistercian monk from Snowmass, Colorado, who was teaching the method of centering prayer. Jackie and I began this contemplative practice of silent sitting for at least twenty minutes twice a day with the intention of placing ourselves receptively in the presence of God. A mental gesture of "returning to a sacred word," is silently formed only as often as needed to reaffirm that intention. It has been the core of our spiritual practice for the past twenty years. During these years she traveled to Snowmass twice for ten-day centering prayer intensive retreats. Twice I took the Greyhound bus to a mesa in Idaho to spend ten to fifteen days in silence at a hermitage. Jackie and I became Benedictine Oblates, a lay affiliation with the Monastery of St. Scholastica. During these years I wrote another little book: *The Practice of the Rosary,* presenting this ancient Catholic ritual as a contemplative practice.

The quieting of our lives also gave space for involvement in our own families. We would regularly drive up the Iron Range to visit my mother in Chisholm, Jackie's mother in Soudan, her sister and brother-in-law in Tower. There had been a time in Duluth when we had wanted to bring our mothers into our home on Arrowhead Road to live with us. It had been an unrealistic notion, addressing our needs more than theirs. However, the right time for this was now coming, as we saw unexpectedly one Mother's Day.

Jeanne and Darrell, Jackie and I took our two mothers out for dinner at a fine restaurant. Jeanne, who lived only five miles from her mother's apartment in Soudan, had born most of the responsibility for her care over the years. Toward the end of the meal, as we chatted about nothing in particular, Frances answered someone's question about her coat with a drawling smatter of unconnected words. All eyes were on her suddenly. Jeanne asked again. Again something like a slow growl and half-words came out. We sat apprehensively in silence looking at her. Frances smiled sweetly back as though all were fine.

In the restaurant parking lot, while Darrell and I helped our mothers into the cars, Jackie and Jeanne snatched a few moments of hurried whispering. Later that day we were on the phone to each other and to my mother in Chisholm. In the next week or two, Jeanne let us know that her mother's speech had returned to normal but that she was showing other signs of failing.

Darrell and Jeanne agreed that Frances would soon be unable to live alone in her apartment. Jackie and I offered to take her to our home, and so it was agreed. I quickly built a wall dividing our upstairs space in half to make a bedroom for Frances. Jeanne reported that her mother apparently had a few more TIAs (transient ischymic attacks) during the period preparing for the move.

A few weeks after she came to live with us she lost all ability to speak. At first she was physically strong enough to go out to an adult day activity program. A blue bus would come for her early and bring her back every afternoon. She looked like a school girl standing out by the mailboxes waiting for the bus each morning.

Most remarkably, as soon as Frances became mute, it seemed as though a great weight lifted from her. It seemed that the silent stroke in her brain that left her speechless had also canceled years of crippling depression. Since her husband's death, eighteen years earlier, she had lived under this weight, only rarely and for short periods emerging into the sunlight of the love her family and neighbors had for her. Once, while Jackie had been pregnant with Sara, we had taken her to Duluth for a two-week hospitalization, which ended successfully only after she had a series of electro-convulsive-therapy treatments.

Now, unannounced, a spirit of serenity was upon her. Even as she was getting ready to leave us, she became very present to us and to everyone who came through our door, reaching out with her thin arms, grasping with birdlike hands. For long periods she would sit with vacant face; then, when a grandchild would come to her, her face would not brighten but its texture would change from stone to soft velour.

Her daughter, Madelyn, came to her from California at the end of the summer. Her daughter Patsy came with her family from Wisconsin. Jeanne and Darrell came often with Melissa and Amanda. Our family photo album records all this almost without caption or comment, all these family group photos with healthy, glowing faces smiling for the camera around the grey face of Frances in the midst, unsmiling, shriveling.

The stroke had shut off her esophagus. She could no longer eat, could not swallow, would gag and choke on the smallest bits of solid food. More than once I had her up on her feet at table, at her back with my arms under hers from behind, gripping my own hand in front and ready to do the Heimlich maneuver, certain that I would snap her frail twig-work of ribs with the first necessary upthrust.

The tenderest pictures in the album are like stills from a silent movie on the day she walked Patsy and family out to the car for what everyone knew was the last goodby–gazing up at me as at a god, turning her head to look at Patsy with deep intimacy, cradling and kissing the tear-stained face of her eleven-year-old grandson, Matt. Then the pictures are of her in the recliner, eyes intense, mouth slack, daughters, granddaughters huddling around her on the bed stroking her hair. Two last pictures in the album: Jackie leaning forward, her mother returning her kiss. Jeanne, eyes closed, kissing her mother's alert, uplifted face.

Jeanne stayed with us that whole week after Thanksgiving, and she and Jackie began the death watch. One night they were startled awake by a sharp crack. The burning votive candle beside the bed had shattered the red glass protecting cylinder around it. Quickly they went to her bed to see if her spirit had left–but their mother still breathed. Two mornings later I was called out of a meeting at Esther House and given the message to pick up Maria at school and go home at once. Jackie, Jeanne, and Sara were at the bedside as we joined them for the countdown. And Vernal, our own hospice nurse, was with us, quietly noting the slowing of breath, the dropping of temperature.

One more picture in the album. Earlier that year Jackie had gone on a fun outing with members of her hospice team to explore a hidden rookery of blue herons tucked back in the swamp. She had done a marvelous photo study of these huge birds on nests and flying like majestic cranes just above tree level. We took the best shot of the series and placed it alone on the final page of the pictures of Frances's last days. It is a shot through black branches against a sepia sky of a giant heron launching straight up from a tangled nest, wings spread out full, long neck and head pointed to zenith, perfectly back lighted by a burst of the sun itself. The caption: "December 2, 1988–11:20 A.M."

....

Jeanne was administrator of her mother's estate. We were all surprised that there was any amount of money there. Matt and Frances Vesel had apparently saved from a modest income for a long time. Each of the four daughters received about ten thousand dollars. Jackie took her share and split it four ways. She put two quarters in college funds for Sara and Maria. She gave me a quarter and kept one for herself.

One day she and I were sitting in her studio doing our afternoon twenty-minutes of centering prayer. The timer beeped, and we both opened our eyes and looked across at each other, taking another long, peaceful breath. I said:

"You know what just came to me now?"

"What's that?"

"I just had an idea. What would you think about you and me taking our shares of your mother's inheritance and taking the girls on a bicycle trip in Europe this summer?"

"All summer?"

"Maybe–whatever I could get off work. What do you think?"

Jackie pondered–but only for a moment. "I think I could get used to this idea. I think it would be great, if we could do it. What about my clients?"

"Well, you could give them notice far in advance. You might lose some of them, but I bet you could build back up to a half-time client-load pretty quickly. I don't think you would have much of a problem. I have carried over some vacation time from Esther House and haven't used any yet this year. Del just gave me a bonus of extra days-off for that special video training project I did for Hecla, Inc. I think I could pull together almost two months. And I could ask to take a month of unpaid leave. We could spend all summer bicycling in Europe, June, July, August."

"Could we go to Slovenia?"

"Slovenia? I was thinking southern England, France, Germany. Slovenia–sure, that's in Europe, isn't it? Your family?"

"You know how Jeanne and Pat and Maddie and I always tried to get mother to go to visit her sister, Ivanka, before she died? She wouldn't do it. I wish she had used this money to go to meet her sister. Well, maybe, now I could go in her place and meet the family over there."

"Perfect! Let's do this. What about Sara and Maria? They are not going to want to leave their friends for three months and be with us. Sara has this new boyfriend."

"Phil, if we decide to do this, I think we consult with the girls but don't give them a vote. If this is a good thing for us to do as a family, we let them know that this is what we are planning. This is a mom-and-dad decision."

....

For four years our family had been settling and moving inward.

Now we began a new phase, moving outward toward the world. In the next ten years we would travel broadly, go on pilgrimage, and live overseas. The death of Frances and her gift of money catalyzed it. We have lived these two movements ever since like a braided strand–going out on adventures, returning to our country home for rest and reflection, then gathering resources and desire to go out once more. So much has happened on our travels about the world that the telling of it will be deferred to the next chapter. However, a quick sketch is needed here to make sense of what took place between these adventures while we were settling back into home on the farm.

With Frances's gift we bought four new mountain bikes and rode Europe for three months the summer of 1990, tenting our way from Belgium to northern Greece and back up to Paris. No sooner were we home than Jackie took a notion to Japan. So we both took courses to learn how to teach English as a second language, found jobs in Japan and a high school for Maria, and spent a year in Osaka (Sara stayed home to begin college). We loved Japan and the Japanese and have gone back three times. Then I got the notion to bicycle to Jerusalem. Sara wanted to go, too, but was just graduating from college and had to find a job to start paying off student loans. So we went to Jerusalem twice that year, once by airplane with Sara and once by bicycle, just Jackie and I. A couple of years earlier Sara had gone to Ghana for two months by herself–I already mentioned that. There would be other outings–to Asia, to South America, to Tuscany–Alaska and Nova Scotia bracketing some ordinary motorings about the lower forty-eight–but these continued wanderings actually belong to the final chapters of this book.

At home, while our daughters were growing up and Jackie and I were earning a living, life continued in a fairly ordinary way. We helped our girls with homework, had them join the church youth group, drove them to swimming practice, 4-H meetings, cheerleading, ballet, friends' houses. We had to discipline and ground Sara more than Maria. There were screeching family scraps, and I would roar like a lion to break them up, ordering Maria and Sara: "Out on the road! You down that way you down the other way stay away from each other and don't come in till I tell you!" Years later they would gleefully reveal that, when I banished them to the road, they would sneak around, join up out of sight of the house, and go for a friendly walk together. There were boyfriends, parties, lots of uncertainty for Jackie and me about how to deal with adolescent girls. They got jobs in town, driver's licences, cars.

Maria had a job at a video rental place that also carried used paperbacks. One evening, just as she was closing, this tall, good-looking Marine in uniform came in looking for a book. She was impressed that he wanted a book. Even more impressed when he asked her if she would like to go for coffee (rather than for a drink). I don't know, I wasn't there, but I hear they fell in love that evening. They started to, in any case, but had a long wait and a long-distance courtship. Rolland was recently back from patrolling waters off Somalia and would be stationed in Okinawa, South Carolina, and Panama yet before they would marry.

Sara finished her college at St. Scholastica in Duluth, Jackie's alma mater, graduating with a master's in the occupational therapy program. Our graduation present to her was the trip to Jerusalem, but she had to make it quick because her friend Brent was waiting–to become her husband.

....

Another ordinary event that took place just after we returned from Japan was that I became clinically depressed. Ordinary but not insignificant. As a mental health professional I knew how common major depressive disorder is. I had often diagnosed it in others; now I knew I had it.

I was not depressed "about" anything. Life was very good by any objective measure. Jackie, Maria, and I had just come home from Japan, picking up life here where we had left off a year earlier. Sara was starting her second year at the local community college. My mom was ninety but healthy and chipper. Our dog was happy to see us. Jackie and I had transferred enough of our earnings from Japan to provide an income-buffer for the startup of a joint counseling partnership we called Guidance Services, buy a new computer and laser printer, and replace all the leaky old double-hung farmhouse windows with new Crestline crank-out windows. I had a good woodpile ready for the coming winter.

One Monday morning in October I awoke heavy and grey. As the mood of sadness and exhaustion continued the next day and the next, Jackie and I speculated that maybe this was "reverse culture shock" from overseas re-entry; or maybe I was worried about job insecurity, or maybe I was just physically exhausted from installing all those window in a race against cold weather. I had finished the last two, in fact, with strong wind whipping snow through the openings I had cut in the wall of the house. Perhaps I had caught a chill.

By the next week, I knew this was persistent depression, not the flu, not a cold, not worry or a blue mood. I got worse by the hour, despairing, crippled, drained of energy. My appetite was gone, and I ate out of duty. My favorite times were centering prayer where I sat in blank silence for a half-hour with no movement, no expectations, and sleep, where the world disappeared. My worst was waking from sleep in sudden and profound anguish at 4:00 A.M. every night with no hope of slipping back into oblivion. When I listened to the radio in the morning while I ate mournful oatmeal and heard about a new production coming to the Reif Theater, I heard it from an unbridgeable distance, as though I were under water, or floating untethered in frigid space, eternally snipped away from all human warmth. When I heard the KAXE announcer interviewing a fellow from the DNR about lake levels, I would feel impossibly worthless, at the sound of two men who had real jobs that mattered, speaking with competence and knowledge. They got paychecks, too. I didn't. I had nothing to offer, could do nothing, wanted nothing more than to disappear.

By November I was able to self-diagnose. I had all the criteria for "Major Depressive Episode": depressed mood, loss of interest and pleasure, weight loss, appetite and sleep disturbance, sluggish psychomotor activity at some times and fiercely anxious agitation at others, unrealistic sense of worthlessness, trouble concentrating, preoccupation with death. I was not suicidal; but it sure would have been wonderful to go in my sleep or even come down with some dramatic terminal illness, which would give some legitimacy to this absurd suffering. The only other symptom listed in the diagnostic manuals that I did not have was "disturbance of menses." (I had not completely lost a sense of humor, preferring what is referred to in the trade as "gallows humor.") I also had not lost my faith. I could not pray, but that was all right. I saw this as a kind of spiritual scouring, a dark night. I could sit quietly in ruin like Job. Yet at times I could not sit quietly but writhed and thrashed and moaned. I knew I was frightening my family, Sara and Maria most, and that knowledge compounded my misery. I was surprised at how physical this illness was. I knew I had become mentally ill, but I felt this sickness not only in my mind but in all parts of my body, a deadness at the center of my head, a doubling of gravity, the supreme effort to raise my facial muscle into something like an appropriate expression when I went out into society.

I needed to be with people and became panicky when left alone, when the girls went off to school and Jackie left the house to go into the studio for four hours with clients. I forced myself to work on curricula for our Guidance Services practice, preparing a course on mental illness for first responders, developing a couples' communication workshop. Eric and Vernal stood by me throughout this time. I felt some relief when Jackie and I would go down to their place for morning coffee and an hour of chatting. But I could not sit long as my anxiety rose like hot water in my veins and I would have to stand and pace about the room, begging their indulgence, as I tried to stay in the conversation. Midwinter, they were planning to go to do a six-month stint of volunteering at Holden Village, a Lutheran retreat center in the State of Washington. The week before they were to leave, they told me they would cancel all their plans and stay home if I needed them to be here. I was overwhelmed at their generosity once more and deeply warmed by this offer of love; but I urged them to go and do what they had planned. Jackie, more than anyone, stood by me, suffering too at seeing me like this, unable to say anything that would help, needing to keep her distance at times in order to avoid being sucked into this vortex.

One night that winter I had a dream. Wearing high-top rubber overshoes I stepped out of the house into the yard which was soppy with running water and standing puddles because it was a glorious spring day. I ka-lumped around to the back of the house and looked up into a radiant blue sky awash in sunshine and saw it alive with swooping, darting birds, exuberantly swirling overhead. Within me burst what I can only call joy–joy which I held and savored like a long drink of water.

As I awoke to the darkness of our bedroom, probably a few minutes later, I knew at once that I was still a profoundly depressed man, that I was still swaddled in the smothering grasp of this dark suffering. I felt no joy, but I *remembered* that joy. It was like no other I have ever experienced. The memory of it burned bright within me–how can I tell this?–like a small light alongside my misery. I could revisit that memory at will the next day, the next week, a month later and still know that light. It was not the beginning of recovery, rather a mysterious companion, perhaps an owlstone.

Why I did not take antidepressant medication earlier I cannot explain. It makes no sense, but I resisted the suggestion stubbornly. Despite my training and considerable knowledge about psychotropic medications, I did not go to my doctor for months. It was not denial or pride; I readily admitted to myself and others that I had this mental illness. Perhaps I thought I could tough it out by myself; but I knew I was far too weak. Why did Jackie not make me go to the doctor and ask for help? I don't know, I am sure she tried. I just cannot account for why I persisted in staying in this blackness for nearly six months, unless, perhaps it was the very pull of this darkness itself keeping me from reaching for a solution.

One day Jackie came home and said, "I stopped to see Kris (our doctor) today and told her about your anxiety and agitation. I asked her to give me something for you. Here, take these." It was anti-anxiety medication, something like Valium. Her directness was welcome. I was grateful for being told what to do and washed a few pills down with water. Ten minutes later I felt the anxiety slide away like a slippery peel. It was like aspirin relieving a headache. Depression remained, but I experienced the relief of panic symptoms. Probably that was the turning point. I knew anxiety and agitation were surface symptoms, major depressive disorder the bedrock. I needed more than Valium and went to see my doctor.

This was Kris Johnson, whom we had known and loved as Kris Nelson at Chester Creek House. We had lived together for years. She had gone away to medical school after Chester Creek, become a family practice doctor, married a doctor, had children, and settled in Grand Rapids. She is a kind and lovely woman. I sat in her office and told her the diagnosis: "Kris, I have clinical depression. I know the criteria, and here they are." She gave me samples of Paxil and told me things I already knew: that I should not expect results for two to four weeks, that the chemistry needed time to built in my system, that I might have such and such side effects.

Almost as silently as the depression had descended the previous October it lifted about two-and-a-half weeks into the Paxil, as though a heavy, waterlogged, wool blanket were lifted from me. I found a job working two days a week as an outreach social worker making house calls to seniors at risk in our county. My partner, Cindy Brummer, and

I began creating an innovative program called Home Visitor. Jackie and I began to see more couples in marriage counseling, develop weekend marriage retreats, and do training. I went out into the woods, tapped the maple trees, boiled down two hundred gallons of sap into five gallons of syrup for Jackie to can, then picked up my chainsaw and went at next winter's firewood. I had a wonderful summer.

In September Eric and I were planning a trip into the Boundary Waters Canoe Area with two of his friends. I was looking forward to it. Without warning I awoke one morning under a cloud of depression. It was back. My life was fine, all was going well, I had no worries. But it had moved back in like dirty weather. Before brushing my teeth that morning, I gulped down some of the Paxil left over from the preceding spring. I phoned Kris as soon as she got to her office and told her I had relapsed. She saw me right away and renewed the prescription.

When I met with Eric and the guys to pack for the trip and sling the canoes up on the car racks, I explained to them that I might be poor company but they should not worry about me. I would do my best to keep up; but I would not be drinking any of their brandy. The weather was clear and crisp, and the leaves were turning colors. It was a great trip and the guys great company. But I could not taste or enjoy any of it, and every portage to the next lake took all my strength. This, more than anything, convinced me of the chemical nature of depression. Everything about me pointed toward happiness. My body was not working.

The medication, however, did the trick; and, within a week after we were back home, the depression lifted once more like rising smoke and blew away. It has never returned. Kris told me I had probably stopped the medication too soon in the spring. Studies suggested, she said, that there is far less likelihood of relapse if the antidepressant regimen is continued as long as nine months to a year after symptomatic relief. I took her advice and stayed on Paxil until the following summer.

This experience, terrible as it was, became very useful in my professional work. I spoke openly and often about it at senior clubs, with clients, and in the support groups Jackie and I led. Whenever I did, I had their attention and their trust. I saw their heads nodding. They thanked me for not being ashamed.

I am not ashamed to speak of failure. One of my favorite short stories from an anthology I have misplaced was called "The Failure," written by a South American writer, I forget which country. It is an unremarkable story of one man's ordinary life trying and failing at many things, maintaining his self-respect and peace of mind, losing most of what he had hoped for and retaining what was important. I forget the specifics, but I know he was loved by his wife...and by others. A lot like Nome Ogrodni, perhaps. Funny, I never made that connection until this very moment as I type these words.

Well, I recall four major failures in my life: teaching religion at Duluth Cathedral High School, failing my oral exams in Transactional Analysis, the moral collapse which nearly broke my marriage, and my clinical depression. I do not embellish these as learning experiences. I do not glorify them as "ultimately working out for the best." They were what they were: breakdowns, great failures, even those I could not help. I know there is one more coming–a final one. It is all right.

....

Jackie had developed a strong reputation as one of the best therapists in the area. All her clients came by way of personal recommendation and word of mouth. She has never advertized her service, nothing more than a notice in the yellow pages of the phone book. Meeting new people out in the community she often hears, "Oh, *you're* Jackie Solem! I've heard so many good things about you." She could go off bicycling in Europe and Asia for three months, drop out for a year to work in Japan, and when she returned have a full schedule of clients again in a matter of weeks.

After Japan we decided to specialize as co-therapists in marriage counseling. It seemed natural. We had weathered a lot in our own marriage, grown up, and were happy together. We both had many years of professional experience. Our inexpensive lifestyle allowed us to offer clients two of us for the price of one. Jackie continued to work by herself with individual clients, and often with families, for she was very good with children and teens. I only joined her when the client was a couple. I supplemented this with home visiting to seniors and contractual social work with the hospital, home health agencies, a physical therapy service, and a foundation leadership program. Our church hired us to run two weekly support groups, one for people in grief, the other for people going through divorce. Although all these jobs took us in many directions,

Jackie and I never let work creep up and make us too busy. We always held it to twenty hours a week.

Working as co-therapists has been one of the finest experiences of our marriage. Marriage counseling, which our colleagues working alone found frustrating and intractable, we found enjoyable. Teamwork distributed the heavy lifting of working with couples in conflict. We brought both male and female viewpoints and were less likely to be seen as siding with one of the clients. Often we would stop the action and say, "Wait, watch this," then turn to each other and have their argument between us in a constructive way. Jackie could stand in for the wife (while she observed) and play out the dispute with the husband. I could do the same with the wife while he looked on. At times when they and we got really stuck, we would invite them to eavesdrop while we talked about them. We would momentarily ignore them, turn to each other, and have our professional case conference right there. We made sure the first two sessions were intriguing and enjoyable, because often one of them had been dragged into counseling very reluctantly. Or one of them may have already decided to divorce and was "here to give it one last chance." In those first sessions we gave them a fun conflict exercise and watched how they did or did not resolve it. This gave us and them a lot of information about their communication and fight styles.

Next we taught the five stages of marriage: romantic blending, differentiation from each other, finding oneself, getting reacquainted, and dancing. Marriage is a developmental process, we taught, like the stages of development every person goes through from infancy through adolescence, young adulthood, mid-life, old age (credit to Ellen Bader and Pete Peterson from whom we learned the five stages). Couples get stuck usually in one of the first three stages or in making the unexpected transitions required by maturing to their next stage. This educational introduction gave them a functional diagnosis, a suggestion of the tasks they needed to work on, and a map.

From this point on it was lab work. We would have them talk to each other, not to us. Then we would coach, interrupt, redirect, cheer on, or roleplay an alternative. They could see that their therapists had been through all five stages, that what we were giving them came from our own marriage struggle, and that we were dancing.

....

The year Frances died, Sara, Maria, Jackie and I took a long, leisurely train trip out west on Amtrak. A year or two later the four of us bicycled in the Canadian Rockies from Banff up to the Columbia Snowfields. Then the girls started going their own way. Sara graduated from college. Maria married Rolland. Jackie and I came back from Jerusalem just in time for their birth of their son, Tristan. Sara married Brent. And we began to take care of my mom. It was the normal progression, the same thing all our peers were experiencing: You finish raising your kids, get them on their way, then turn around and begin looking after your aging parents.

My mother lived in her own apartment in Chisholm until she was ninety-five. Then one day she fell, trying to bring her laundry up from the basement. She agreed it was time. We brought her to an assisted living residence in Grand Rapids. As the director took us for the tour, Mom learned that residents could not smoke in their rooms. She had always smoked cigarettes since she was a young woman–three quarters of a century. I thought to myself: What now? This isn't going to fly. After the tour, the three of us sat alone talking it over.

"Well, Mom, what do you think?" I asked her.

"It's nice. It will be all right."

"What about smoking? Are you going to go all the way down to that airless little room or outside, even in winter?"

"I guess I will have to quit."

She did, cold turkey. Another surprise came a few days later. Staff called me to say my mother had put all her tattered photo albums from when she was a young flapper out to be picked up with the trash. They had rescued them and thought I might want them. I did. I asked her why she had done this. She said simply, "Oh, I don't have much room here for those things. You can have them if you want them."

She was not confused. Meanings were changing for her. She remained alert, elegant, clear minded. She was, as always, a great conversationalist, interested in the other person. During the next five years she fell twice and went to the hospital each time. After the first fall we asked her to come live with us. With misgivings she agreed to do so. She was able to shuffle about our farmhouse with a walker. Jackie tended her intimate personal care, including assistance with colostomy care. She lived with us for seven months, the length of time Frances had; but at the end she did not die but insisted she go to the nursing home. I told her she was not eligible. Too healthy, did not require skilled nursing care. I was a social worker for the elderly; I knew the regulations on these matters. Grumpily she said, all right then back to the assisted living residence. After a month there, she fell the second time and got her ticket into the nursing home. Still, she healed quickly, though confined now to a wheelchair. At age ninety-eight she opted to have cataract surgery and lens replacement in both eyes and was delighted with the result. As we sat in clinic waiting rooms, I would ask her what she thought of her life, how she saw things now. I asked her about her thoughts on death and what would come after that.

"Oh, I don't know about all that," she would reply vaguely. "I don't know what to think about all those things we have been told. When my papa was dying, I remember him saying–it was probably the last thing he said to us–'It's so mysterious, so mysterious....'"

I was surprised at this because she had always been such a devout and well-educated Catholic, always interested in religious discussion. I had thought old people tended to get more pious as they neared death. I did not see that with her. She seemed at peace even as meanings appeared to be changing for her.

We had a big birthday party for her at the nursing home when she turned one hundred. She seemed to like it and was very engaged with everyone. Nearly a year later she began to die but remained lucid up to her final week when she became a hospice patient. The last time she spoke to us was to plead, "Don't go! Don't go!" as we sat by her bed giving the hospice nurse intake information. We tried to soothe and reassure her, but the next time we visited she was in a coma. We sat watching with her as long as we could that Saturday; but late in the afternoon we had to leave briefly to go to church, for Jackie and I were scheduled to speak from the pulpit at all the Masses that weekend about Catholic teaching on human rights and social justice.

As soon as the Mass was over we hurried back to the nursing home. Her room was empty. The bed was stripped. I went to the nursing station to ask where my mom was.

"Mrs. Solem passed away about an hour ago," I was told. "We could not reach you, but we did speak to your brother, Quinn. She is at the funeral home."

I called the funeral director and he said we could come right over. He

ELEVEN

Bicycling to Jerusalem

*T*he road broadened to a palm-lined boulevard as we approached the edge of Damascus. We were surprised to see a barren hump of mountain rising from the plain on our right with the white city clinging to its skirts. Bicycling was smooth, the traffic light. Gradually the mountain disappeared behind our shoulders, and we were drawn into a river of jostling, fuming cars and trucks as we headed in, keeping our eyes on signboards that read "Old City."

Damascus claims to be the oldest continuously inhabited city in the world. Aleppo and Jericho dispute this, but ancient hieroglyphs name "Dimashqa" as one of the cities conquered by the Egyptians in the fifteenth century B.C.E. Cuneiform notations from Ebla and Mari date it even a thousand years earlier. It has always been an important city, taken and re-taken by conquerors including King David, the Assyrians, Nebuchadnezzar of Babylon, and Alexander the Great. By the time Saul of Tarsus met Jesus on his way there, Damascus was capital of a Roman province, and later it became a Christian city, then a Muslim one. The Mongols swept in from central Asia and razed it. Next came the Egyptian Mamelukes, then the Ottoman Empire. In World War I it was an important base for the Germans and Turks; after the war the French were in control. Since 1946 it has been the capital of an independent Syria.

It is a city of fascinating contrasts. Dense traffic, load-bearing don-

keys, Bedouins mixing in crowds of city folk sporting the latest cool fash-
ions. Jackie sneaked a quick side-photo of two women totally covered in
burka cautiously lifting black veils to peer through plate glass at a display
of lacey pink lingerie. Everywhere the wail of Arab pop music blending
with the quivering soar of legendary Egyptian singer, Oum Foultoum.

We edged out of traffic and came to a stop curbside. Pointing ahead,
I asked a man, "Old City?" He shrugged and moved away. An older man
came over.

"What are you looking for?" in English.

"The Old City. Is the Old City straight ahead on this street?" I held
out my guidebook map.

"This is Old City! You are in Old City!"

"No, here," and I pointed to the center of the map where an area of
blocks and streets were ringed by the sawtooth markings indicating ram-
parts and city walls.

He grabbed the map and looked at it like something new. Then
shoved it back to me. "Old City! Here is Old City!" jabbing a forefinger
down at the ground. We were gathering a crowd. I had to retrieve the
guidebook politely from groping hands.

I knew this was not original and ancient Damascus. No city walls so
far, and overhead direction signs beckoned us on to "Old City." Repeatedly we asked others as we rolled slowly forward and each time were
given contradictory or patently wrong information about where we were
on the map. Street signs were no help. Either they were in Arabic script
or, when legible in Roman characters, referred to something other than
the actual street. We knew that locals often do not use street names but
had informal ways of referring to the neighborhood. They were unable
to read the map but tried to do so anyway and cheerfully gave us misin-
formation.

Jackie agreed to stay put with the bikes in the shade of a building
while I wandered off, map in hand, up and down streets, around corners,
like a surveyor taking sightings. I returned a half-hour later pretty sure
I knew where we were. I had found the Hejaz Train Station only eight
blocks away, sighted the satellite dishes on the roof of the Telephone
Building.... There was Jackie in the usual crowd of onlookers, but at the
center were two tan-uniformed, white-helmeted policemen.

"This man speaks English," she said happily as I came up.

Indeed, one of the officers understood what we wanted and apparently could read the map. We pointed out the area where the guidebook suggested "accommodations–low-end." The two cops spoke in Arabic for a few moments. Then the first one said, "Follow this man." His partner straddled a motorcycle, fired up, and rolled off into the back streets.

We had a unique tour of Damascus, waddling and twisting through serpentine streets with our heavily loaded bikes, sweeping out onto fast avenues, cutting recklessly across swimming traffic to keep up with the motorcycle cop, who looked back and slowed to keep us following. We made u-turns on multi-lane streets and did other things that surely seemed illegal, but who were we to doubt our leader? If this were a shortcut, it was beginning to seem we had crossed half of Damascus; when suddenly he pulled up at the end of a narrow, arbor-shaded lane and pointed. Half a block away was the Al Haramain Hotel, our first choice in "accommodations–low-end." A crisp, friendly salute, and the law was gone.

We booked a triple for the equivalent of $8.50 and were told the price would drop to $6.50 if we wanted to change rooms tomorrow when a double-bed room would become available. The hotel had once been a dignified Damascus home of some elegance with a charming courtyard and marble fountain with swimming goldfish, high ceilings and doors, windows trimmed with faded traces of carved molding. Now it was active, full, friendly, but shoddier than what we had been used to, poor light, no towels, W.C. in the hall, shower in the basement. It was like a low-budget youth hostel. The staff were Syrian and Sudanese. The other guests, new Zealanders, Australian backpackers, a German family, seemed to prefer sitting out on the mix-and-match stuffed furniture in the common areas, reading, writing, chatting, to staying in their austere bedrooms. The conversation was of travel, food, exchange rates, rip-offs, encounters; and there was the frequent hushing of voice whenever reference was made to the neighboring country, Israel. Although Israel was on nearly everyone's itinerary, we all knew that in Syria it was neither wise nor safe to acknowledge this or even pronounce the name. Jerusalem would sometimes be referred to as "the big J" and Israel as "the place we are not supposed to go to."

We rested, washed, and did laundry in the sink. We had hauled our bicycles up to a third-floor balcony outside our room and chained them together. This was also a good place to dry our wash on clotheslines in the direct afternoon sun. As shadows lengthened and the heat of the day lifted, we walked to the Old City, seeking the Soufanieh neighborhood.

....

What had brought us here in the spring of 1998? We live on a dead-end gravel road, and I had a daydream. I would often pretend that one summer day I would pack my bicycle panniers, strap on a tent and a sleeping bag, count a few hundred dollars into my wallet and grab my passport. I would roll my bike down to the end of the road and turn east. Without timetable, without adequate funds, I would head for Jerusalem. It was only a daydream, perhaps the bachelor fantasy of a middle-age husband and father. I often took this trip in my mind, a solitary pilgrim pedaling to New York, camping in fields, stopping for days to do day-labor, flying the ocean and continuing on the other side for months, a year, till I walked my bike through the Jaffa Gate. My family listened to this entertainment at times, would smile indulgently and nod. Of course it was just a daydream: I had a wife, two daughters, an elderly mother to care for, a dog, and a job.

One balmy day in August, Jackie and I were bicycling an abandoned railway bed in Wisconsin, planning to tent overnight in Frederic and make the return trip to St. Croix Falls in the morning. She was saying how much she loved this. We had been talking about taking Sara to Jerusalem for a graduation present after New Years. I started again:

"Would you—would you ever consider bicycling to Jerusalem with me some day?"

"I would if I had a motor."

"You would? You mean it? Are you serious?"

"Sure. If I had a motor. I couldn't think of it otherwise."

"Really? Do you really mean it? I mean—they make motors, I'm sure of it. I used a Solex bike with a motor in my student days in France. If I find one, you'd go?"

"Sure."

"I'll find one!"

"Okay."

The interesting thing about this conversation is that Jackie already had an internal motor. A short time before, she had a pacemaker implanted in her chest to correct a malfunctioning A/V node in her heart. The problem might have been genetic, but one specialist speculated that an accident eight years earlier during our European bike trip with the girls might have been responsible. That three-month trip, financed by her mother's legacy, nearly ended as soon as it started.

Jackie, Maria, Sara, and I had just landed in Brussels at the end of May in 1990 with our four new mountain bikes disassembled and packed into the narrow factory shipping boxes in which they had arrived at the bike store. The airline had accepted them as luggage without extra charge. We bolted and screwed them together in a corner of the baggage claim area, loaded each bike with four homemade panniers, threw away the cardboard shipping boxes, and headed out across the greening Belgian farmland to Louvain (Leuven in Flemish) where I had done my four years of theology and been ordained.

My schoolmate, Father Tom Ivory, was now the rector of the seminary there. He received us, housed us, and fed us with warm hospitality for two days. On the third morning we loaded up and headed out for Holland to begin our bike trip in earnest. About twenty kilometers on, as we passed through the first town, Jackie's front wheel caught a shallow gutter, went into a wobble, and I watched her dive forward over the handlebars and slide to a stop on her face, hands, and chest. I dropped my bike and ran to lift her. The girls managed to haul the two stricken bikes away from the lane of traffic, and the three of us gathered round her and sat her on a low brick wall in front of a house. She was badly skinned on the knee and chin, and one finger was bleeding. She was dazed and disoriented; it seemed a long time before she could tell us in which of the panniers the first-aid kit was kept. We swabbed and swathed her wounds, anointed her with love, and gradually she struggled up, complaining of some pain in her chest. The bike shifting gears were bent and scraped, but no major damage showed there.

We rode on. Jackie's shock subsided, but she quivered as she began slowly riding. Our spirits lifted; we stopped to eat and once again began to laugh and have fun. After another twenty kilometers, we stopped at St. Truiden, the halfway point to Maastricht, our day's destination. There we bought groceries for supper and took a break at an outdoor beer café. As we got ready to leave, Jackie began to gasp with pain in her chest, saying she did not know if she could go on. We waited and her pain and shortage of breath grew worse. I went into the café and asked the proprietor and patrons in what fragments of Flemish I could remember from my student days where we could find a doctor. They talked it over among themselves and agreed that the hospital would be best. One of the customers drove Jackie and me to St. Joseph Ziekenhuis while Sara and Maria stayed at the café with our bikes and gear. Jackie was probed and questioned by several doctors, then wheeled away for an x-ray. The verdict was: bad contusion but no fracture. She was given a foot-wide elastic bandage to stretch around her chest and back and discharged. The bill was eighty-five dollars, less than we had feared. We returned to Maria and Sara, then biked to a campground at the edge of town and spent a stormy, windy night in our tents.

The doctors had said she should expect the healing to take six weeks (half our trip) and should rest and wear the bandages. Huddled in our tent that night she and I talked over our prospects. I suggested she keep bicycling, if she could, to keep her blood flowing to the area of contusion. She agreed and threw the elastic wrap away. Within a week she was pain-free.

Perhaps that was not the end of it, we are not sure. We rode on into Germany, spent a week in the Black Forest, took the train to the top of the continental divide in Austria and coasted down to Innsbruck, crossed the Alps by train to arrive in Kranj, Yugoslavia where we and our impounded bikes were rescued by Jackie's Slovenian cousins. Leaving the bikes in Vido's barn, we switched to buses for three weeks, crawling through the stony mountains of Bosnia-Herzegovina down to Dubrovnik, taking a ship on the Adriatic around forbidden Albania to northern Greece, by bus again on high, tortuous, mountain roads–Joanina, Metsovo, Meteora–down to beaches on the Agean Sea and on to Thessaloniki. A night train took us through Macedonia, Serbia, Croatia, back to the cousins in Slovenia. There we reclaimed our bicycles and rode them out of Yugoslavia, across northern Italy, and up to Paris where we found a way to re-box them for the flight home.

Jackie had experienced no more pain from her fall in Belgium at the beginning of that summer. However a question about it came up a year later. By then we were living in Japan, Maria, Jackie, and I. Sara had stayed home to begin college. Our four bikes had been hanging from hooks in a shed at home on the farm for only two months when morning coffee with Vernal and Eric planted the idea of going to Japan. This time Jackie was the instigator and I had to be talked into it. By February, however, she was spending a month at St. Giles College in San Francisco taking a month-long intensive in Teaching English as a Foreign Language (TEFL), while I stayed back to take care of Maria, now in the eighth grade. In March I took my turn at St. Giles. We wrote inquiries to all thirteen international schools in Japan to decide where Maria would start high school and selected Osaka. By summer Jackie had interviewed in Minnesota with a board member of the International Counseling Center in Kobe and I had phone-interviewed with a Japanese business-English teaching company in Osaka. We quit our jobs at home, and on August 6, 1991, we landed in Japan, our home for the next thirteen months.

When we found an apartment and registered as residents at the Ikeda City Hall, we learned we were eligible for full coverage under the Japanese national health program. We also were on the list to receive news and notifications from the city, which we were unable to read. Our new friend, Masako Kawamura (who became Jackie's best friend) translated: "This one is for a routine total health checkup. Take it. It's free–cost you no money. Doctor Nakayama's office is just here–right across the street from your apartment. Go there for your free health exam!"

We all went for our checkups. We spoke no Japanese. The doctor spoke no English. When he came to Jackie, he became very agitated and let her know he wanted to phone Kimura Sensei, the priest at the Episcopal church we were attending. His urgent message to the priest was: "Get a translator in here! This woman is in trouble!"

This doctor had administered the first electro-cardiogram Jackie had ever had. It had detected a malfunction in her heart's firing system. This prompted a series of evaluation and monitoring at the nearby Osaka heart research hospital, the best in the country. Her visits there continued throughout that year and were covered by national health insurance. The best specialists in Japan told her that she would soon need a pacemaker but recommended she wait until she returned to the United States. She was not yet a candidate for this procedure, they explained, but soon would be and she would know without question when that moment came.

One day, a year after we were back home from Japan, Jackie was carrying two bags of groceries from the car to the house. Halfway across the yard she slowed and stopped. Then set the groceries on the ground and rested a bit. Then picked them up carefully and continued on into the house. As the Japanese doctors had predicted, she knew the time had come for a pacemaker.

....

So when I asked her if she would bicycle to Jerusalem with me, she said she would if she had a motor. A second one–mounted on her bike. The one inside her chest had been working fine and had given her vigorous health and normal energy.

I found a bicycle motor on the internet and ordered it. It mounted behind the seat with a spring-loading connected by cable to a lever bolted to the handlebars. The bicycle could be pedaled normally; but, when approaching a steep hill or a mountain ascent, the rider could pull back the lever and lower the motor drive-wheel against the rear tire to jump-start the engine. The drive-wheel against the tire would then take over, and the bicycle temporarily became a motor bike.

It worked so well when Jackie tried it out that I could not keep up with her. I had been studying possible routes on maps of Europe and Asia and noticed that there were quite a few mountains between Minnesota and Jerusalem. I ordered a motor for my bike, too.

....

This was not to be my bachelor fantasy nor even a great bike ride. We told ourselves we were preparing for a year of pilgrimage, entering into an ancient tradition of arduous journey to the holy place. Our haj. Perhaps it seemed odd that we would begin by quickly going there–the three-week trip to Israel with Sara–and then return home to pack our bikes and start again on the three-month trek to Jerusalem. However, being in Jerusalem was not the point, going there was. Canterbury Tales is not about Canterbury.

Moreover, a year of pilgrimage did not just mean these two trips to the Holy City. Nested within them were a scattering of sub-pilgrimages, side-trips to other places of sacred reputation, not all of them Christian. This had been a thematic interest of our earlier travels also. Our 1990 summer bike trip with Sara and Maria had taken us far off the bicycle path to spend a week in Medjugore, a famous Catholic pilgrim destination where six visionaries were reported to be receiving daily messages from the Blessed Virgin Mary. During our year in Japan, we had spent much of our free time visiting temples and shrines in Kyoto and Nara, learning all we could about Shinto and Japanese Buddhism. On return visits to Japan we lodged with Catholic monks, wandered among the homeless of Tokyo meditating on the sacrificial life of service of saintly Satoko Kitahara, traveled to the north on a route approximating the pilgrim road of the haiku poet, Basho, and arrived in Akita to spend days of prayer at a convent where Sister Agnes Sasegawa had received heavenly messages confirmed by a weeping wooden statue of the Blessed Virgin. Other times we stayed overnight in a Buddhist temple on Mount Koya and visited some of the eighty-eight temples of the pilgrim circuit on the island of Shikoku, including the temple birthplace of Kobo Daishi, sainted founder of the Shingon Sect of Japanese esoteric Buddhism.

All this reflected the Janus quality of our spirituality during this final decade of the century, the pairing of our movement toward a quiet, contemplative life on the farm with a repeated launching out into the world, far and wide, straining to see the living faces of those who had seen the other world, hear what they had heard, stand in the places where great things had happened. It all was about direct experience, interplay of the inner and outer life. During this decade Jackie and I both had a growing fascination with a peculiar subculture of Roman Catholic mysticism. Since childhood this had been part of our religious folk heritage, but in these days there appeared to be a worldwide flourishing of paranormal phenomena: visions, heavenly messages, locutions, miracles, healings, emanation of tears, blood, oil from statues, pictures, and the bodies of living persons. If we heard of such things among shamans and Hindus we were mildly curious, but these reports were from our kind of people, impressively credentialed, and a few of them authenticated as supernatural by the highest authority of our church. We wanted to go and see for ourselves.

So our bicycle ride to Jerusalem would start in Paris with morning Mass at rue du Bac, the convent location where, as the pope had declared, the Mother of God had appeared to Saint Catherine Labouré in 1830. Some said this event was the beginning of "the Marian Age," an era of many private revelations from heaven extending to our own time. On our way up to Jerusalem we would meet the seers of Medjugorje during

Holy Week and Easter, interview an alleged priest stigmatist in Slovenia, go with Orthodox pilgrims up the mountain to Prislop in Romania, visit the tomb of Shayk Yusuf, a Muslim or Alawi saint, where miraculous healings take place, meet a Syrian woman whose body exudes pure oil and occasionally an agony of blood patterning the wounds of the crucified Christ.

These turned out to be stops along the way, not our reason for going. Our "mission statement," so to speak, I typed on a sheet of paper:

> *We are Christian pilgrims going to Jerusalem. We are from the United States of America. We live in a small town called Bovey in the State of Minnesota (near Canada). As we go to Jerusalem, we are praying for peace for the world. We greet you in peace and friendship. We ask God to bless you and your family and to bless all the people of this good country.*
>
> — *Philip and Jackie Solem*

I translated this into French and German; and, as we traveled, we found people to translate from those languages or from English into languages ahead we would not speak. A pilgrim in Bosnia wrote it out in Romanian. A young woman we met at a café in Ljubljana translated into Bulgarian. Jackie's cousin, Janez, gave the Slovenian version. And a young priest at the border town of Letenye turned my German into Hungarian. We also carried a laminated collage of photographs from home: our house and yard, our daughters, my mother, and on the reverse side a hand-drawn outline map of the United States with Minnesota highlighted and a big arrow pointing to "Bovey." Over the years, updated versions of this photo/map sheet would carry us past hours of language barrier with laughing, pointing, smiles, nodding in Arabic, Hindi, Mandarin, Turkish, and Serbo-Croatian. All it required in subsequent trips would be to remove my mother, add sons-in-law and grandchildren.

....

Bicycling to Jerusalem took from March to June, 1998. There was snow on the ground when we left Minneapolis, springtime in Paris when we landed. Our first week crossing France into Germany was plagued by constant breakdowns, repairs, redesigns of our overloaded packing. A snowy, cold winter in Minnesota had prevented us from road testing our motors and luggage system. Bolts sheared off, tires went flat, my motor broke. We found rest and good food with German friends from my seminary days and rested the bikes, too, with a train ride over the Alps into Slovenia. We stayed with Jackie's cousin, Vido, at the gostilna and made the rounds of the other cousins, Franz and Ivan, and their families. Leaving the bikes in the barn there once again, we took train and bus through Croatia down to Bosnia for Easter. There were hundreds, maybe thousands of pilgrims in the village of Medjugorje as usual. The first person we met by chance as we stepped off the bus was an acquaintance who lived thirty miles from us in Minnesota. The second was woman in the crowd going into the church who said, "Do you remember me?" I had sat next to her at a dinner in Cairo three months earlier when Sara, Jackie, and I had been in Egypt. The third was Oscar, a young man from Costa Rica, whom we had met at the Church of the Holy Sepulcher in Jerusalem, whose parents in Cairo had invited us to that dinner, and who planned to start college in Minnesota in the fall–across the street from my old seminary.

All the other pilgrims had come in tour groups. We were the only ones camping in a tent, cooking on a butane single burner, washing up from a plastic basin. It was a rainy, cold week. We met the visionaries and heard their stories, walked from village to village through the vineyards and tobacco fields, prayed a lot of rosaries, climbed the stony mountains. Easter was disappointing, cold, wet, spiritually unremarkable. We were ready to get back to Slovenia, back to our bikes and the road east.

The day we said goodby to Jackie's relatives in Cerklje was one of our hardest. We started in rain. When I stopped to change to a wet-pavement drive wheel on my bike motor, I discovered that the repair done in Germany had been botched and I could not loosen the bolt. Jackie's bike was all right. We rode through the day in driving cold rain. The landscape was beautiful but mountainous, and we were on a tertiary road in the countryside, far from lodging. We could not think of trying to camp in a field in this steady downpour. No one knew of hotels or rooms for rent, only rumors: "Perhaps at Trojane? Only twenty kilometers ahead (in the wrong direction)." No choice but to press on.

Jackie's motor worked off and on. I had to pedal and often dismount, walk, and push the bike uphill for a kilometer or more. At the top of a mountain pass, just as Jackie was about to start a long, fast descent, I watched the sidewall of her rear tire blow. With no shelter from the pelting rain, we huddled while I removed the wheel and changed the tube with blue, shaking hands.

Finally we had definite word of a hotel an hour or two ahead in Vransko. I flagged down a passing police car to confirm this. Yes, they said, a hotel in Vransko. At dusk we rolled into the small town and were directed to a large, pleasant building that looked like a rural inn. Shaking with cold, glad to be here, hoping they would not be full, we entered and asked the woman at the bar for a room. "Nein," she said, "wir haben kein Zimmer." No rooms. They did not, never had, rented rooms! Five or six people along the way had directed us here, but, no, there were no sleeping rooms in Vransko.

We refused to accept this answer but just stood and pleaded and looked miserable. Someone suggested we go on to Zalec, only twenty kilometers, not far. We asked if there were not a church, a priest, in this town, but the people at the bar seemed mystified by this question. They were all very sympathetic, obviously felt sorry for us and said they could see how exhausted we were, but.... Jackie said, "I don't *want* to go to the next town!"

We wandered onto the street in the growing dark, asking anyone we could see. Two women were talking on the street, and one responded to us in fragments of German-English. They pondered our problem and agreed there were no legally registered rooms for rent in town. One of them, speaking only Slovenian, took us to the tavern and talked to the bartender and patrons, made a phone call, then suddenly invited us to go with her to her house. We left our loaded bicycles outside the tavern and went with her. She had phoned ahead, we discovered, to check with her sister with whom she lived.

Thus we met Sonja and her sister Milenja, who spoke cultured German. They sat us in the kitchen, gave us wine, spread the table with food, and heard our story (in German). These two sisters lived together in this large house at the foot of the mountain beside a swift stream. They were retired. Sonja had been chief judge in Celje, Milenja an art museum curator. Their brother, Boris, a doctor, had lived with them here until his death some years back. We assumed we were being sheltered for the night, but they made no move to show us our room and Sonja was frequently on the phone. She left the house and shortly returned exultant:

"Everything is arranged–*nasdravja!*" and they both lifted wine glasses to toast us. We would stay at the priest's house.

They piled us into their small car, stopped at the tavern for us to get our belongings from the bikes and lock them in a shed, and drove us to meet the priest, a cheerful, lively, middle-aged comic. There were two priest houses. He lived in a small one, part of a row house along the street. The one he let us into was a very large house with three sleeping rooms, a kitchen, full bath, and much more, the home of a former pastor then in retirement elsewhere. We were given the keys; our beds were already made up for us; the heat had been turned on. The place was ours. We stood alone there when they had gone, then just wandered about. I kept saying, "What just happened to us? What happened?" It was Clamart all over again–Clamart, the suburb of Paris, where an empty church hall had been given to Jackie, Sara, Maria, and me for a full week at no cost when our money had run out and we were at one of our darkest hours.

We stayed on in Vransko for two days until the weather cleared. We were Sonja's and Milenja's guests for meals. They worried about us and urged us to forget about the bicycles and take a car or a train to Jerusalem. The tavern owner had his expert mechanic take a look at the locked up drive-wheel on my motor. In a half-day of careful work with a blowtorch he undid the bad repair done in Germany and had the motor back in operation. While he worked, we wandered down to the most beautiful corner of the village, a sheer mountain wall, a cave from which flowed a stream of clear water which ran over a small dam in a steady sheet, old abandoned buildings shut down by the Communists after the war and now back in private ownership being readied for renovation. We enjoyed the emerging sunshine, flowering trees, chickens strutting, people in their gardens, a walk through the hops fields.

We spoke to the priest only a few times. He was always brisk and lighthearted. Once he brought us a plate of potica, a Slovenian pastry we had both grown up with on the Iron Range. Finally we were packing the bikes and getting ready to go on. The priest stopped by and we thanked him repeatedly. He asked something in broken German-Slovenian-English that I thought sounded like "cash." When we did not understand, he turned and walked off. Suddenly Jackie said, "We should offer to pay something for our stay here!" I hurried after him, but he had gone into his house. While I deliberated about whether to ring the bell, he suddenly emerged and came toward me. I thrust into my pockets and brought out a wad of Slovenian bills and asked what we could give for our stay. He walked up to me and tucked a 10,000 SIT ($61) bill into my shirt pocket. As I stood stunned, he said "Slovenisches Abschied" (Slovenian farewell), laughed, and walked back into the house.

We rode into the most perfect spring day, warm, clear, blue sky, on level terrain along a valley between mountain ranges. Along both sides of the road farmers were preparing miles of hops fields, tall poles imbedded in the ground with a structure of gridwork at rooftop height holding strings dangling to the soil like giant bean trellises, so many strings suspended across the landscape that it appeared a mist was hovering far into the distance.

The priest at Vojnik told us to camp where we liked alongside the church, and his aged housekeeper with a kind face wrapped in a babushka brought us in and fed us. The next bicycling day was as lovely as the last though we moved into hill country and had to engage the motors frequently. Then we began to meet headwind and Jackie decided to use her motor steadily, even on the flats. Pumping as hard as I could, I kept falling behind and decided to engage my newly repaired motor. All the while I worried I might be overdoing it, using the troubled machine more than necessary, wondering if it would hold up, wondering if it would take us all the way to–

Clack! Ping! Roaaar! Over my left shoulder I watched my blue neoprene drive-wheel skitter across the roadway behind me. This was it. The end of the motor. I stopped and went back to retrieve the piece and looked under the motor mount to make sure. This time the shaft had sheared right at the surface of the motor. When Jackie slowed, turned, and rolled up to me, I showed her the wheel.

"How do you feel?" she asked.

"Neutral," I said. "No feeling one way or the other. Only the thought that my motor is finished and our trip now will change. We are back to the plan we worked out in France, just before Metz."

We biked on to Ptuj, a historic and picturesque town on the Drava River and found refuge at a Franciscan monastery where we stayed several days, for I had come down with a bad cold and spent half the time in bed. We boxed the motor and mailed it home from there. I would pedal the rest of the way to Jerusalem with more reliance on trains and buses than we had planned.

In a single day we left Slovenia, crossed a finger of Croatia, and entered Hungary. We asked the priest at Letenye if we could camp in his yard. He knew only Hungarian, so I spoke some Latin to him and showed him the English paragraph about our pilgrimage and translated it into Latin. He answered with a stream of Hungarian, went into the house and returned with 4000 Forints ($20) which he pressed into my hand while he led us across the street to a hotel.

Our fortunes continued to improve for awhile. The priest at Inke took us into his house and fed us. In Kapsovár we had a clean and cozy apartment with full bath, two beds, stove, fridge, pots and pans and access to all pools and saunas at a thermal bath complex for eight dollars a night. It was such a good deal that we stayed two nights and soaked our aching muscles, napped, read, studied the maps.

I discovered there the cause of all our bicycle and motor breakdowns. They were all related to an ill-fit between expensive tires I had special ordered before leaving home and high-quality replacement rear wheels I had bought at the local bicycle store in Minnesota. I had noticed by feel that the new wheels were slightly narrower and had asked the store mechanic about it. He had assured me it would not be a problem. In fact, the tires fit on the rim, but poorly. As they rode, they distorted, giving an upward jolt against the engaged drive-wheel with every rotation, eventually snapping the shaft. They also frayed on the sidewalls and blew out frequently. In the middle of Hungary we threw away the expensive tires and bought new Czech-made ones for one-fifth their price. It was the end of breakdowns.

At this wonderful thermal bath I hung my laundered jeans and shirt on the iron fence outside in the sun and wind. It took a good while for the jeans to dry. In the apartment Jackie and I spread the maps of each country ahead on the couch and discussed possibilities for the route. After a while I got up and said, "I'd better go get my jeans outside." Gone! The fence was bare. Nothing to do, I thought, I'm down to one pair of cotton slacks and sweat pants. I scouted all about the fence hoping maybe they had just blown off, but I had buttoned the jeans around a rail, so I knew this was wishful thinking. I turned to go back to the room and caught a glimpse of an old man sitting on a bench facing the street, his back to me. He glanced back. On impulse I walked over to him, saw a fabric bag beside him, looked in. I said in English, "I'm just looking for my jeans," bent down and picked my dried jeans out of the top of his bag saying. "Köszönöm, köszönöm." ("Thank you, thank you"). He looked up at me sheepishly, toothlessly, as if to say "no problem." I felt no reproach, only gratitude that I had not lost my everyday traveling jeans, and went in.

In Bonyhád the priest turned us down and we had to stay in a costly hotel but we gave a half-hour interview there through a translator on Rádio Bonyhád. In Felsöszentiván, at the end of one of our longest days bicycling across the Great Plain of Hungary, the priest said it was "impossible" for us to camp next to his house, next to the church, in any of the open fields nearby, timidly wished us success, shook my hand, and shut the door. We asked at a store and were told there was no camping available, and we should go back twenty kilometers to Baja where we had crossed the Danube or forward eighty kilometers to Szeged.

Just then, Jackie spotted a woman of whom I had asked directions to the church disappearing around a corner on her bicycle. Jackie engaged the motor and raced after her. When I caught up, breathing hard, I told the woman in German what had happened with the priest and what we needed. Again the hopeless response: no hotels or rooms or camping places. No possibility even of freelance camping illegally, for there were no woods, only flat, open fields. She began to say she was sorry...when, "well, maybe...." She said we should follow her and led us to a shabby, unkempt house at the edge of the village and called repeatedly at an open window. A middle-aged man came round the house and she spoke to him to a moment. He replied, "Ja" and beckoned us into his yard.

This was Robert. At once he opened his very run-down house and yard to us. He showed me his room and said we could sleep inside in his bedroom with him–or outside in our tent (we chose the tent). He lived with his bent, misshapen father, Ludwig, who was friendly and animated and slept in the adjoining room. Robert, who spoke broken German, overwhelmed us with hospitality, pressing wine on us, offering us his kitchen, his bathroom, introducing us to his brother-in-law, who came to inspect, having already heard about us in the village. We grew less and less comfortable with his insistent cordiality when he wanted us to go out to a pub with him. The effect of the wine was beginning to show, but he remained friendly and humbly accepted our oft-repeated "no."

He had to show us his large garden, which he said was his life. As we crawled into our tent beside his cluttered house, Jackie commented to me that we are truly beggars on this journey and receiving this kind of hospitality from the poor is emotionally costly.

It was a sleepless night. Robert got drunker on wine and he would show up outside the tent while we were trying to sleep whispering, "Philip, Philip. Pasz auf–wein trinken? Philip?" (Philip, hey look, how about some more wine...?) We were not afraid of him, but I worried that the brother-in-law, whom we did not like, might come back. At 2:30 in the morning, I went out to pee, and Robert came out of his house. I had to have a conversation about his "terribly old dog" who was blind and deaf. I suppose we got a few hours sleep. All night the countryside was awake with barking dogs. The roosters started crowing and triggering neighboring roosters from 2:00 A.M. on, about once every hour. We were glad to see 6:00 A.M. We ate bread and jam and tea inside the cluttered, dirty house with old Ludwig while Robert was out shopping for rolls and vinegar. We decided that we had been taken in by the village out-cast, perhaps the only person more desperate than we had been yesterday. We said a friendly goodby with heartfelt thanks to Robert. He stood by his fence gate weeping as we left.

Days later, as we approached the Romanian border, our anxiety began to rise. We had listened to dire warnings from their neighbors in Slovenia and Hungary and even from some Romanians we had met en route against biking and tenting there. The country was desperately poor and still in shock after the depredation of its fallen tyrant, Ceausescu; and villages we would pass could be wild and dangerous.

The day we decided to cross and make a seventy-kilometer sprint to Arad, the first city on our route, we were stopped by a cold, relentless rain and a signboard that indicated only trucks and buses were allowed at this border crossing. We would have to go fifty-six kilometers north to cross at Battonya. Once again we were rescued from the road, soaked and shivering, and given unlimited hospitality by a priest and his household. For three days we lived with them in Apátfalva waiting for the rain cell to pass. They dried us out and warmed us up, invited us to their table, took us with them about the neighboring parishes they served and honored us as pilgrim visitors, and took us on a full-day outing to the Hungarian National Historical Memorial Park to show us the history of their country. All this without speaking a full sentence to one another. Hungarian is almost totally foreign to us, less familiar than even Japanese. To hear it spoken, it sounds at times vaguely like Finnish, to which it is distantly related. We spent three days in close company with these people and could share no more than a word borrowed from Latin, French, German, English, always a word, never a phrase or a sentence. Drawing pictures to explain a complex thought was usually more effective than charades. I was reminded of the story Sara told when she returned from her summer alone in Ghana, how for days she had communicated richly with the boys in the school for the deaf by teaching them how to knit. Which brought back the memory of Jackie sitting for hours with only a phrase or two of Spanish and chattering with the *campesinas* of San Salvador over sewing and embroidery.

When the sun came out, they drove us with bikes in a trailer to the border at Battonya. From there it was an easy ride into Romania to Arad where we took a night train to lift us into the mountains of Transylvania and the city of Sibiu at the center of the country. A friend in Minnesota had given us the name and phone number of an Orthodox theologian in Sibiu. Sebastian Moldovan took care of us for several days, installing us in guest rooms at a convent of Orthodox nuns, showing us around the city, talking theology with us in his study. I was intrigued to recognize among the books he was using to prepare a doctoral dissertation texts in French which I had studied twenty-five years earlier at the University of Louvain and articles written by some of my Belgian seminary professors.

Some of the easiest bicycling of the trip came next. We left Sibiu through a narrow pass near the top of the Carpathian Mountains and coasted for nearly a day alongside the Olt River toward the Danube River plain. The first night we stayed at an Orthodox monastery, the second two nights we lay sick in a shoddy hotel in Dragasani. Weakened by this bout with food poisoning, we staggered our bikes to the train station and bought tickets to Bucharest. Our plan at this point had been to continue bicycling east to the Black Sea in order to catch a ship from Romania past Bulgaria to Istanbul. We had read about this ferry in our guidebook; but I decided to confirm it before crossing half the country and phoned the port in Constanta from the Bucharest train station. No, I was told, the ferry had been cancelled this summer. There was no passage to Istanbul. So we turned south and crossed the Danube into Bulgaria at Ruse.

By now we were falling seriously behind schedule and daunted at the prospect of trying to struggle through the Balkan Mountains. At noon we went to the Ruse train station and booked tickets to Istanbul. The wait on the platform was tense, for there were rough-looking men lounging about, inspecting our bikes and gear, loudly asking how much they cost ("What dollars?") We refused to speak to them. I worried how we would jam our bikes into a packed Bucharest-to-Istanbul train. Jackie was nervous about the aggressive men. Suddenly it all changed: the train rolled in. Jackie snagged an empty compartment; I quickly shoved our panniers, tent, and sleeping bags through an open window to her; I dragged our bikes into an empty car and strapped them to the window rails along the passageway, after taking off the pedals and swiveling the handlebars sideways.

We rode with ease and security through the beautiful, mountainous Bulgarian countryside into the night. The conductor came by and charged us extra because we were in a sleeping car but also gave us pillows and sheets. At two in the morning everyone left the train for two hours at the Turkish border. I had to buy entry visas for both of us, and when I gave the man at the window a U.S. hundred dollar bill, he held it up to a dim bulb, squinted, and tossed it back at me, a scrap of paper, counterfeit. I carefully cut my last hundred from where I had duct-taped it to the inside of my belt and pushed it across to him. Again he lifted it to the bulb, squinted for a long moment, then nodded and stamped the visas into our passports. At four in the morning a conductor rousted us out on the rolling train to inspect our tickets and to charge us extra for the bicycles.

"Twenty dollars!" the man said.

"No! Too much!" I said. "I won't pay twenty!"

"Twenty dollars!" he insisted.

"Too much!" I shouted and dug out a U.S. bill. "I'll give you ten!"

"Twenty dollars."

"Okay, ten dollars and ten German marks ($15)"

He took it.

Istanbul was a great relief from the tension of Romania and Bulgaria. Turkey felt safe, clean, orderly. We found an inexpensive room with a glorious rooftop view of the city and the Sea of Marmara, the passage to the Bosphorus, and, only two blocks away, the Aya Sofiya (Hagia Sophia) and the Blue Mosque. We stayed for five days, watched the Sufi whirling dervish ritual, nine men floating, arms out loosely, rotating on and on in trance, and, for the only time during the pilgrimage, became tourists.

With a motor we would have taken on the mountain climb to the tabletop of central Turkey, but, as it was, we took a night bus down to Cappadocia. Göreme in Cappadocia is remarkable for its scenery and history. It is a village in the midst of bizarre natural cone formations of tufa volcanic ash rock weathered over eons into fairyland forests. Houses are built into these cones, against them, all around them. The Hittites once settled here as did the early Christians after them. There are remains of hundreds of Christian churches carved into the soft rock. Seljuk Turks and after them the Ottoman Turks burrowed into the tufa and honey-combed the cliffs and fairy chimneys to make homes, tunnels, passage-ways and storehouses. We rented a room and were given a cave at the top of one of these pillars, which we reached by climbing iron steps to a small door and entering on hands and knees. The room was a hemi-sphere. A window had been cut on one wall and glass put in. The door was a plug of planks, two feet by three feet, cobbled together. About the walls were rows of niches made by some cave dweller from a previous century as pigeon roosts. Here we slept in great comfort atop the pillar of stone. There was in the room but a double mattress with sheets, pillows, and blankets on top of a rug. Ten dollars a night.

We resumed bicycling east across Turkey when we came to the Med-iterranean at Adana and made a brief side-trip to nearby Tarsus, where the Apostle Paul came from. Continuing east to Ceyhan, we met a man named Ismail Ergün who took us to his home for tea then guided us to the top of a rock outcrop outside the city where we pitched our tent alongside the ruins of a Crusader fortress.

The next day we rounded the bend along the Mediterranean and be-gan heading south for the first time since leaving Minnesota. We were closing in on Jerusalem. We camped near the beach, swam in the sea, cooked our simple meals on our single-burner stove, and politely de-clined invitations from people who came to invite us for tea and con-versation–endless glasses of tea for hours on end with conversation in Turkish–too exhausting for us after a day of bicycling.

Were it not for the protracted military standoff between Israel and Hisbullah on the southern border of Lebanon, the simplest path would have been simply to follow the seacoast south. However, we had determined this way would be blocked and we would have to bypass Lebanon. At Iskenderun we turned inland, away from the sea and began the steepest ascent so far, over the Amanos Mountain Range. We had not been able to find detailed maps of this part of Turkey, so we did not know what we were in for. Jackie's motor was not strong enough to carry her and I could not pedal. We pushed the bikes ahead, heavy step by heavy step, in sweltering heat, stopping often to rest, leaving the bikes standing by the roadside while we slipped down into pine groves and threw ourselves on the ground or on rock slabs. As we pushed the bikes forward again, huge trucks roared and grunted up the grade in their lowest gears. After a few kilometers, we were looking down on Iskenderun and the brilliant sea behind it and then up at the road which snaked and rose ever upward out of sight. We were spent and took refuge in the shade of a concrete bus stop shelter. Young university students coming out to the road to catch a dolmus (van) stayed to talk with us in schoolroom English and tried to help us hitch a ride with a climbing truck. All the laboring trucks on the highway passed by, unwilling to break momentum by stopping. Finally, from a side road, a loaded van emerged; and the students flagged it and negotiated a ride for us up the mountain as far as Belen, where we hoped to take a hotel. The workmen rearranged the junk in the van and jammed our bikes in and somehow wedged us in also. On and on we climbed, looking down sheer slopes into narrow valleys. How could we have made this on foot?

In Belen we paid the men three million Turkish lira ($12) for the ride and ate at a restaurant. There we learned that there were no hotels or rooms for rent in town. We were given misinformation by a waiter which led us to understand that we were very near the mountain's summit and could coast down to a town in the valley beyond and find a hotel.

Encouraged by this error, we decided to press on, even though it was now midafternoon. I helped Jackie start her motor, got her moving up the mountain road with a running push, and shouted after her: "Don't stop for me! Whatever you do, don't stop till you get to the top!" When she was out of sight, I began pushing my bike. It was my most desperate hour on this trip. I had no energy left but had to push on. Often I stopped, dropped the kick stand and braced the wheel against rolling back, and lay down on the gravel in the skeleton shade of the bicycle frame, while cars and trucks ground past me, farting out black clouds of fume.

An hour later, as I plodded forward, an orange truck came slowly down the hill, turned around, and pulled in front of me. I knew Jackie had sent it. The man got out and said, "Madame," pointing upward ahead. He helped me load my bike in the back of the truck, then drove the five or six kilometers to the summit where Jackie was waiting. He spoke only Turkish. His truck was nearly junk, and he could scarcely get it in gear, but he drove us to a restaurant and insisted we eat and drink. We spent the next hour struggling with our rescuer who insisted on taking us to his house to meet his wife and children (would we camp there?) and instead took us deep down a valley siding to show us some apple trees and a stream. He would not understand or listen to what we wanted. He wanted us to pick apples.

"No!" Jackie shouted at the man. "No, I don't *want* any apples! No, I'm *tired!* I want to go back up!"

He kept gesturing toward the apples down a steep slope at the side of the road.

"No!" she screamed. "Take us back to the restaurant!"

Crestfallen, the man, fairly drunk, protested, "Okay, problem-no-problem, Madame." He pointed to the stream. There were villagers beside it but no village in sight. "I house–childris, camping..." he tried again.

"No!" she yelled furiously. "Take us to the restaurant!"

He looked defeated, disappointed, angry: "Madame problem-no-problem."

He managed to grind the truck into gear and lift us back up the gravelly switchback to the restaurant. Glassy-eyed and swaying, he indicated many bewildered apologies, and we were conciliatory; but as quickly as possible we moved our gear to the flat rooftop of the restaurant and set up our tent there. Toward evening the proprietor joined us on the rooftop to sit quietly and peacefully with his two sons. Honoring the gift of their presence for a few minutes, we then climbed into the privacy of our tent, wretched with fatigue.

Early the next morning before anyone was awake we glided away, down, down the mountain onto the broad plain of the Orontes River and, thirty kilometers later, coasted into Antakya–ancient Antioch. By chance someone directed us to Barbara, a German woman living alone, maintaining a tiny Christian presence in this ancient city where the term "Christian" was coined. She invited us in for tea, and we talked of many things, our work, our faith, our travels, our pilgrimages. She had once bicycled from Germany to Jerusalem, we were astonished to hear. She asked where we were staying, then offered the loan of the empty house next door which she was responsible for. For four days we lived in this old house with airy rooms, mats on the floor, enclosed courtyard, kitchen, bathroom, shower, on the beehive back streets of Antioch.

When we crossed the border from Turkey into Syria, we had to be very careful about what we said. Before leaving on this trip we had been well informed that we dare not mention Israel or Jerusalem at any time while in Syria. Syrians refer to it as "Occupied Palestine." At the border, when I presented our passports, the unsmiling man behind the grill asked:

"Where are you going?"

"Damascus."

"Where after Damascus?"

"On to Jordan, Amman."

"After Jordan, where?"

"We could go down to Al Aqabah to take a ship to Egypt. Or a plane to Cairo from Amman. Or maybe just fly back home to New York."

He paused. Nodded (correct answer). Bang, bang, stamped the passports and slid them back to me.

Syria was our favorite country on this trip. Everywhere we heard "Welcome!" which seemed to have many meanings: Welcome to Syria! Please come and buy something. You're welcome. Or Goodbye. We quickly became comfortable and oriented in Aleppo. This has to do with getting familiar with manners and customs, styles of approach by and to people, a testing out of how open and welcoming the people are, successful use of the money, adjusting to the sound of the language and the look of unreadable writing, and many indefinable things. Everyone we met was surprised–at times amazed–that we were American. French, Germans, Turks, Russians, Armenians, Kurds–but American? Regularly we encountered the legendary honesty of the Syrians and, for the first time, had no sense of guardedness, no worry about leaving our bicycles and baggage unattended. We were never approached by beggars or hustlers. Several times–in shops, by a cab driver–I was made to know I had over-paid and correct change was handed back.

As we bicycled south toward Damascus on a wide highway, we stopped for a midmorning rest and shade under some yew trees to drink water and eat a few handfuls of pistachio nuts. Soon we had men at our elbows, greeting and speaking Arabic. Three of them had seen us bicy-cling and had come from three different directions. We were not sur-prised, for we were used to waving and frequent calls to come for tea. These men, too, gestured to the village on the slope, about a half-kilome-ter from the highway, urgently inviting us to tea. We had been wanting to meet village people and had heard from Barbara that we would easily find lodging with them. Even though it seemed too early to stop for the day, we decided this time to accept and see where it led. We followed the man on a motorbike up the road to Kseiba, population 3000.

We were beckoned into a yard surrounded by a cinder block and adobe wall and welcomed by a number of men, youths, and some women and children. Shortly, Jackie disappeared to the back of the large house with the women; and I remained on the porch while more men gathered and we were all served glasses of tea. Only one of them, Hammed, spoke an isolated word or phrase of English, awkwardly pronounced. The clus-ter of men and boys carried on loudly and vigorously with each other, discussing, arguing, at times roughhousing, drawing me in every now and then referring to "Clinton!" and "Sadam Hussein!" (much laughter). I did not try to communicate, only sat and watched and responded when I could. They were warm and affectionate with one another. The men were boisterous. Younger boys and small children watched silently from their places in the circle. More tea and more tea. Then a demi-tasse of coffee just for me. Jackie appeared wearing a long, blue dress the women had lent her. Much laughter. They dressed me in a long, silk, beige jella-ba, which men wear, and a keffiyeh headdress scarf with rope ring atop. I wore this for the rest of that day and the next morning; for they took away my shirt, jeans, and socks. Apparently we had been invited to stay the night.

The rest of the day they showed off their village and showed us off to the village, taking us out into the fields to meet the workers, to a little house to visit a suffering, dying grandmother with henna tattooed face, neck, and hands, to meet Bedouins camped in a large tent near the house, to see a herd of goats, to admire their "forest," a grove of what looked like stunted jack pine and view the panorama of the rolling plains in the sunset. For meals we sat on the floor around a huge silver tray and dipped mouthfuls of egg mixture and something like cold tabouli and tomato-cucumber salad with tear-offs of flatbread, two feet in diameter, folded in quarters like a newspaper for easy handling and placed on the marble floor beside each person. Only the men, Jackie, and I ate together. Jackie, as a Western visitor, had access to both the women's and the men's world. I was restricted to being with the men.

In the evening, more people gathered to sit about the house and talk endlessly. We showed pictures of our home and family. Supper was served to only about six men, Jackie and me in the same fashion, boiled chicken pieces on a mountain of steamed white rice washed down with liquid goat milk yoghurt. There was no furniture in the room, only a TV, carpet and pillows. People moved in and out freely, the ebb and flow of extended family, kind, laughing, sensitive with each other with fluid touching of one another and hand-holding among the men. When they could see we were getting very tired, they rose and beckoned us to a large room with a mattress bed made up and demonstrated how to turn the key in the lock from the inside.

In the morning, after we had washed up, we were led to sit on a carpet and pillows along the marble, pillared porch that ran along one wall of the house facing an enclosed orchard of berry, apple, and olive trees. The air was fresh and clean. Swallows swooped and darted. Hammed's face seemed thoughtful and concentrated. He was composing an English sentence. Leaning toward me he carefully spoke and pointed: "The birds believe in God."

Breakfast was served the same way, huge disks of pita, salty feta cheese cubes, green olives, fresh tomatoes, peppers, yoghurt. Then tea and more sweet, sugared tea. Then tiny, sweet cups of coffee. My shirt and jeans were returned to me cleaner than they had ever been–and pressed with creases down the legs of my jeans like dress slacks. Our bikes had not been unloaded since we had arrived. All our needs had been cared for. With many a goodbye and thank you in Arabic-English, we blessed them and they blessed us. Waving, we rolled out of the yard, out of the village, down the main highway to Damascus.

Bicycling through the Middle East was by far the easiest part of the trip. We had no more mechanical troubles; the weather was good; the people were warm and respectful. In Damascus, while we were walking along Straight Street, looking for the Soufanieh neighborhood where we knew the stigmatist, Myrna Nazour and her family lived, Jackie's eye was caught by ornate brass and gold ware in a shop window and said, "Let's ask in here."

The shop was cluttered with hanging lamps, brass bowls, gleaming metal screens, and shining gold far into the dark recesses of the room. At a desk near the door sat a woman in a fine, ankle-length dress with a silk scarf closely wrapping her head and neck. She greeted us in cultivated English and at once offered tea. Yes, this was her shop, she said. She thanked us for our compliments on her wares. How had she learned such good English? Well, she had exchanged lessons with a young woman from Texas living in Damascus, Arabic for English...and on we chatted easily and pleasantly while her assistant brought tea. The Soufanieh area? It was not far, but she could not exactly give us directions. Yes, she had heard stories of this Myrna but did not know much about it...She was fascinated with the story of our trip. All the way from Paris? On bicycle? And you are Americans? Then she became grave, and her assertive manner turned apologetic and tentative:

"Please forgive me, I wish to ask something that perhaps is very personal."

We were surprised. What would this be? "Yes, certainly, go ahead."

"If it is not impolite for me to ask–but–were you not afraid on such a long trip?"

Oh, this again. The fear question. We had been asked this far less cautiously a hundred times by friends, family, and strangers from the moment we began talking about plans for this trip at home, all along the way, in every country.

"Well, yes, of course we have had our fears but..." we began the stock response.

"I mean–were there not–animals?"

We stopped. Blank. Never before had we heard this. "Animals?"

"Yes, I think on such a long trip with bicycle you must have gone through many forests. Were you not afraid of the animals?"

Both of us sat dumbfounded. Animals. We have been harried and worn down by warnings about terrorists, traffic, thieves, hostile governments, border guards, nighttime gassing of train compartments, bad roads, bad water, bad food, bad people, war, bombings, kidnapings. This woman was asking if we were not afraid of wild animals in the forests. Then it became clear. A city dweller. She lived in the Old City which was wrapped in greater Damascus, which was in dry, unforested Syria. She had heard stories of dark woods, fierce animals. The world out there is a dangerous place.

As we left Syria and entered Jordan, it was a relief to be able to speak of Israel and Jerusalem without whispering. We could walk up to someone on the street to ask directions and simply say, "We want to go to Jerusalem." Our urgency to pass through Jordan quickly came with the awareness of nearing our goal. After a night in Amman, we waited the next morning at the border, for our passports to be checked and our bicycles loaded on the bus for the short crossing of the King Hussein/Allenby Bridge into Israel. The bridge is a well-worn, iron structure, about a hundred feet long, over the muddy, brown Jordan River. Then came the final ascent: Jericho to Jerusalem.

On the Mount of Olives, Jackie and I stood straddling our bicycles, looking across the Kidron Valley at the walls of Jerusalem. The glorious golden Dome of the Rock on the Haram al Sharif shone in the sunlight. We rode down, then steeply upward again to the walls, and entered through the Herod Gate. Leaning the two bicycles against the wall, I kissed the stone and, for the second time this year, we recited the opening lines of the psalm:

I rejoiced when I heard them say, 'Let us go to the house of the Lord.'
And now our feet are standing within your gates, O Jerusalem!

Our bed that night was in the back room of a Palestinian family home in the Old City's Arab Quarter. Our plans had been to spend the next ten days revisiting The Holy City, Galilee, and Judea, places we had seen with Sara only five months earlier. First, however, we needed to phone our daughters to let them know we had made it and were safe.

Maria's pregnancy was close to term, her due date only two weeks away. When Jackie reached her on the phone, Maria said at once:

"Oh, Mom! Could you come home? I'm scared!"

"Are you all right, Honey?"

"Yes, I'm all right, I'm fine. Could you come home?"

We went to the airline office and changed our tickets to an earlier flight home, limiting our stay in Israel to a few days in Jerusalem and a brief visit with our Sri Lankan friends in Herzliya before going to the airport in Tel Aviv. Because of our trip here with Sara the previous January, we felt we had already had the pilgrimage dessert before the meal.

Maria's and Rolland's first child, Tristan Michael Miller, was born five days after we landed in Minneapolis/St. Paul, two days before we had been originally scheduled to return. Jackie was with them in the delivery room. I was listening at the door.

....

Back home on the farm, Jackie and I reflected in the quiet and carefully integrated these experiences. For example, I reminisced about a fragment of labored conversation, somewhere in Eastern Europe, as we had been slowly pushing our heavily loaded bikes forward up a grade so steep it had even overwhelmed Jackie's motor. I remember saying to her between gasps for breath:

"You know, even with all the trouble we have had–breakdowns, flat tires, weather and cold, being so discouraged and miserable at times, I have never once thought, 'Why are we doing this? Maybe we should quit.' Not once, even at the worst times."

"Me neither," she said, puffing and pushing. "Hard as it's been, we know why we're doing this. And we know where we are going."

"Right (puff, pant). Right. But you know what I have also been thinking? I think (puff, puff) this is the last time I want to make this kind of trip. This is enough for me."

Jackie was fifty-seven years old, I fifty-eight at that time. We were no athletes, not even avid bicyclists. There would be other travels together, none so hard as this one, but each an adventure with its own risk and uncertainty. Some tame, such as walking in Tuscany, tenting all the way to Nova Scotia with our friend Florence, or taking the inside passage to Alaska with Masako and Teruo. Some across broad sweeps of continent from Buenos Aires to Tierra del Fuego and back up to Iguazú Falls on the border of Brazil or across India, China, Japan by land and sea in two months. (On this latter voyage, a half-year of careful planning to hop over the Himalayas from India into Kyrgystan and take a train across western China along the Silk Road changed in a half-day with the sudden fall of the Kyrgyz government and rioting in the streets of Bishkek, our transit destination. On the spur of the moment we decided to fly instead from Delhi via Thailand into southern China, ride for three days down the Yangzi River, and take the ferry from Shanghai to Japan.) Always we would return to the quiet of our farm and everyday duties to fold these experiences inside and ponder them. These journeys through the world far and wide have always been journeys of the inner life.

Isn't this the image: We start again, go out and make another loop, a trip away from home, another probe of death, another journey to the edge of the world where ships fall off. Probing death is like poking a sleeping beast, running up, poking, running away squealing, excited to see if it will rear up, maw open, and chase! Why probe death? Why not stay away, stay home where it is safe? Hard to say, except that most of us probably get restless and want to leave home for a while, take a break, get away.

Don't many children's tales go this way? Tales of travel, tales of adventure, meaning danger.

Sara would say, "Tell me a story, Dad. Make it scary."

"Did I tell you about the alligator girl who went to Hole-in-the-Day Bay?"

"About it!"

"Well, once upon a time there was a little girl named Ali who lived with her mom and dad and her dog, George, in a pretty house in the valley...."

"Make it scary, Dad."

And, even as I would pick up the pace of the adventure, she would keep her little hand on the throttle. Of course Ali traveled out of the valley far away from Mom and Dad; and maybe George would have to stay home because he couldn't get time off his job herding sheep. The plot would thicken, the tension build. There would be darkness, far-off sounds coming closer, strange appearances, the way lost, and....

"Dad? Not *too* scary."

....

It starts early, this leaving home. Nonsense nursery rhymes of baby-hood give way to stories, and stories mean travel. Travel means leaving home and coming home. Most of the stories I told Sara ended with the girl or boy sitting by the fire or at the kitchen table with cookies and milk given by a kind big-person.

What would it be like, I wondered, to leave home and not come back? What would it be like to set out with no planned route and no return date, an open-ended trip?

What would it be like to "call in well" to your job some morning (I got the phrase from Tom Robbins's *Even Cowgirls Get the Blues.*)?

What would it be like to leave all like Paul Gaugin and go off to the South Sea Islands to live out your days painting?

What would it be like to leave your nets and your dad in the boat and follow the burning-with-life man?

What would it be like to be doing a repair on the outside of the space shuttle, to slip loose from the tether, and to tumble silently off into space?

....

Nearly all the stories I told her were travel tales, an expandable for-mula. I just had to start with a whimsical set of characters, a quick de-scription of home-base, and then start walking. Neither she nor I knew what was going to happen, what kind of dangers would be met, or when we would round the bend and turn homeward. We always ended up safe back home.

I did not tell her yet the other ending. There will come a day when I leave home, door ajar and banging in the wind, never to return. There will be one day a straight-line trip out, no loop. Some day I will leave this place.

TWELVE
....

This Water Lives in Mombasa

N ow we were noticing, with every turn of a season, every return home from travel, that our neighborly community at the farm was flaking away, fading. People were dying or moving on. Gayle died in the log house across the field after a long struggle with cancer, only forty-two years old. The orange school bus no longer rumbled down the road each morning. All our children grew up, moved away, started families. Marie Karjala lost a foot to gangrene, hung up her barn boots for the last time, and went to the nursing home. Jackie and I had to pry her brother Waino's clutching fingers loose from the farmhouse in which the two of them had spent a lifetime and convince him to follow her, even as he was determined to spend another winter alone in the smoke-blackened house with a hole in the bottom of the empty fuel oil tank and the only heat coming from kindling in the kitchen wood stove. Eric and Vernal had disassociated with the American enterprise during the Gulf War in 1991 by temporarily moving to Canada. After that brief war, they returned to the farm; but when our nation committed itself to ever more war-making after 2001, they left the country once again, took permanent residency on the Queen Charlotte Islands off the coast of British Columbia and became Canadian citizens. They return to this Minnesota farm regularly for several months at a time; but now their austerely simple home in the log barn across the yard stands empty for most of the year.

We were alone. Gary remarried, and we could look across the fields to see smoke rising from his and Wendy's chimney. Charlotte depended on us for animal care and we on her for house-watching when one or the other was away. But the vibrant sense of extended family in close community had passed.

More often, activities with friends and family took place elsewhere-scheduling holiday rotations at our children's homes, caring for grandchildren in St. Paul and Kansas City, large family reunions with Jackie's relatives, or smaller ones with our immediate family at a midway restaurant in Duluth or a campground outside of Ely. We went to be with our children's children–Tristan, Cecilia, Kyla, Gavin–these new loves who had come into our lives; but our small house in remote north country was seldom the gathering place.

Yet it was very good to be here alone. We had come twenty years earlier for this as well as for the warm sense of community now gone. We had come to slow down, go inward, reflect and give thanks. We had entered old age and spoke more often of retirement, Social Security, and Medicare. For years I had looked forward to getting old. I thought it would be a fine thing no longer to have to go to a job to earn money. Jackie would say that she did not yet see a time when she would want to stop being a therapist and spiritual director, she so loved her work of helping people grow and find their way.

I, on the other hand, had invented in my mind what I called The Institute for Doing Nothing. People laughed when I talked this way while I was still in mid-life, never quite getting my point. The point was not that we at the institute would not do anything; it was that we would labor vigorously at doing nothing *useful*. And by "not useful" I meant not necessary, not necessarily applicable, not financially profitable. The IDN would be independently wealthy, of course, so finances would be no worry and no staff would be occupied with raising funds or writing grant applications (that would be "useful"). And we would have a comfortable, beautiful, new complex, probably in Colorado or someplace in the foothills of the Rockies; and there would be big conference rooms where institute members could gather and brainstorm and exchange ideas, and quiet meditation rooms, state of the art research labs, and a splendid library, and lots of garden space and walking paths. And members would more likely grow flowers (which are useless but delightful) than vegetables, and invent things for the sheer pleasure of discovery and launch expeditions around the world and down into the deep sea. And....

Well, Jackie would periodically ask me to explain to her one more time how we were going to live on Social Security without pension and without savings (we had given and traveled it all away). I would go over the projections once again: how long we would have to work before applying, what our very manageable expenses would be with no debts, no house payments, only one car, Medicare replacing the hefty self-employment health insurance premiums we had been paying, and so on. I told her that in my ten years of outreach home visits to the elderly in Itasca County I had met many people getting along fine on less Social Security than we would have. In fact, in ten years, I had met no seniors who were without food, clothing, or shelter. Some of them fretted about their finances, it is true, as they served me coffee in their warm kitchens and pushed a plate of cookies toward me. None of them *really* were "choosing between groceries and medication." Jackie would trust me and be reassured until the next time she began to wonder how we were going to get along in old age without money...and I would patiently get out the folder and go over it again.

At the end of 2004 the plan went into effect, and it worked. I stopped working as Jackie's co-therapist in marriage and family counseling and ended all my piecemeal social work jobs. She gradually cut back her therapy work to two days, and then to one, a week. At the same time she resumed training with her former art teacher, Sister Mary Charles, an accomplished iconographer, and began to accept commissions from churches to paint religious icons in the Byzantine tradition. On the side she continued a sporadic business of selling her stunning photo greeting cards which carried this inscription on the back of each card:

White Stone: Jackie Solem lives in rural Northern Minnesota and has recorded many theophanies in various places in the world. Seeing is believing.

One day not long ago, as we lay in bed in the morning light talking, I was telling her about my urgency to get started on next season's firewood and plans to start tapping the maple trees. She commented on how hard I work.

"You think I work hard? I don't think of myself that way. I'm a re-tired guy."

"My gosh, you work hard! You don't realize how much you get done!"

"I don't know. I think of myself sitting around reading books and thinking deep thoughts, that's all."

"You do that and...," here she took me on a verbal tour of the house, the rooms remodeled, the septic installed, the furniture built, the well pounded, the windows installed, wiring and plumbing replaced, the cords of wood cut, split, stacked. I pulled my hands out from beneath the blankets and raised them in the air to flex my achy, arthritic fingers and thumbs. They backed up what she was saying.

"But I'm glad I am done working," I said. "At a job. I don't have to peddle papers anymore, don't have go collecting for my route on Satur-day mornings, don't have to get up now and go to school. The government just puts money in our checking on the second and fourth Wednesdays of every month whether we work or not."

"You know, Phil," she said, "you have your Institute for Doing Noth-ing now. You do work very hard, but you have all the time you want to read and watch your astronomy videos and think and go to your phi-losophy discussion group with your friends. And we travel and see the world."

"I guess that's right." It had not occurred to me that way. "Jackie, you are a member of the Institute, too, much more engaged and still earning money; but you are doing it because you like it. So you are doing noth-...I don't mean what you are doing is *useless*...wait...let me try to say this right...." (Be careful.)

....

These past ten years–ever since we returned from Jerusalem–have been a period of great activity and growth. Even though we had no sav-ings and our income was receding, we managed to go on a major trip every year–across Asia, north to Alaska, south to Tierra del Fuego, east to Nova Scotia, west to California, with Europe, North Africa, Mexico and Central America still in the planning stages. Our outer life gained momentum with retirement; and we seemed to want to go ever farther abroad to see the world, smell baskets of spices in open markets, smile into the soft eyes of henna-lined faces, taste curry, mole, asado, chianti, exult at thrumming chanting under the tinkling of a hundred bells, watch flame and smoke rise from corpses alongside the river which is a goddess.

The energy of inner life has kept pace: for me, unexpected migration, for Jackie a period of consistent spiritual deepening.

"We have begun to complete the circle of this generation." Jackie says to me. "Our parents have died; we are the elders now." Older she is and regarded as an elder in the Anishinabe sense, a grandmother, a wise woman. People who know her well or who have only heard her reputation come looking for inspiration and guidance. They know her to have uncommon spiritual depth and warmth.

I who live with her have two images. I see people coming to her one-by-one or in groups, and I see her reaching out to gather them and to talk eagerly about things that truly matter. I am struck by how intently she looks at people, clear and interested. They trust her. They sense that she wants them to have life and a spirit of liberty and to come free of their entanglements. They feel how interested she is in them. The other image is of her sitting on our bed for two hours each morning, legs outstretched, surrounded by a tumble of books, a writing pad and pen, a journal book, and, on her lap, propped into a pillow, a board-icon of the face of Christ into which she is gazing. Or when I tiptoe past to get a shirt from the closet, she is still there, straight and motionless, eyes closed in wordless prayer. Always there is a sprawl of books about her, art books, human development books, mostly spiritual books–*The Soul of Rumi, All Saints, Holy Bible, Spirituality and Health, Encounters with Silence, The Brain, The Lives of the Forgotten Desert Mothers, The Enneagram, The Questions of Jesus, Meister Eckhart, Medjugorje Day by Day, The Courage to Create, Living Buddha Living Christ, The Hidden Heart of the Cosmos*....

She continues to accumulate an ever growing library of this sort, more than she could read, but kept for some indefinite future nourishment and even more "for other people whom it might help." Along one wall of our bedroom are shelves of art books–color study, painting, calligraphy, photography, iconography. She has always loved art since childhood and tells me, "Art is my way of contemplation." I tore out all the walls of our upstairs a few years ago, leaving only the bathroom enclosed. My design was to build a light-filled art studio for her supplies, her large easel, her books, her paints–with our bed in one corner and only a little space for wardrobes. I was pleased to think of myself as a kept man sleeping with the artist in the artist's loft. No need of a bedroom.

She earns a little bit of money from the sale of her photography and from church commissions for icons. However, most of her earned income these days is from her work in the little studio outside our house as a therapist and spiritual director. Jackie has not fully retired from her profession, as I have from mine. She loves that work still; and nearly all the income from it is reinvested in art, photography, and programs of psychological and spiritual growth. For example, a few years ago, she asked me what I thought about her entering a two-year certification program in spiritual direction. My pragmatic response was that she had plenty of experience and skill in that area already and certainly did not need more credentials. Moreover, it would be very expensive and not very cost-effective, and so on. As her interest continued, I came to understand that her eagerness to make this major investment in energy and money was not about her profession but about her life. She then spent the next two years of intensive home study, peer supervision, and two summertime residencies with the Shalem Institute in Bethesda, Maryland. Another time she spent one weekend a month for the better part of a year in the study of psychosynthesis. Recently, she has been traveling to California and to Minneapolis for advanced training in the Enneagram and has been organizing local conferences and personal development groups based on this process of "integrating body, mind, and spirit." I have had people tell me that they have been drawn to this method and signed up for these offerings primarily because it was Jackie who was organizing them, so thoroughly do they trust her.

As she and I have been sharing the life review of these memoirs in which I interview her, then write, then read her the drafts, she tells me she is putting together the pieces of our life and of her own life with new understanding–even those which we seemed to have dropped or misplaced–such as the finding of Angela, the little foster granddaughter whom we tried to adopt and had to give up, letting her disappear from our lives. Letting her disappear until one day, after twenty-five years, we found her again, grown up. We met her and the good parents who raised her–in *Ely!* to our surprise.

She returns to her memory of little Gerry in Soudan, Minnesota, always scanning the environment, trying to understand what is going on here, how people say they believe *this*, but do *that*.

As a young nun, she recalls, she had the romantic fantasy that she would die young and that saintliness meant that the world was to be eschewed, so that when something lovely or good came her way, she tended to anticipate its loss with the inevitable bursting of the bubble. She wondered if she had to choose between the joy she found in art and beauty and self-abnegation in the service of God.

As she matured, she decided to move past her ambivalence and enter life fully with zest and courage. The habit of scanning, ever scanning, remains, the internal questions about "what if this?...and on the other hand what about that?" persist, but they are less often the old sense of bewilderment and more dependably an attitude of balance. She tells me she recognizes implicitly that anything good has an underside which keeps her keenly alert to the suffering of others. This, perhaps, is what drew her to her work as a therapist. As she sits with people to hear their stories and their trouble, she watches the interplay of light and dark, joy and pain, the yin-yang of all experience. One of her most successful early photographs was of an exquisitely lovely, misty rose with a single hard, dangerous thorn thrust up into the foreground of focus.

This pairing of opposites has left her always scanning in an effort to weigh what was going on about her, a habit of ever preparing for what might threaten. She directs much attention to prevention, maintaining health, inquiring into alternative medicine, experimenting with vitamin supplements. She begins all travel plans by choosing the right clothes, the right health and safety aids, the needed comfort snacks (while I am mapping itinerary and getting visas and air tickets). She cannot bear the sound, sight, or narration of wanton violence and will leave the conversation, the room, the theater, if it erupts. She says she prepares for the possible impact of violence upon her calm spirit by taking it on selectively in small doses–by listening deeply to people's pain in therapy, in grief support group, in muted, confidential conversations. Violence of any sort overthrows balance and survival. She anticipates it in fantasy before our most daring travels, lies awake imaging the worst, going cold with fear–then moves ahead with faith and a decision for trust, which transmutes it all into courage. At that point, her step forward–into marriage, into adopting a child, into giving away her house and home, into getting on a bicycle and riding into the Middle East–becomes a calm act of certainty.

This attitude toward the world forms the terrain of her spirituality: a steady awareness of the presence of God and a conviction that the life she is living is Christ in her. Her appreciation of life in the moment is where her attention is focused when she is not entertaining fears. She does not strive toward definitions, as I do, but returns again and again to the words "presence" and "experience" when speaking of God and spirit. Her daily spiritual practice goes toward introjecting the personality of Christ into her thoughts and behavior as best she can. She says she does not go seeking the cross as he did in his life but, rather, opens herself each morning for at least two silent hours of prayer, which carries her through the day "under the eye of this loving Being." She speaks of wanting to be loyal to his mother, Mary, and loyal "to the spirit of him who yielded everything to the Father." With amusement and delight she tells this dream: "I am walking from Tower back to my house in Soudan. Clasped under my arm is a big, red piece of steak. I pass under the bridge that passes over the highway forming a cross at right angles to it and stand there. And the caption appears in the dream: 'My meat is to do the will of Him who sent me.'" She laughs, "Isn't that *wild?*"

....

For me, however, this has been a period of spiritual migration. A few years ago I began journaling again to come to terms with a new flurry of substantial doubts about my religion. Surprisingly, these arose shortly after Jackie and I returned from the arduous prayer journey up to Jerusalem full of faith and devotion. In my thirties I had been in a period of near total unbelief for about six years, as I have told, then suddenly leapt back from it to solid ground, as from a raft going over a falls, as I watched my moral integrity and marriage going into free fall. Following conversion and re-attachment to conservative Catholicism I had found myself one day listening in appreciative surprise to my very Catholic, ninety-eight-year-old mother's musings with uncertainty and doubt "about all those things we have been told." Two years after that, as Jackie and I looked down at her still body in the mortuary, it was odd that I was thinking not of the resurrection of the body but of a candle extinguished.

World travel altered my world view, and I began to entertain impossible thoughts.

For example, in Japan I struggled to make sense out of Shinto, a national religion that has no meaning outside of Japan. Shinto has shrines, an ordained priesthood, elaborate ritual, prayers and blessings, local *kami* deities, but no God, no theology, no belief system. When I asked who or what hears these prayers, the question had no meaning for my Japanese friends. "This is not religion," I was told. "This is just what we Japanese do." Elsewhere I asked a panel of saffron-robed Tibetan Buddhist monks who had been speaking of compassion, ritual, and meditation also to say a bit about God. Their response was brief: We do not speak of god. This is not something our practice or monasticism is concerned with. In India Jackie and I saw the flat stone in the temple of Mathura where the Lord of the Universe became incarnate as Krishn in 3228 B.C. while his parents were imprisoned by a demon king. We had seen a similar flat stone in the church at Bethlehem where the Son of God was born. The stories were similar: prophecies of long-awaited saviors, virgin births, births of the divine ones in squalid circumstances, slaughter of the innocents by King Kans/King Herod, flight to Gokul/to Egypt.

I had always been interested in other religions and read widely: the Upanishads, Dhamapada, Bhagavad Gita, The Qur'an, Talmud, Zoroastrianism, Zen, analyses of primal mythologies. As a young theology student in Louvain I had been led underneath Catholic dogmatism to an appreciation of the archetype substrata implicit in all religions following the work of Mircea Eliade. And now in these later years, I turned again to the study of myth and followed the work of Joseph Campbell.

However, it was a revisit to the sources of my own religion which raised the most troubling questions. For the first time I read a translation of the full text of the Dead Sea Scrolls and was shocked at how much of what I read there deflated the sense of uniqueness in the Jesus story. Similarly, when I listened on tape to a lecture series on "Lost Christianities," I wondered why, in my thorough theological training, I had not been exposed to the astonishing diversity of beliefs among the earliest Christian communities, those closest to the founding, concerning basic questions of faith: the reality of Jesus, the number of gods, even the malice of god. As I read various studies of Jewish history—the development of Judaism without the revisionist lenses of Christian interpretation—the meaning of the Old Testament suddenly looked very different. When Jackie and I took our turns teaching the Catholic Faith in our parish church to people considering conversion to Catholicism, I found myself spelling out that very little of it went back to the time of Jesus. Most of what they would learn, including the compilation of the Bible itself, had taken form after the first three hundred years and some of it very recently.

What I wrote in my journal shows that I was progressively questioning the very notion of the supernatural. I had been interested in a scientific explanation of this world ever since I was a boy. I remember my dad telling me there was a *fourth* dimension, time. I could hardly believe it. When I was not yet in high school I had pulled from his small library behind the glass doors of the bookcase a severe, thin volume called *Relativity and Space* by Steinmetz, which I seem to recall had a publication date of 1923, only seven years after the publication of Einstein's General Theory of Relativity. It was a technical text full of mathematical formulas and indecipherable paragraphs, but I poured over its mysteries straining to connect space and time, gathering that it had something to do with light and only dimly beginning to grasp that there is no fixed point in the universe–that everything is in position and movement relative to every other thing. That we see everything from a point of view: *"However, when you stand over here...."* It was the beginning of a lifelong fascination with the very large and the very small, the Big Bang, the black holes, electron shells, quarks, neutrinos and the expanding universe. Here were explanations of the origin of the world and of life itself, every bit as shimmering and mutable as the myths but relying on observation, documentation, testing and validation–not on say-so.

I had time in these retirement years to think more deeply on what this world was all about. It was not just scholarly study and ancient texts. As I strolled the road before our house day after day, the movement once again from belief to unbelief came gradually through observation of the grasses, the seasons, the evidence of death scattered everywhere in nature. I was looking outward and upward constantly and thinking about sleeping and waking and sleeping, the evaporation of memories, the passing of time, aging and watching my mother dying and dead. Alongside the vastness of this world, which I would see as I squatted to contemplate the head on a stalk of timothy grass on which wee bugs were crawling–which I would see when I then looked up at a sea of grasses and then out beyond them to the continent, then to the seas, and outward to the Hubble snapshot of a tiny slot of sky containing untold galaxies in spacetime halfway to the expanding edge of the universe–alongside all this, my religion and all the others seemed folk tales. The question, "Who made this?" seemed absurd, absolutely the wrong question. My heart and my mind shrank from the crassness of wanting to package this existence.

And the "who?" question arose in smaller flourishes. Here was one. Jackie and I were sitting one evening with our grief support group, as we have every Thursday for fifteen years. As I listened to people in the group speaking of their images of God (a person, a man, the Big Guy, *He* always *he/him,* who was powerful, loving, whimsical, beyond question, unpredictable, unreliable, ignoring heartfelt prayer, cruel, detached, intimate and caring, tender, always there for us, ignoring us, making a mockery of our most painful hopes and dreams, absent, irrelevant), I said to myself: This is what it means to believe in a personal God. They are talking about *someone.* I do not believe there is this God. This, I think is what Joseph Campbell means when he says, "God is a concept." These portrayals of God are adapted, as always, to the occasion; and the occasion here (grief) calls for Him to be unloving (He killed my child!) and unresponsive (All those prayers wasted!) and remote, even absent ("What I am *so* worried about is that there is no one to take care of my six-year-old Devon, that he is all alone and needs his mom now and no one is taking care of him!"). A few moments later that same mother, a born-again Christian, would say God is Love and Devon has gone up to God and is at peace now, pain-free and just perfect.

At that, I thought of God as a Japanese *furoshiki.* This is a large cloth, perhaps two feet square, which women use to bundle and carry things, placing them in the middle and gathering the four corners. A suitcase, box, or even a paper bag hide their contents. But a *furoshiki* graciously takes the shape of its contents.

I do not think I have lost my faith. I do not even like to use the words "disbelieve" or "unbelief," as though belief were the normal fixed point from which to judge. The polarity of belief I think is not unbelief but lucidity. The past five years have felt like a seeing-more-clearly, neither loss nor disillusionment. I must have anticipated this in the story about Saint Nicholas which I told my little daughter, Sara, making the distinction between what is story and what is real. I think that bedtime tale was not only an honest and sober explanation to her at that time, but also a parable kept in reserve for myself, as a lamp on the journey of my own old age.

Although I have led with my inquiring mind, this is surely a journey of the heart. I know we need myth and ritual and poetry and song as well as lucidity, data, and logic. Of course rationality and the scientific method are not the only way to know the world. They had nothing to do with my falling in love with my beautiful Jackie. Today I remain a practicing Catholic Christian primarily because of my bond with her–not only because she remains firmly grounded in her faith but because this shared faith brought us to marriage and sustained us during our most difficult and dangerous times and gave us great courage and joy all through the years. I love Jackie more than my thoughts, more than my conclusions.

Not long ago I heard an interview with the eminent physicist, Freeman Dyson, by Krista Tippett on the NPR radio program, *Speaking of Faith.* She asked him about belief in Christianity. He answered that he is a practicing Christian but not a believing Christian. That formulation made sense to me; and, for the time being, I use it when I am asked to account for myself. I do not know the road ahead, but there is no need to. I am also comforted by the knowledge that this distinction is not so strange, that the Shinto take it for granted as do most Buddhists and many observant Jews who subscribe to no creed. For that matter, I suspect it is the condition of many, if not most, of my co-religionists at Mass on Sunday morning, good practicing Catholics who quietly keep within a second set of books.

....

Clearly Jackie and I have diverged in the way we see things. This is not a bad thing. As we have instructed the couples we worked with in marriage counseling, differentiation from one another while maintaining the bond is a principle of healthy marriage. Perhaps our different styles of thinking and feeling, which have always been at play in our relationship, have naturally led to such differences in our spiritualities today, late in life. Jackie has inclined toward large themes of thought, clothed in language that is allusive, suggestive, and global. I, too, am drawn to large themes, but in categories and detailed with information, historical references, enumerations, distinctions. Both of us love abstractions; but hers run more toward emotion and beauty on the light side and indignant generalizations on the dark, while I love to step to the whiteboard of the mind to make lists, draw arrows, and lace my expositions with poetic cleverness and a cascade of metaphor. Both of us live in a mental world of dualities. Hers are both/and. Mine are either/or. Jackie holds the duality of fact/myth, spirit/flesh, God/human, maybe yes/maybe no. She holds both and struggles, always testing to see "how does this fit here?...then how does that?" She expects the "fit" to lie somewhere in the paradox, even when she cannot see it or account for it. I, on the other hand, am asking: "What is real here, what is true?" My expectation is that there is a resolution of the paradox or contradiction eventually.

We have long conversations about the big questions of life and the universe. Usually, when we finally run out of words and thoughts, we emerge rested, energized, and joyful. Sometimes we bruise each other and take offense and have to just drop it. It is not surprising that we have come to such different views of the nature of reality and the meaning of life. We really are not at odds, because she is refreshed by my clarity of thought and I am warmed by the love and beauty of her vision. She says that she has come to a stronger sense of her inner authority at this point in life and knows that she has to rely on her own mind and spirit to say what is true. Aware of the dramatic swings out and back that I have made with strong certainty in my life, she worries at times that I can quickly leave behind some relationship, belief, or value that shortly before was very important to me. She wonders that what I have called "my spiritual migration" away from a supernatural understanding of life may undercut the shared spiritual ground of our relationship. At the same time (an example of her both/and), she says that she utterly trusts me because she sees how I behave and how I love her. This dance and dialogue which we maintain is exciting to both of us; and both of us consider it to be a continuation of our spiritual journey, our fascination with the unpredictables of the inner life.

....

The day we married, when Jackie had slowly descended the wide staircase flanked by her sisters, we first greeted our guests around the ellipse of tables. Then she pointed to two banners, large enough to be carried in procession, hung facing us across the wedding hall. She had made these at home a week earlier. Each was a plain field of deep green; on one was sewn the yellow shape of a flame, on the other the image of a sun.

"The candle flame" she announced, "is a traditional wedding symbol familiar to us all—two burning tapers leaning together to make a single flame. But the sun is Philip's and my own symbol. My family name, Vesel, means 'happy' and 'blessed' in Slovenian. In Norwegian, Philip's family name, Solem, comes from 'sol-hjem,' meaning 'sun-home.' Today we come together before you to form the House of the Happy Sun."

Then the Dale family began to sing:

Walk slowly...breathe softly...take off your shoes...when opening any new door....

Symbols, the elements of myth, have stealthily made their way into our marriage all through the years. Rarely have we consciously contrived them, as we did with the happy sun and the gesture of waiting on tables at our own wedding. Most have surfaced unbeckoned from deep places through unknown trapdoors and stood waiting in shadow and behind curtains to be recognized in their own time.

Such an epiphany came this past winter while Jackie and I were at home, treating ourselves to a private Meryl Streep film festival. We had collected some of her old movies from the video store and the library and were watching one or two a week, delighting in the kaleidoscope of roles and accents she has played over the years. At the time, Jackie and I had been collaborating on these memoirs for months; and I had already written most of the chapters. No doubt this had us in an aroused condition of receptivity when two minor scenes in *Out of Africa* switched on a cascade of memory and insight into our personal symbol-world.

In this 1985 film portrayal of Isak Dinesen's memoir, the Danish Baroness, Karen Blixen (Meryl Streep), makes a courageous but ultimately doomed effort to develop a coffee farm on marginal land at the foot of the Ngong Hills in Kenya. During an early scene of the film, she is making an inspection of the property and laying out plans to her head servant, a competent, dignified Somali named Farah Aden:

Baroness Blixen: *Now, if you put a dam here to stop the water, then I can make a pond here. Do you know how to make a pond?*

Farah (shocked): *Msabu! This water must go home to Mombasa !*
Baroness: *Yes, well, it can go home after we make a pond.*
Farah: *Msabu, this water **lives** in Mombasa !*

That scene remained with me more forcefully than any other in this lyric and melancholy film — that and a partner scene at the end. The next day, as I returned to this writing, I suddenly saw how often themes of water, running and pooled, have appeared in the poetry of our marriage. In writing *Owlstones* twenty years earlier, I had knowingly intended Ravenna Rosealice and Nome Ogrodni as figures of our own inner lives and relationship. Yet, for the first time, I saw the reflection of House of the Happy Sun in my naming "Brighthome" the ancestral estate whose saving was the pretext for the tale. And I noticed that the story's tension would pool for a while at the seaside town of Quiet Waters, where Nome and Ravenna would marry. And I saw that Brighthome had been built along the lovely Sula River , whose flow would ultimately bring the dissolution of the house itself, leaving its survivors to run on with the tale into uncertainty.

Only then, while reflecting on that fragment of dialogue from *Out of Africa* and its concise wisdom spoken by the Baroness (make a pond for a little while) and by Farah (this water must go home) — only then did I remember a song I had written for Jacqueline one year after we married, one year before we decided to have children. I went looking for the song among old papers, afraid it had been misplaced. But there it was with old letters saved: *"WATERSMEET — for Jacqueline, Christmas, 1971"*:

I worry and often wonder / how empty my life might be,
If the springs would die and the wells run dry / and my soul could sing no melody.
Watersmeet, the waters grow / when raindrops fall, the runlets flow,
The pools brim over, and so I know
They are larger and fuller with the water of another
And we call it a river.

Run on then, river of my life.
Flow gently out to the sea.
And I will follow, and I will lead,
For I am you, and you are me.

I met you in star-filled evening. I loved you in early morning.
And the day took a great new meaning, and my heart could sing new mel-
ody.
Watersmeet, my river grows. You came beside me and joined my flow.
Your eyes brim over, and so I know
I am larger and fuller with the life of another,
So they call me a lover.

Run on then, river....

I daydream and often wonder / what puzzles our lives would be,
If your eyes shined and your form would change, and your body would sing
new melody.
Watersmeet, the waters swell, the current swift where children dwell,
And sons and daughters, mysterious waters,
You'd be larger and fuller with the life of another,
And they'd call you a mother.

Run on then, river of my life.
Flow gently out to the sea.
And I will follow, and I will lead,
For I am you and you are me.

....

Now, even though our story has not ended, this telling of it has–with the refrain of the song. It ends with the last page of *Owlstones*, where Nome and Ravenna are leaving Brighthome behind and passing beyond Hite's Farm into the Outlands. And it ends with the following scene, toward the end of *Out of Africa*, a brief complement to the earlier one, which brought our own symbol-world into focus:

It is years after the previous conversation with Farah. What happens now suggests that the Baroness has incorporated his wisdom into her own. Absolutely drenched in long Victorian dress and muddy boots, she is fiercely struggling with a long-handle spade alongside a half dozen Kikuyu workmen in a blinding downpour to save the dikes holding in the pond, the main reservoir for irrigating the marginal plantation. The water is spilling over the top, and they are shoveling side by side, desperately pushing mud in to gaps as fast as they can. They can hardly see through the violence of the rain. A large piece of bank melts and slurries away; the water pours through. The workmen scramble. Resigned, she straightens and leans wearily on her shovel—calls out:

Let it go! Let it go. This water lives in Mombasa, anyway.

Printed in the United States
107621LV00003B/217-255/P